MARKET REFORM IN SOCIETY

MOISÉS ARCE

MARKET REFORM IN SOCIETY

POST-CRISIS POLITICS AND ECONOMIC CHANGE IN AUTHORITARIAN PERU

THE PENNSYLVANIA STATE UNIVERSITY PRESS

UNIVERSITY PARK, PENNSYLVANIA

Publication of this book has been aided by a subvention from Louisiana State University.

Library of Congress Cataloging-in-Publication Data

Arce, Moisè's.
Market reform in society : post-crisis politics and economic change
in authoritarian Peru / Moisè's Arce.
p.   cm.
Includes bibliographical references and index.
ISBN 978-0-271-02542-1 (hardcover) | ISBN 978-0-271-02543-8 (paper)
1. Peru—Economic policy.
2. Structural adjustment (Economic policy)—Social aspects—Peru.
3. Economic stabilization—Social aspects—Peru.
4. Peru—Economic conditions—1968– .
5. Peru—Social conditions—1968– .
I. Title.

HC227 .A772 2005
306.3 0985—dc22
2004012427

TO MY PARENTS,

Jaime Arce and Haydeé Esquivel,

and

TO MY WIFE,

Jennifer McGarr,

for their love and support

CONTENTS

ACKNOWLEDGMENTS

One of my earliest exposures to Peruvian politics as a child occurred on the day my father and I went to our city's main plaza to participate in a political rally for presidential candidate Fernando Belaúnde. I saw thousands of people excited to see Belaúnde, and my father lifted me up to see him as he walked by, flag draped over his shoulders, making his way through the plaza. As the story goes, the election of Belaúnde as president of Peru ended military rule and marked the beginning of the country's transition to democracy. In reality, various political and socioeconomic problems would tear the country apart in the years ahead. Since the early 1980s, Peru has seen three different national currencies because of hyperinflation, escalating political violence with a death toll of approximately 69,280 people, the collapse of the traditional political party system, and most recently, massive corruption caught on videotapes made by Fujimori's chief security advisor. Little did I know back then, on the day of that political rally, that I would be studying and writing about these phenomena many years ahead.

This book began in the early 1990s when I was a graduate student at the University of New Mexico. This was also the beginning of the Fujimori era, which appeared to bring a sea change in economic policy, including the transformation of the political landscape. In many different ways, this book traces the Fujimori regime, as it climbed the "higher hills," as Przeworski might describe it, of economic reform in the early 1990s to the continuation of politics as usual toward the late 1990s. Societal actors broadly defined were important in shaping the direction of market policies that were originally implemented in a top-down, autocratic fashion. These interactions between state and societal actors as they affected policies are at the heart of this book.

At the University of New Mexico, I was most fortunate to receive the mentoring of Karen Remmer and Ken Roberts. There they helped me to turn my inside knowledge of Peru into a finished political science product and I continue to learn from them today. I am most appreciative of their continuing guidance over the years. I also thank Erik Wibbels and Caroline Beer for their friendship, encouragement, and continuing support.

At Louisiana State University, I am extremely lucky to have as a mentor Cecil Eubanks, who has taught me many valuable things about research, teaching, and professional development. Mark Gasiorowski and Cameron Thies are great colleagues who continuously challenge almost every good idea I think I have. Stacy Haynie and Wayne Parent were particularly helpful in seeing this book to completion. Stella Rouse and Nathan Willingham provided valuable research assistance.

For their knowledgeable recommendations over the years, I express sincere thanks to Cynthia McClintock, Max Cameron, Francisco Durand, Carol Wise, Catherine Conaghan, Ken Coleman, Christina Ewig, Julio Carrión, Efraín Gonzales de Olarte, Javier Iguiñiz, and Catalina Romero. I have also benefited from numerous anonymous reviewers from various journals and I acknowledge their suggestions here and elsewhere. Naturally, responsibility for any remaining shortcomings in this book rests solely with me.

I would like to thank the following organizations for providing the funding that made my research possible: the National Science Foundation, the Social Science Research Council, the Fulbright Scholars Program, the University of New Mexico Office of Graduate Studies, the University of New Mexico Latin American Institute, the Commission for the Promotion of Peru (Promperú), Louisiana State University Council on Research Summer Stipend Program and Faculty Research Grant, and Louisiana State University College of Arts and Sciences.

Excerpts from Chapters 2 and 6 appeared previously in "The Sustainability of Economic Reform in a 'Most Likely' Case: Peru," *Comparative Politics* (April 2003), and material from that article is reproduced here by permission of *Comparative Politics*. An earlier version of Chapter 4 was published as "The Politics of Pension Reform in Peru," *Studies in Comparative International Development* 36, no. 3 (Fall 2001), copyright © 2001 by Transaction Publishers, reprinted by permission of the publisher. I thank these publishers. Special thanks also go to Sandy Thatcher and Penn State Press for seeing the project through to publication.

I thank my parents, Jaime Arce and Haydeé Esquivel, for their generosity. Their sacrifice in sending me to the United States to study put me on a path I might not otherwise have traveled, for which I am very grateful. I thank them also for helping me to keep my ideas on Peruvian politics firmly grounded in everyday reality. To Jennifer McGarr, my wife, for reading every page, more than once, since the beginning of this project, and for the joyful life we, including the little one on the way, have together.

FIGURES AND TABLES

AAFP	Asociación de Administradoras de Fondos de Pensiones
	Association of Pension Fund Administrators
ADEX	Asociación de Exportadores
	Association of Exporters
AFP	administradoras de fondos de pensiones
	pension fund administrators
AMSSOP	Asociación Médica del Seguro Social del Perú
	Medical Association of the Peruvian Institute for Social Security
AP	Acción Popular
	Popular Action Party
APRA	Alianza Popular Revolucionaria Americana
	American Popular Revolutionary Alliance Party
ASBANC	Asociación de Bancos
	Peruvian Banking Association
BCP	Banco de Crédito del Perú
	Credit Bank of Peru
BCRP	Banco Central de Reserva del Perú
	Central Reserve Bank of Peru
C90	Cambio '90
	Change '90
CADE	Conferencia Annual de Ejecutivos
	Annual Conference of Executives
CCD	Congreso Constituyente Demócratico
	Democratic Constitutional Congress
CIAT	Centro Interamericano de Administraciones Tributarias
	Inter-American Center for Tax Administrations
CLAS	Comités Locales de Administración en Salud
	Local Committees for Health Administration

COMEXPERU	Sociedad de Comercio Exterior del Perú
	Peruvian Society of Chamber of Exporters
CONFIEP	Confederación Nacional de Instituciones Empresariales Privadas
	National Confederation of Private Business Organizations
COPRI	Comisión de Promoción de la Inversión Privada
	Commission for the Promotion of Private Investment
CUT	Central de Unión de Trabajadores
	Workers Central Union
DGC	Dirección General de Contribuciones
	Directorate General for Taxation
DL	decreto legislativo
	legislative decree
EPS	entidades prestadoras de salud
	health promotion entities
ESSALUD	El Seguro Social de Salud
	Peruvian Institute for Social Insurance in Health
FEDEVAL	Federación de Vendedores Ambulantes de Lima y Callao
	Federation of Street Vendors of Lima and Callao
FENTRACOM	Federación Nacional de Trabajadores Comerciantes en Mercados y Anexos
	National Federation of Merchants in Markets and Subsidiaries
FREDEMO	Frente Democrático
	Democratic Front
FTMS	Federación de Trabajadores del Ministerio de Salud
	Federation of Health Ministry Workers
FONAVI	Fondo Nacional de Vivienda
	National Housing Fund
FONCODES	Fondo Nacional de Compensación y Desarrollo Social
	National Compensation and Social Development Fund
IAT	Instituto de Administración Tributaria
	Tax Administration Institute
IDB	Inter-American Development Bank
IEAN	impuesto extraordinario a los activos netos
	extraordinary tax on net assets
IES	impuesto extraordinario de solidaridad
	extraordinary solidarity tax
IMF	International Monetary Fund

INDECOPI	Instituto Nacional de Defensa de la Competencia y de la Protección de la Propiedad Intelectual
	National Institute for the Defense of Competition and the Protection of Intellectual Property Rights
INEI	Instituto Nacional de Estadística e Informática
	National Institute for Statistics and Information
IPE	Instituto Peruano de Economía
	Peruvian Institute of Economics
IPSS	Instituto Peruano de Seguridad Social
	Peruvian Institute for Social Security
MIMDES	Ministerio de la Mujer y Desarrollo Social
	Ministry of Women and Social Development
NM	Nueva Mayoría
	New Majority
ONP	Oficina de Normalización Previsional
	Pensions Normalization Office
OSINERG	Organismo Supervisor de la Inversión en Energía
	Supervisory Board for Investment in Electricity
OSIPTEL	Organismo Supervisor de Inversión Privada en Telecomunicaciones
	Supervisory Board for Private Investment in Telecommunications
OSITRAN	Organismo Supervisor de la Inversión en Infraestructura de Transporte de Uso Público
	Supervisory Board for Infrastructure Investment in Public Transportation
PAC	Programa de Administración Compartida
	Shared Administration Program
PPC	Partido Popular Cristiano
	Popular Christian Party
PRI	Partido Revolucionario Institucional
	Institutionalized Revolutionary Party
PRICOS	principales contribuyentes
	major taxpayers
PRONAA	Programa Nacional de Ayuda Alimentaria
	National Food Assistance Program
PRONASOL	Programa Nacional de Solidaridad
	National Solidarity Program

RER	Régimen Especial del Impuesto a la Renta
	Special Income Tax Regime
RUS	Régimen Unico Simplificado
	Special Simplified Regime
SAFP	Superintendencia de Administradoras de Fondos de Pensiones
	Superintendency of Pension Fund Administrators
SNE	Sociedad Nacional de Exportadores
	National Exporters Society
SNI	Sociedad Nacional de Industrias
	National Industries Society
SNP	Sociedad Nacional de Pesquería
	National Fishing Society
SNMPE	Sociedad Nacional de Minería, Petróleo y Energía
	National Mining, Petroleum, and Energy Society
SUNAD	Superintendencia Nacional de Administración de Aduanas
	National Superintendency for Customs Administration
SUNAT	Superintendencia Nacional de Administración Tributaria
	National Superintendency of Tax Administration
SUTEP	Sindicato Único de Trabajadores de la Educación Peruana
	Sole Union of Workers of Peruvian Education
UEIT	Unidad Especial de Investigación Tributaria
	Special Unit for Tax Audits
VAT	value-added tax
VV	Vamos Vecinos
	Let's Go, Neighbors

Since the mid-1980s, Latin American countries have increasingly turned from the state to the market to achieve sustainable economic growth. This trend was accelerated by the debt crisis in the early 1980s, which spurred governments across the region to adopt policies involving the privatization of state enterprises, market deregulation, and trade liberalization. Much of the literature on the politics of market-oriented or neoliberal reform has emphasized the origins of this change, exploring the reasons why countries adopt market policies and the political and social conditions that help or hinder their implementation (Haggard and Kaufman 1992, 1995; Nelson 1990). The study of market transitions also has been predominantly state-centered, focusing on the role of political leaders and technocratic elites during economic restructuring (Dominguez 1996; Teichman 2001). Political leaders and technocratic elites are widely perceived as market vanguards crafting reforms in a highly autonomous and insulated policy-making environment with limited input or interaction with social forces.[1]

Studies on the political effects of market-oriented policy reform have begun to appear only recently. Interestingly, this current wave of marketization has led to two sets of important, albeit contradictory, propositions about the political and social consequences of reform. Originally, the literature suggested that reforms run into serious political obstacles largely because of asymmetries in costs and benefits. Market reforms, scholars argued, entail concentrated and immediate costs for specific social groups and dispersed, long-term benefits for the rest of society. Based on these premises, dominant chief executives were seen as pivotal to overcoming "policy stalemates" and pushing through politically costly reforms (Haggard and Kaufman 1995, 156–57). Therefore, successful reform appeared to require the marginalization or defeat of market foes, in particular, organized labor and labor-based parties. As Schamis (1999, 237)

---

[1]. For recent contributions on the consequences of economic reforms, see Snyder 2001; and Chalmers, Martin, and Piester 1997.

aptly noted, much of the politics of economic reform was read simply as "the politics of neutralizing the losers." Consequently, scholars emphasized the disorganizing or weakening effects of neoliberal policies on societal groups.

This dominant perspective, however, came under scrutiny on the basis of additional evidence. In Mexico, for instance, the deregulation of coffee production as part of a broader framework to retrench the state at the national level induced "reregulation" practices, that is, the creation of new regulatory frameworks at the subnational level. Whereas the introduction of deregulation was initially portrayed as eliminating benefits, the politics of reregulation is about reinstating them (Snyder 1999, 202). In other words, rather than imposing concentrated costs on powerful interest groups or producing diffused benefits for the rest of society, as the earlier view of neoliberal reform would have it, reregulation created "concentrated gains and targetable, excludable benefits." Furthermore, as noted by Schamis (1999), economic-reform initiatives, such as trade liberalization and privatization, spawned the formation of "distributional coalitions" even prior to their initiation and, consistent with Snyder, concentrated gains or rents following their implementation.[2] Further, the political-economy literature originating from postcommunist countries suggests that winners (for example, state managers who become private owners), not losers, represent the main political obstacle to the progress of economic reform. By blocking further reforms, these short-term winners extract rents at the expense of society at large (Hellman 1998).[3] Thus successful economic reform appears to revolve around the capacity of governments to "restrain the winners" (233), rather than, as in the past, "neutralize the losers" (Schamis 1999). Seen in this light, rather than solely disorganizing groups, reforms have also led to the empowerment of traditional elites, the formation of "distributional coalitions" (Schamis 1999) and even the establishment of "crony capitalist projects" (Snyder 1999, 200). In a nutshell, where economic reforms are framed as involving concentrated losses, the research emphasizes the disorganizing effects of market policies on social groups, such as labor; but where reforms are framed as entailing concentrated gains, the emerging literature has identified a structural pattern involving the strengthening of other actors, such as the business sector (Díaz 1997; Teichman 2001).

This winners-losers trade-off characterization of neoliberal reforms, however, disguises a richer causal story that cannot be captured by reducing the

---

2. Economic liberalization, Schamis (1999, 244) notes, "may not be enough to eliminate incentives for rent-seeking behavior; indeed, it may just as well generate new ones."

3. For an interpretation offering an alternative to Hellman's analysis, see Frye 2002.

effects of marketization to a single policy reform; a specific economic sector or social interest; or as Remmer (1998, 8) noted, "a simple collective action dilemma whose resolution depends upon state actors." While there is no denying that market reforms may have empowered some groups at the expense of others, marketization is all these things and more. These current propositions tend to overlook the complexity of market policies as well as the variable impact of different reforms on interactions between state and civil society. In a sense, prevailing views regarding the impact of market reforms ignore how capitalism, borrowing Schumpeter's (1975, 82–85) term, represents a force of "creative destruction."[4] Neoliberal reform policies can create new bases for democratic politics by strengthening or even triggering new patterns of societal organization; but they can also destroy or undermine the capacity of other societal groups through outright political exclusion or clientelism.

As market economics increasingly dominate the developing world, it becomes imperative to assess the political and societal consequences of neoliberal reform. How do market reforms affect social interests? Which societal groups are strengthened and which are weakened by neoliberal policy change? Are new sets of actors emerging? If so, what are their feedback effects on reform processes?

In this book I probe these questions for the case of Peru, which has been often held out as a prime example both of the autocratic imposition of neoliberal reforms and of the widespread disintegration of civil society and representative institutions (Cotler 1994; Tulchin and Bland 1994; Panfichi 1997). Peru experienced one of the deepest economic crises in the region in the late 1980s coupled with far-reaching social turmoil resulting from prolonged guerrilla warfare. Peruvians reacted by rejecting the entire traditional political party system and voting into office Alberto Fujimori, who was elected to the presidency in 1990 as an independent candidate and political outsider. Defying his campaign promises and bypassing majoritarian preferences, Fujimori launched an extreme variant of the economic program that is advocated by the so-called Washington consensus: a broad array of policy changes entailing, among other factors, fiscal discipline; trade liberalization; privatization of state enterprises; and a general preference for the market rather than the state in determining prices, interest rates, and capital flows (Williamson 1990). The absence of a congressional majority, however, was a critical limitation early in

---

4. More specifically, "creative destruction" denotes a "process of industrial mutation . . . that incessantly revolutionizes the economic structure from within, incessantly destroying the old one, incessantly creating a new one" (Schumpeter 1975, 82–85).

the Fujimori regime. Partly in response to this political shortcoming, on April 5, 1992, the president delivered a self-administered coup, or *autogolpe*. The autogolpe enabled Fujimori to implement major market reforms via numerous presidential decrees. In the post-autogolpe period, the president maintained a strict and disciplined congressional majority, which continued through the end of the 1990s. Certainly, the Peruvian state—especially in the early Fujimori years—demonstrated a far greater capacity for relatively autonomous decision-making than did other states in Latin America, even with respect to business.[5]

Social mobilization, in particular through unions, which was strong throughout most of the 1980s, declined considerably as a consequence of the protracted economic crisis and the ensuing political violence. The economic crisis led to massive factory layoffs, widespread unemployment, and an informalization of the workforce, all of which, in turn, severely fragmented and atomized the labor movement. Predictably, labor offered "token resistance" to Fujimori's neoliberal project as calls for general strikes to protest government policies were poorly followed by the rank and file (Roberts 1998, 264).

My findings, based on fresh evidence that extends to the end of the 1990s, reveal that some sectors of civil society in Peru have managed to influence and reshape reform policies that were originally introduced by insulated technocratic elites with limited societal input. Since the early 1990s, the implementation of some market reforms has provided incentives to adapt and form new societal organizations and to engage in collective action. Certainly, not all market reforms have generated an organized response from civil society, and some traditional forms of collective action have been weakened. The analytical puzzle, however, does not merely revolve around determining which market reforms are more prone to trigger a societal response and which sectors of civil society are more prone to react. Also critical are questions regarding how these societal responses or lack of responses affect the stability and long-term viability of market-oriented reform projects.

To the extent that some sectors of civil society have managed to contest or negotiate market policies in an unlikely setting such as Peru, where vigorous market reforms have gone hand in hand with an autocratic style of policy formation and widespread disintegration of established political parties and other societal organizations, there is every reason to assume that the same is

---

5. As noted by Manzetti (1999, 250), Fujimori, unlike other Latin American presidents, "did not ally himself with big domestic economic groups and instead dealt with them from a position of strength." In Chapter 2, I expand on this theme.

happening elsewhere. The Peruvian process of neoliberal restructuring thus has profound implications for an analysis of the political consequences of market-oriented reforms throughout Latin America.

The central thesis of this book is that neoliberal reforms induce a variety of societal responses, including the creation of new societal organizations, reflecting the variable content and asymmetrical distribution of the costs and benefits of the policies implemented. This argument builds on theoretical work in the field of public policy. While this literature helps explain how different types of policies lead to different patterns of political responses, politics can also feed back into market-reform projects, strengthening reforms in some areas but weakening or diverting them in others. In this vein, the book advances an interactive approach to capture the two-way relationship between state reformers and collective actors in civil society. Specifically, I argue that the feedback effects of societal responses on reform processes are shaped by the exigencies of the new market model, such as the fiscal health of national economies, as well as points of institutionalized access available to societal groups with which to "talk back" to the state.[6]

LOOKING AHEAD

This book is an appraisal of the Peruvian process of economic reform, focusing specifically on how societal actors respond to market policies, and the feedback effects on those responses on reform processes. It provides important challenges to the accepted wisdom about economic reform. First, existing literature focuses almost exclusively on state structure and autonomy, not social interests. The analysis shows that there are competing interests that play a fundamental role in the process of reform even within the state. Second, to the extent that attention has been paid to societal groups, studies have been narrowly confined to the response of social interests to a specific set of policies. In contrast, here I analyze a broader spectrum of reforms, which are more representative of the neoliberal project (see also Melo 2003). And finally, existing research has taught us much about policies typical of the first stages of economic reform, policies that are targeted primarily to set macroeconomic stability. I seek to improve on existing literature by examining policies charac-

---

6. The term "talk back" is taken from Conaghan (1996, 34). When institutional channels through with to "talk back" to the state are absent, Conaghan writes, "citizens are reduced to 'masses' easily manipulated by elites" (51).

teristic of later stages of neoliberal restructuring, which include attempts to revamp state institutions that facilitate sustained economic governance. Fundamentally the book is about Peru's most recent experimentation with markets and its societal consequences.

Chapter 1 presents the central argument of the book and the theoretical framework that informs it. I outline the changes that occur as market reforms shift from initial to later stages and explain the pivotal importance of state reform for the long-term sustainability of market reform projects. Although neoliberal reforms are intended to shrink the state, the state still has a crucial role in providing and enforcing the regulations and policies for societies and markets to function (World Bank 1997; Heredia and Schneider 2003), including "safety nets" to protect the most vulnerable sectors of society (Graham 1998).

Chapter 2 provides a historical narrative of the Peruvian process of economic reform. There I explore the various political and economic factors that led to the election of Alberto Fujimori and the introduction of neoliberal reforms. In this chapter I also analyze the process of state reform, which has been central to the success of the market-oriented policies currently in place. To advance market reforms, Fujimori enlisted the support of three important sets of actors, or "policy carriers" (Silva 1993, 529): technocrats, who dwelled in international lending circles and had close ties to members of the private sector; the business elite, representing primarily the export and financial sectors; and personal loyalists, who were connected with Fujimori through personal, familial, or social ties. Among the personal loyalists, some were interested in promoting technocratic policy management (technocratic loyalists), while others were primarily concerned with advancing party politics (populist loyalists). As is documented in this chapter, each of these groups dominated different phases of economic reform, and while all of them were instrumental to the Fujimori regime, the relative importance of each waxed and waned according to the electoral calendar and the progress of the market agenda.

In Chapters 3 to 5, I analyze and compare three sets of important policy reforms with widely varying impacts on civil society. Chapter 3 focuses on tax reform; Chapter 4 examines pension privatization; and Chapter 5 explores social-sector reforms, contrasting targeted poverty alleviation with health decentralization. The three chapters trace the implementation of the reforms from their initiation to the early 2000s and analyze their effect on the behavior of collective actors in civil society. The focus is on state reform because of its pivotal importance to the broader sustainability of the neoliberal reform project. As similar policy initiatives have become key components of reform packages all over Latin America (Graham and Naím 1998), the theoretical significance of their impact on Peru has broad implications. Where appropriate, each of these in-depth case studies offers a comparative perspective of similar reform processes and policy outcomes in other Latin American countries.

Chapters 2 through 5 are based largely on primary sources, including interviews with dozens of policy makers as well as with societal actors central to the reforms. Changes in policies implied the inclusion of societal demands in the planned reforms, and these changes were assessed by comparing the original and final design of reforms. The changes were confirmed with interviews, journalistic accounts, and leading sources concerning the scope of economic reforms undertaken by Fujimori.

In the final chapter I reexamine the distinctive societal impact of neoliberal reform and extend the framework advanced in this book to other policy reforms. I analyze the prospects for the sustainability of market reforms following the collapse of the Fujimori regime and suggest how democratic institutions can contribute to the deepening of economic reforms throughout Latin America. While the Peruvian economy has performed comparatively well vis-à-vis other countries, corruption and adjustment fatigue began to appear particularly during the last years of Fujimori's second presidential term. Despite these shortcomings, the analysis points to a cautiously optimistic prognosis for the Peruvian process of economic restructuring.

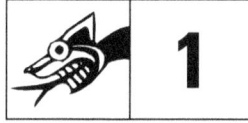

RETHINKING THE CONSEQUENCES OF NEOLIBERAL POLICY REFORM

The political and social consequences of neoliberal policy reform have remained largely undertheorized. In fact, while authors of cross-regional studies have pointed out that societal groups fail to account for the initiation or lack thereof of market-oriented reforms (Geddes 1995), research on how groups are strengthened, weakened, or even created by neoliberal policy change is still limited. Existing scholarship has also dealt extensively with the role played by political leaders and technocratic elites during market restructuring, while, surprisingly, devoting little attention to social interests, much less treating the possibility that collective actors in civil society may choose to support, oppose, or modify the boundaries of reform policies that are already in place.

In the first section of this book I outline extant propositions regarding the impact of economic reforms on social interests and their limitations. The second section is where I develop the central argument of the book, which revolves around the ways in which different types of policies induce different patterns of political responses and around the feedback effects of those responses on reform process. The final section of this chapter justifies the selection of cases and provides an overview of the three sets of market policy reforms central to this book, which collectively illustrate the variable impact of neoliberal reform on different sectors of civil society.

FROM CAUSES TO CONSEQUENCES

Scholars initially emphasized the destructive sociopolitical consequences resulting from marketization. The early literature suggested that most, if not all, neoliberal reforms were executed in a top-down fashion with little input from legislative bodies, civil society, or other sets of actors. Reform was consequently seen as undermining democratic accountability as well as decision-making processes (Przeworski 1993). A related line of arguments suggested that neoliberal reform threatened the organizational bases of representative institutions and large-scale secondary organizations, particularly political parties and labor unions (Zermeño 1989). As suggested by Roberts (1998, 270), "The globalized, neoliberal variant of capitalism . . . is both a product and an accelerator of the fragmentation and weakening of popular collective subjects, the labor movement in particular."[1] Reform is thus seen as contributing to "low intensity citizenship," a phrase that O'Donnell (1994) and others have used to characterize many emerging democracies (Oxhorn and Starr 1999; Smith and Korzeniewicz 1997; Kurtz 2001). In many ways, the presumed disintegration of traditional actors is associated with the retreat of "corporatist citizenship regimes," which became the primary mode of interest intermediation between state and society prior to marketization (Yashar 1999).

Recent literature, however, has adopted a more nuanced position that looks at how new, more autonomous, pluralistic forms of organization emerge to respond to and shape the process of economic reform. Chalmers, Martin, and Piester (1997, 567, 571), for instance, suggest that societal recomposition is taking place in the form of "associative networks," which they define as "nonhierarchical structures formed through decisions by multiple actors who come together to shape public policy." These networks, among other things, "(a) relate diverse types of organizations and people, (b) frequently change in response to new situations, (c) generally privilege cognitive politics and (d) rarely exhibit a sharp hierarchical form." Administrative and political decentralization to subnational units is one of the main forces contributing to the emergence of these "associative networks." Along these lines, Yashar (1999, 86) notes that decentralization programs "have devolved varying degrees of power to more local units . . . and, in turn, have created a more localized space for agglomerating individual preferences, calculating decisions, and implementing programs." Recent studies thus redirect our attention to the emergence of new forms of interest intermediation, while at the same time old corporatist structures of representation appear to decline (Hagopian 2000). In all, the prevailing neoliberal discourse, and decentralization initiatives in particular, as

---

1. For a discussion of labor during economic reform, see Murillo 2001; and Levitsky and Way 1998.

Yashar (1999, 86) notes, have led to the creation of "neoliberal citizenship regimes," rendering democratic politics increasingly "more liberal and more local."

With the rise of "neoliberal citizenship regimes," and following recent contributions by Snyder (1999) and others, the analysis presented here brings social interests back into the analysis of market transitions. It examines the variety of ways in which social actors may respond to economic restructuring as well as the potential for the emergence of new patterns of societal organization or "associative networks" in response to policy reform. This line of analysis contrasts with much of the early discussion regarding the imposition of neoliberal reforms and the pervasive social atomization resulting from marketization, which placed societal actors in the role of "passive recipients" of state initiatives, incapable of contesting or modifying the implementation of market reforms. In other words, while recent literature suggests a shift toward more pluralistic and local forms of interest organization, it still remains unclear how and where to expect an organized response to marketization, much less the impact of such responses on reform processes.

Prevailing propositions on the consequences of reform also tend to overlook the complexity of market policies as well as the variable impact of different reforms on interactions between state and civil society. As suggested by Remmer (1998, 7), "Market-oriented reform involves a multi-dimensional and, potentially, not fully coherent process of policy change." Undoubtedly, different sets of policy reforms impose different patterns of costs and benefits on different sectors of civil society. The incidence of costs and benefits of a reform policy, in turn, may be expected to shape the incentives to adapt or form new societal organizations and to engage in collective action. Seen in this light, existing generalizations about the winners and losers of reform suffer from a whole-reform bias, treating marketization as a single entity rather than a package of many different policies.

Finally, prior efforts to theorize about the political consequences of market reforms have been limited by their tendency to look primarily at reform policies that take place during the initial stage of neoliberal restructuring, which are intended primarily to set macroeconomic stability. The emphasis placed on the early stages of policy reform is problematic because important changes occur as market reforms shift from initial to later stages. Broadly speaking, macroeconomic-stabilization policies targeted at reducing fiscal deficits and controlling inflation define the initial stage of neoliberal restructuring. Such policies take place largely in an insulated policy-making environment, providing state and technocratic elites with substantial autonomy from societal groups. Stabilization policies are easier to execute, and their results are often immediate. In contrast, later stages of neoliberal restructuring—dubbed "second-generation" reforms—entail the strengthening of a state's organizational resources via the construction of new and more effective state institutions, such as independent central banks, regulatory commissions, extractive institutions, and compensatory organizations. The politics during this later stage of reform are more complex and less predictable than those of the initial stage. Among other things, later reforms are more difficult to implement, take much longer to achieve results, involve a broader array of actors, and require the cooperation of a wider range of societal groups (Naím 1995; Graham and Naím 1998; Pastor and Wise 1999). Thus, while initial reforms were perceived to disarticulate collective actors, "second-generation" reforms may spawn new ways of organizing and mobilizing civil society.

The distribution of the costs and benefits of market reform policies changes significantly as the process of reform moves onward. During the initial stage, it is difficult to identify clear winners and losers, given that the burdens of macroeconomic stabilization are widely shared by most of society. In contrast, the burdens of subsequent stages involving such reform policies as state reform are largely borne by specific groups (Nelson 1999; Tulchin and Garland 2000). Thus the consequences of market-oriented reforms during later stages of neoliberal restructuring require additional analysis.

An understanding of the political consequences of marketization entails addressing two analytical issues overlooked by existing perspectives regarding the impact of neoliberal reform. The first issue speaks to the interaction that takes place between state reformers and collective actors in civil society—however localized the interaction may be—during economic restructuring. The second revolves around the complexity and potential variability of market reforms as well as their mixed societal impact. To address the first analytical issue, I will advance an interactive approach to explain how market-oriented reform policies shape the behavior of collective actors and, simultaneously, how collective actors in civil society support, oppose, or modify the boundaries of reform policies already in place. To address the second analytical issue, I disaggregate the complex concept of market-oriented reform by exploring three different sets of policy initiatives involving state reform in contemporary Peru: tax reform, privatization of social security pensions, and social-sector reforms in poverty alleviation and health decentralization.

THE SOCIETAL CONSEQUENCES OF ECONOMIC REFORM:
A THEORETICAL FRAMEWORK

Policies as Producers of Societal Responses

What, then, have been the political consequences of neoliberal reform? In what areas and under what conditions have neoliberal reforms strengthened, weakened, or even created new patterns of societal organization? Building on theoretical work in the field of public policy, I argue that different sets of policy reforms have induced very different patterns of societal responses, reflecting the variable content and asymmetrical distribution of the costs and benefits of the policies implemented.

Lowi (1964, 1972) argued that public policies may be categorized into three different types: regulatory, distributive, and redistributive. Lowi's main thesis is that "policies determine politics." In this sense, regulatory policies, such as those involving a governmental choice regarding "who will be indulged and who deprived" on the basis of some general rule, are most likely to be associated with interest-group politics. Distributive policies, particularly those allocating public resources to specific societal groups, are most likely to result in clientelistic politics. Redistributive policies that seek to distribute wealth from one group to another are most likely to lead to class-based political activity. Although the boundaries between these three categories are difficult to draw (Wilson 1973, 327–30; Greenberg et al. 1977), Lowi's framework remains a useful conceptual tool in the study of public policy.

In a similar vein, Olson (1965) and Wilson (1973, 1980) suggested that the incidence of the costs and benefits of a policy shapes the incentives to form political organizations and to engage in collective action. These incentives are likely to be strong particularly when there are high per capita costs to avoid or high per capita benefits to reap. Wilson (1980) suggests a fourfold typology in which costs and benefits may be either widely distributed or narrowly concentrated (Table 1):

a. When both costs and benefits are widely distributed, a government agency is not likely to encounter opposition from any important interest group, because its goals are settled by the support of popular majorities. This type of policy pits the general public against itself. Both costs and benefits have a low per capita value. Majoritarian politics are the likely outcome.

b. When costs are narrowly concentrated and benefits are widely distributed, a government agency is likely to encounter a dominant interest group

Table 1   Wilson's typology of policy situations

Costs of Reform	Benefits of Reform	
	Concentrated	Diffuse
Diffuse	Client Politics (c)	Majoritarian Politics (a)
	Dominant societal group favorable to reform	No important societal group continuously active
Concentrated	Interest Group Politics (d)	Entrepreneurial Politics (b)
	Two or more groups in conflict over reform	Dominant societal group hostile to reform

SOURCE: Adapted from Wilson 1989, 76–78; and Sharp 1994, 921.

hostile to its goals. This type of policy pits the general public against special interests. Costs have a high per capita value, while benefits have a low per capita value. Entrepreneurial politics are the likely outcome.

c. When costs are widely distributed and benefits are narrowly concentrated, a government agency is likely to encounter a dominant interest group favorable to its goals. This type of policy pits special interests against the general public. Costs have a low per capita value, while benefits have a high per capita value. Clientelistic politics are the likely outcome.

d. When both costs and benefits are narrowly concentrated, a government agency is likely to encounter two or more rival interest groups in conflict over its goals. This type of policy pits special interest against special interest. Both costs and benefits have a high per capita value. Interest-group politics are the likely outcome.

While Lowi's framework suggests how the content of a policy shapes the political process, Wilson's implies how the incidence of costs and benefits shapes the extent and nature of organizational activity in a policy area. Together they help explain how different types of policies lead to different patterns of societal responses.[2] While these societal responses can affect the ultimate direction of the reform process, weakening or diverting reforms in

2. Among others, some examples of the broad use of Wilson's typology include those by Sharp (1994), who studies the dynamics of issue expansion and public opinion; Baron (1994), who investigates electoral competition and campaign contributions in the United States; and Schneider and Ingram (1993), who study the social construction of target populations and its effects on public policy. Pierson (1993) has criticized the works of Lowi and Wilson for being "extremely parsimonious." In Pierson's view, first, individual policies are likely to have not just one outcome, but rather a multiplicity of consequences; and second, the impact of policies is likely to occur in interaction with other variables. In this book, I address these shortcomings by tracing the evolution of these policies since their implementation.

some areas but strengthening them in others, the feedback effects of these societal responses on reform processes are generally constrained by the exigencies of the new market model, among them the fiscal health of national treasuries, as well as points of institutionalized access that are available to societal groups so they may "talk back" to the state.

Feedback Effects on Reform Processes

Discussing the importance of a state's fiscal health, Teichman (2001, 215) notes: "Once having made the transformation from statism to a greater reliance on the market, the logic of the new economic arrangements mightily constrains policy choice." In the neoliberal era, in fact, the pursuit of fiscal discipline has "locked in" (Kaufman 1999, 357) the course the government can take with respect to tax policy. Macroeconomic equilibrium implies that state actors are limited in the extent to which they can finance or increase government spending. Broadly stated, market restructuring has constrained the capacity of societal actors to modify policy reforms as well as the capacity of state actors to accommodate societal demands.[3] These fiscal (or budget) constraints potentially can dissipate as countries move from crisis situations to periods of economic recovery and stability.

More important, under the new economic model, control over some basic macroeconomic policies has become increasingly centralized under executive authority. Governments have empowered central banks and insulated finance ministries as well as other important state agencies (Maxfield 1997; Boylan 2001). This type of centralization was perhaps more acute in Peru than in any other country in Latin America, particularly during the regime of Alberto Fujimori. In Peru, for instance, the ministry responsible for managing the economy—the Economics and Finance Ministry (hereafter Finance Ministry)—regulated taxation and social security policies alike. In contrast, the president had almost exclusive control over poverty-alleviation efforts and health administration. These policies were thus centrally administered.

In addition, during the Fujimori regime, potential points of access for policy negotiation or influence, including the Congress and the judiciary, were eliminated or increasingly marginalized (Conaghan 1996). As many scholars

---

3. Research on countries of the Organization for Economic Cooperation and Development (OECD) has noted that the fiscal health of national economies continues to limit the range of options pursued by policy makers in their attempts to modify existing tax structures. For further discussion, see Swank 1998.

have noted, the 1992 autogolpe allowed Fujimori to redesign the nation's democratic institutions, strengthening the power of the presidency and thus limiting institutional checks and balances.[4] While some sectors of society were hurt by the lack of representative forums for influencing policy, others, particularly the business elite, were able to reap substantial benefits by negotiating directly with line ministries, in particular the Finance Ministry. In fact, business groups, as Lindblom (1977) noted, are likely to occupy a "privileged position" in capitalist democracies given their financial resources and capacity to determine economic performance. Moreover, the business elite tends to be more organized than any other sector of society. By these means, prior organizational efforts on the part of social actors positively affect the process of contesting or modifying the boundaries of decree-driven policy reforms.

Given this backdrop of centralized executive authority and limited institutional channels for policy influence, state actors still require the cooperation of groups within and outside the state to implement policy change. As Silva (1993, 529) notes, "[S]tate structure cannot explain the content of policy"; rather, policy necessitates "carriers." As is elaborated in Chapter 2 in this volume, these "policy carriers" became the interlocutors for the transfer of societal preferences.[5] Further, by occupying different positions within the cabinet, where much of policy discussion took place, they helped strengthen reforms in some areas, while diluting them in others.

The set of policy initiatives addressed below illustrates the variable impact of neoliberal reform on civil society (Table 2). In essence, reform policies involving narrowly concentrated costs (for example, taxation) and benefits (such as pension privatization) provided incentives to adapt or form new societal organizations and to engage in collective action. The opposite is true for reform policies involving widely distributed costs and benefits (for instance, poverty alleviation). In the former case, collective actors in civil society have managed to reshape the boundaries of reform policies that were initially implemented in a nonconsultative fashion. In the latter case the state, as opposed to collective actors in civil society, has determined the final fate of the reform process. This arrangement holds true also for policies involving concentrated

4. Explaining welfare retrenchment, Huber and Stephens (2001, 23) write: "A dispersion of political power enables potential losers to mobilize opposition and effectively resist cuts, whereas a concentration of political power enables governments to implement cutbacks despite widespread political opposition." The Fujimori regime could be characterized as a system with few or no veto points, thus allowing dramatic policy change.

5. Teichman (2001, 16) characterizes these interlocutors, or "conduits of policy influence," as "policy networks."

Table 2 Comparison of reform policies

Policy Reform	Policy Impact	Potential Winners	Potential Losers	Societal Response	New Organizations, Associational Activity	Policy Outcome
Tax	Concentrated costs Diffuse benefits	Unidentifiable	Formal and informal business sector	Opposition by business associations	Yes	Dilution
Pension	Diffuse costs Concentrated benefits	Business sector	Weakened formal, organized labor and pension bureaucracy	Support from the pension industry	Yes	Deepening
Poverty Alleviation	Diffuse costs Diffuse benefits	Unidentifiable	Unidentifiable	Societal indifference	No	Stop and Go
Health	Concentrated costs Concentrated benefits	Grassroots committees	Health bureaucracy	Opposition by health bureaucracy, support from grassroots committees	Yes	Partial Implementation

benefits and costs (such as health decentralization), as both potential winners and losers have incentives to organize and exercise political influence. The final section of this chapter contains a discussion of these policy reforms.

THE CASES

The three sets of market policy reforms that are the focus of this study were initiated by the Peruvian executive between 1991 and 1994, and their core objectives, which centered on the introduction of a market-friendly or market "conforming" (Swank 1998) approach to economic governance, remain in effect today. The new thinking about taxation, for instance, places greater emphasis on collection efficiency than on vertical equity. Not only in Peru, but across Latin America, marginal income tax rates and brackets have been significantly reduced, while at the same time, taxes on consumption, in particular value-added taxes, have become "the work horse" of newly reformed Latin American tax systems (Tanzi 2000). More important, whereas in the past, progressive taxation was justified in an effort to redistribute income and reduce inequality, today international lending institutions, such as the World Bank, advise nations to pursue such goals by means of better-targeted poverty-relief programs rather than through fiscal policy. The Peruvian targeted poverty-alleviation program, the National Compensation and Social Development Fund (FONCODES), is a case in point. The market orthodoxy also has been the overriding rationale behind social security privatization and health-decentralization reforms. Private-pension schemes are designed to provide citizens a "choice" in retirement plans, just as health decentralization has been promoted as a method to give consumers a "voice" in the management and delivery of services.

These reforms capture the maturation of ideas surrounding the "Washington consensus," which has guided the process of market-oriented reform across Latin America. The Fujimori government began by attempting to increase tax revenues—for this purpose, revamping the tax office—to reduce mounting fiscal deficits, and from there to sustain the stability effort. The government subsequently sought to reduce the role of the state through major privatization and deregulation programs. In terms of privatization, the reform of the social security pension system was especially critical. Private retirement accounts were seen as key elements in the development of the country's private financial market. Moreover, to address the "social question," which—as many observers correctly noted—had been largely neglected by the "Washington consensus," the Fujimori government began promoting social-sector reforms. Initially, and consistent with the neoliberal orthodoxy that advocated a "lean state," the Fujimori regime began implementing social programs to alleviate poverty. These programs were seen as essential to the long-term viability of neoliberal reforms, the consolidation of democracy, and the political survival of Fujimori—a reform-minded political outsider lacking a clear organizational base of support (Mauceri 1997; Roberts 1995). Moving away from this "reductionist" phase that had focused mostly on targeted assistance, the Fujimori government adopted a more nuanced understanding of social policy and turned to the promotion of health and education reforms. While the education reform stalled (Graham 1998, 100–105; Ortiz et al. 1999), the health reform program, including both decentralization and the introduction of competition in the provision of services, moved forward. In most respects, health and education reforms are currently viewed by international lending institutions as the foundation for sustainable economic growth (Nelson 1999; Tulchin and Garland 2000).

The present analysis focuses explicitly on state reform because of the latter's pivotal importance to the broader sustainability of the neoliberal reform project. In fact, the bulk of these policy initiatives has entailed the creation of new, better-equipped, more autonomous state agencies outside the traditional line ministries. As such, they exemplify efforts to create "islands of competence" within a state that is otherwise riddled with bureaucratic paralysis.[6] It goes without saying that each of these policies has brought about important changes in the relationship between state and civil society. Historically, Peruvians have been unaccustomed to paying taxes, because tax evasion was hardly ever prosecuted. Poverty relief was traditionally carried out through price controls and subsidies, which were biased in favor of urban and middle-class sectors of society. In addition, the state had a monopoly in the administration of social security pensions as well as health services. By dramatically augmenting tax revenues, privatizing social security pensions, decentralizing health services, and introducing a targeted program of poverty alleviation, the Fujimori reform program fundamentally altered these established patterns. As similar policy initiatives have become key components of reform packages all over Latin America (Graham and Naím 1998), the theoretical significance of their impact on Peru is revealed as having much broader implications.

6. The phrase "islands of competence" is from Geddes (1994, 23). See her (1990, 225) discussion of "pockets of efficiency" within the Brazilian state. Most observers would probably agree that autonomous bureaucratic agencies in the developing world are nonexistent or scarce (see Snyder 1999, 178).

Taking into account that the perceived distribution of the costs and benefits of a reform policy may be sufficient to trigger collective action, and that such distribution can potentially change over time, I have classified each of the policies presented below from the point of view of those who bear the costs and enjoy the benefits. More specifically, if a policy generates concentrated costs for a well-defined societal group and concentrated benefits for another societal group, it will lead to organized conflict as each group has an incentive to organize and take political action. There will not be significant political activity when policies have widely distributed costs and benefits. Finally, if a policy generates concentrated costs (benefits) to a specific, easily identifiable societal group and dispersed benefits (costs) across the general public, taking action to reduce those costs (obtain those benefits) will generate little opposition. Thus to differentiate the policies, one must consider whether a policy that provides benefits to one societal group generates opposition by another societal group, and whether a policy that imposes costs to one societal group generates support from another societal group (see Table 2).[7] Benefits and costs can be tangible as well as intangible (Wilson 1980, 366). Aside from their magnitude and distribution (incidence) across different segments of society, considerations about the fairness and unfairness of a proposed policy are particularly relevant to political action. Politically, magnitudes are captured by phrases such as "windfall profits," "tax burdens," and "unmet needs." Ultimately, the distribution of these costs and benefits produces different kinds of politics.[8]

7. This section draws on Baron (1994, 34–35), who applies Wilson's typology to a discussion of electoral competition and campaign contributions in the United States. Alternatively, in a study of welfare policies in Sweden, Anderson (2001) describes four different logics of retrenchment according to the type (diffused or concentrated) of costs and benefits and their distribution among affected groups, explaining: "The costs of retrenchment are considered to be concentrated if potential losers are represented by organized groups or they form an important voting bloc. Costs are considered to be diffuse if potential losers are not identifiable, divided into rival groups, or not organized at all. The benefits of retrenchment are considered to be concentrated if potential winners are represented by organized groups or they form an important voting bloc. Benefits are diffuse if the group of potential winners is not identifiable, divided into rival groups, or not organized at all" (1070). Anderson's framework is well suited to studying subsets of policies within a broader welfare program. Moreover, this framework presupposes a level of societal organization, including labor's mobilizing political parties, typical of advanced welfare democracies, and thus uncharacteristic of the Peruvian case. Consequently, it will be difficult to apply Anderson's framework to the cross-sectoral analysis of reforms advanced in this book.

8. Social constructions can help determine a priori the beneficiaries and losers of a proposed policy. Using Wilson's typology as an example, Schneider and Ingram (1993) discuss how welfare recipients were socially constructed as lazy or shiftless, thus facilitating top-down retrenchment policies. Similarly, in a cross-sectoral study of policy reforms in Brazil, Melo (2003, 214) writes: "Actors behave on the basis of ex ante expectations and bounded rationality, and these expectations are socially constructed." However, when policies are new or innovative, as are some of the ones

Tax Reform

Tax reform was one of the first policy initiatives introduced by President Fujimori and was viewed as critical for increasing the government's limited revenue base and restoring macroeconomic stability. The core of this reform,
which began in early 1991, was aimed at tax collection by simplifying the tax
system and restructuring the tax office. In terms of the tax system, the reform
streamlined a number of the less significant taxes and eliminated a series of
tax exemptions given to certain economic sectors. It also flattened rates and
reduced income tax rate levels. On the administrative side, there was an attempt to create a modern bureaucracy, through recruiting personnel on the
basis of merit and offering them wages comparable to those paid in the private
sector. The reform successfully restructured the existing tax agency, the National Superintendency of Tax Administration (SUNAT). The new, more autonomous tax office had its own budget, which amounted to a fixed percentage
from the revenues collected (Durand and Thorp 1998; Durand 2002b, 18–28).

At the outset, it was widely perceived that the reform would bring benefits
to all or most of society, and that all or most of society would pay. Such expectations were developed largely through the effort of the tax office to extend
taxation to those working in the informal sector, a sizeable group in the nation's economy. However, as the economic situation improved, and the tax
office succeeded in broadening the tax base, mostly by rigorously enforcing tax
laws and controlling tax evasion, the tax reform process entered a new phase
characterized by increased opposition and demands for more flexible tax enforcement—in short, a "post-reform tax [revolt]" (Durand 1994b, 13).

The tax reform sparked little organized support, and had no identifiable
winners, but there was strong organized resistance and opposition from business organizations, in both the formal and the informal sector. In theory, the
broadening of the tax base suggests that the costs of the reform would be more
widely dispersed. In practice, tax enforcement among small businesses has
been difficult to implement given their sheer number and informal status. As
a result, the burden of the tax reform fell primarily on large (formal) businesses. In fact, less than 2 percent of taxpayers' filing returns accounted for
about 80 percent of the revenues collected by the tax office (see also Arias
1995). Thus the Peruvian tax reform exemplifies a policy initiative involving

---

discussed in this book, it becomes more difficult to characterize groups as potential beneficiaries or
losers. This subject matter is beyond the scope of this manuscript.

concentrated losers and dispersed winners (see Table 2). Consequently, the reform generated intense lobbying by business groups for tax cuts and flexible tax enforcement (Durand and Thorp 1998; Durand 2002b, 28–36; Estela Benavides 2002, 83–87).

Acquiescing to business demands, the government offered a series of tax concessions and cuts, seemingly without paying attention to the costs of implementing such handouts. The bulk of these concessions materialized when the economy began to show signs of recovery. As in the case of social security reform, discussed below, these concessions were facilitated by the Finance Ministry, which during the 1993–98 period had been led by a business leader (Jorge Camet) and staffed by similarly business-minded advisors. The president had appointed Camet primarily as a means to court business and develop closer ties with that sector.[9] The first evidence of this process revealing the willingness of the state to accommodate business demands came in late 1996, when the government announced a broad tax amnesty and reintroduced a series of tax incentives to promote certain economic activities such as tourism, education, construction, and agribusiness. While these concessions benefited business organizations, they also resulted in a gradual loss of policy efficacy, thus diluting the efficacy of the initial reform. Government revenues as a percentage of GDP have stagnated since 1996 at 14 percent. State officials originally hoped for a tax collection equivalent to 18 percent of GDP by 1994. To this date, the tax concessions granted by the Fujimori regime have proved difficult to eliminate.[10]

Informal-sector actors also contested the policy change, albeit with an opposition that was less sporadic than that from large businesses. In 1993, when the tax office attempted for the first time to enforce tax compliance in markets selling food products, associations of market vendors responded by organizing a series of strikes and refusing service to the public.[11] The tax revolt led to the

9. The January 1993 appointment of business leader Jorge Camet to the ministry in charge of managing the economy—the Finance Ministry—is constructed as clear-cut evidence of closer government-business relations. However, it should be recognized that Fujimori's dealings with business leaders preceded the second runoff of the presidential election of 1990 (see Durand 2002a, 323). Likewise, Fujimori's first meeting with Vladimiro Montesinos, who subsequently became his chief security advisor, also took place before the 1990 runoff (Bowen and Holligan 2003, 105–7). However, as is elaborated in Chapter 2, Montesinos's power increased only in the mid-1990s as Santiago Fujimori—the president's younger brother and main advisor—withdrew from government.

10. In early 2002, the government of Alejandro Toledo sanctioned another broad tax amnesty into law. See "Desagio se aplicaría a deudas vigentes desde el año 1996," *El Comercio*, March 6, 2002.

11. "El cierra puertas de mercados fue generalizado," *El Comercio*, July 22, 1993, A12.

establishment of a simplified tax system with a fixed monthly quota, instead of a sales tax with a reduced rate, which was the intention in the original government plan to "formalize" small businesses, including market vendors. It was the concentration of market vendors in a specific location that provided them with a powerful negotiation tool in their dealings with the government. Put another way, the workplace concentration enabled market vendors to overcome their dispersion by numbers, and thus organize collective resistance.

To summarize, large business groups, which are organized and represented by the National Confederation of Private Business Organizations (CONFIEP), have been quite successful in attenuating their tax burden.[12] They have exploited their organizational coherence as well as their personal ties and easy access to state officials in order to obtain those policy changes that were most suitable to their interests (Durand 2002b, 28–36). In contrast, small businesses, mostly representing the informal sector, organized a series of tax revolts, thus spurring popular discontent with the reform process. Approximating Lowi's understanding of redistributive policies resulting in class-based political activity, tax reform has come to represent a classic conflict between "haves" and "have-nots" as larger businesses have demanded more effective taxation of smaller ones and vice versa.

The Privatization of Social Security Pensions

Peru was the second country in Latin America, after Chile, to privatize social security pensions. The reform began in December 1992, when President Fujimori decreed the creation of a private pension system of social security. The private pension system, similar to that of Chile's 1981 pension reform, was set up to supplement the insolvent pay-as-you-go regime with a capitalization system based on individual retirement accounts managed by pension fund administrators (AFPs) and regulated by a new state agency called the Superintendency of Pension Fund Administrators (SAFP). The goal of the reform was to increase national savings and to shelter workers from the bankruptcy of the state-run system by allowing them to choose their own pension fund managers from among competing pension companies.[13]

12. On CONFIEP, see Durand 1992.

13. The literature on pension reform has identified a variety of privatization outcomes. Mexico, El Salvador, and Bolivia, for instance, replicated the Chilean pension model, in which private initiative completely replaces state participation with respect to social security pensions. Argentina and Uruguay adopted mixed social security systems, wherein workers make contributions to both a public and a private scheme and receive benefits from both systems. In contrast, Peru and Colombia introduced parallel social security systems; in these countries, a private pension system was set up to compete with the traditional public system. See also World Bank 1994.

The pension reform provided benefits to an easily identifiable group (the pension industry), while spreading the costs in the form of monthly contributions over a large number of workers. While some of these workers were already unionized (thus eliminating some of the impediments to collective action), the costs arising from pension contributions were insufficient to induce workers to exercise further political influence. The social security system's state of complete disarray at the outset of the reform also gave the pension industry the upper hand in advancing privatization. First, at the time of the reform, the national pension system only took in loosely organized formal-sector workers, or about a third of the entire Peruvian labor force. Second, in the case of retired workers, the bulk of pensioners earned an average of U.S.$68 per month—equivalent to about a fifth of a monthly living wage.[14] In contrast, a group of selected state employees had better retirement plans as a result of a special pension regime that adjusted their earnings to current wages. To this date, the reform has not affected the privileges of those employees.[15] Finally, the unionized social security bureaucracy that managed the national pension system opposed the privatization effort largely because of job losses. These unions, however, were highly discredited by the public because of extended strikes and widespread corruption. To name but one example, the social security bureau employed forty-five thousand workers, a figure that represented an almost 100 percent increase over the number of workers employed by the state agency five years before the reform. In summary, at the time of the reform most active workers were eager to opt out of the bankruptcy of the state-run pension system, the bulk of pensioners protested their meager pensions, and the social security bureaucracy feared job cuts. As one would expect, these societal actors failed to coalesce into a broader coalition capable of preventing the privatization process from taking place.

The dual pension system initially established by the social security reform provided strong incentives for workers to stay in the public system, which limited the prospects for the AFPs. As a consequence, business leaders with a stake in the new pension system, mostly investors from the banking and insurance sectors, chartered a new business organization called the Association of Pension Fund Administrators (AAFP), which was quickly incorporated into the ranks of CONFIEP.

---

14. IPE 1997b.
15. See "Vive la cédula viva," *Perú Económico*, May 1997, 4–5.

Acquiescing to the AAFP's demands, in July 1995, the government leveled the playing field, by equalizing workers' contribution rates in both pension systems. By 1997, the balance had shifted even further in favor of the private scheme. The passing of favorable legislation revealed the political might of the AAFP in contrast to that of the loosely organized formal-sector workers. The potential winners of the reform were thus better organized than the potential losers (see Table 2).[16] In short, the pension reform led to the creation of a new "stakeholder" (Graham 1998), an association of AFPs (AAFP), which has successfully lobbied for the deepening of the reform process.

The Peruvian private pension system, however, is one of the few reformed Latin American pension systems that does not offer a minimum-pension guarantee to its affiliates. In other countries, the government guarantees a minimum pension, which is only paid if funds in the worker's retirement account are insufficient to pay the minimum-pension level at retirement. During the Fujimori regime, the AAFP repeatedly pointed out that the minimum-pension guarantee was the only remaining incentive that could prompt a significant number of workers to shift to the private pension system, yet the government delayed the implementation of such a policy. The business sector insisted that the government was ultimately responsible for the minimum pension, but government officials remained unconvinced. In essence, the overall policy trajectory followed by the pension reform has been characteristic of other policies, in that business leaders have continued to exert pressure on government to change policies further.

SOCIAL-SECTOR REFORMS

Targeted Poverty Alleviation

In accordance with the growing consensus regarding the need for neoliberal reforms to incorporate poverty-relief dimensions, the Fujimori government created another new state agency called FONCODES in mid-1991.[17] FONCODES

16. In addition, while pensioners and private-pension companies anticipated benefits, those of the companies were substantially bigger, more visible, and more rapidly realized than those of the pensioners.

17. Targeted poverty-relief programs were not initially considered among the set of policies advocated by the so-called Washington consensus, but increasingly came to be seen as a vital adjunct to the market reform policy agenda (see Edwards 1995, 59).

simulated the demand-driven mechanism of other poverty-alleviation programs in Latin America, such as Bolivia's Emergency Social Fund, whereby
base-level community organizations, or *nucleos*, design and implement projects they think are best suited to their local needs.

Although FONCODES has successfully directed funds to the poorest Peruvian
districts, it provided little incentive for nucleos to remain organized beyond
the completion of the small projects themselves. In fact, most base-level community organizations that participated in the program tended to be project
specific, that is, they did not engage in a sequence of repeated projects. On
average, these organizations lasted approximately four months, which amounts
to the period required for the execution of the projects. The absence of enduring organizations or stakeholders suggests that the impact of FONCODES on civil
society has been mostly direct, immediate, short term, and highly contingent
on a constant flow of relief funds, indicating that across time the benefits of
the projects were widely dispersed.

While FONCODES was set up as a separate state agency outside the traditional line ministries, it never took over the universe of social-assistance programs funded by the central government. Quite to the contrary, as is
elaborated in Chapter 5, conflicts between FONCODES and the Ministry of the
Presidency, which directed other social-sector programs, were frequent. Thus
the creation of FONCODES did not impose visible costs upon an easily identifiable group of the public-sector bureaucracy. Consequently, the costs of the
program would be widely dispersed and born by society at large in the form of
privatization revenues or by international donors, most notably the World
Bank and the Inter-American Development Bank (IDB). This pattern of unidentifiable winners and losers has yielded very little in terms of collective
action or policy feedback. Given the absence of an organized response from
civil society either in favor of or in opposition to the program, state actors have
been able to utilize the program mostly to their own advantage, molding the
program according to the electoral needs of the executive authority (see Table
2). The boom-and-bust cycle of relief funds surrounding elections speaks to
this process (Graham and Kane 1998; Schady 2000). Not surprisingly, by the
end of the 1990s, the social program rapidly fell prey to Fujimori's growing
electoral machine. Such findings conform with the central theoretical expectations of this book inasmuch as the costs and benefits of the reform process
were both widely distributed among society.

Health Decentralization

To give users a voice and to improve the delivery of health services, the Fujimori government decided to decentralize the health administration in early 1994. Under the decentralization program, base-level community organizations have legal and financial responsibility for the management of health posts, most of which were originally built or rehabilitated by FONCODES. These organizations are also known as Local Committees for Health Administration (CLAS). The CLAS receive public resources to pay for existing personnel, who are in turn evaluated by CLAS members on an annual basis. The CLAS also generate their own revenues, which come from fees paid for medications and services. These revenues, however, are not sent back to the government but instead are retained for use in the local facilities—primarily to improve the existing health services, or to contract additional personnel or hours on a private basis.

As was true for most of the reform policies implemented under Fujimori, there was no prior discussion or debate in either the Congress or the president's cabinet on the decentralization initiative. In fact, the reform began as a pilot program, but demand to create more CLAS facilities rapidly increased, and the numbers expanded from 584 health establishments in 1998 to 1,244 in 2001 (Cortez 1998; Ewig 2001, 260).[18] The idea of a pilot program appeared to imply that the government was only testing a program, while at the same time retaining the possibility of expanding it silently in the future. Moreover, in the absence of institutionalized points of access for societal actors to influence the political process, state reformers managed to control opposition to the program by maintaining a very "low profile" (Ortiz et al. 1999, 22). State reformers within the Ministry of Health, as Ewig (2001, 160) notes, were unwilling to discuss the project broadly, a reflection of their "lack of interest in democratic consensus in general" rather than of strategic political motivations.

As expected, the reform sparked strong and better-organized societal opposition from various sources. Regional health authorities opposed the CLAS reform because it reduced their bureaucratic control over substantial financial resources. Public-sector health workers—grouped in the Federation of Health Ministry Workers (FTMS)—objected to the reform because private contracts eroded their monopoly over public-sector employment. Finally, medical asso-

---

18. In 1994, the pilot program included 300 CLAS establishments (Ortiz et al. 1999, 24).

ciations and guilds opposed the reform because of its potential to "privatize [the] financial administration" of the health centers (Ewig 2001, 159). Health decentralization has thus created concentrated losses for the health bureaucracy.

Equally important, the reform took place during a time when the Peruvian Institute for Social Security (IPSS), the state agency in charge of managing the national health-care system, had already undergone a substantial reorganization process that, in turn, helped improve its overall performance. In fact, approval of the IPSS increased from a dismal 17 percent in March 1989 to 51 percent in September 1993, and later to 60 percent in September 1994.[19] To be sure, the timing of the CLAS reform was strikingly different from that in which state actors began privatizing the national pension system. In other words, the improved public perception of the postcrisis IPSS led indirectly to greater credibility for social actors who opposed the CLAS initiative, in particular, and the health reform in general.

Unlike the FONCODES experience, however, the CLAS program created incentives for local committees to remain organized in part because the administration of health posts is permanent. Stated otherwise, the CLAS initiative provided benefits that mobilized a well-defined societal group, which survived beyond the initial start of the program. Therefore, the health-decentralization process created concentrated beneficiaries, or "stakeholders," on the part of these local committees, leading to a classic interest-group conflict between health administrators who opposed the reform and grassroots organizations that supported it (see Table 2). As a consequence, the decentralization initiative placed the government in the role of arbiter. This outcome is consistent with the central theoretical expectations implicit in this book inasmuch as both the benefits and the costs of the decentralization program were concentrated on specific, easily identifiable groups. Largely in response to pressures from international lending institutions, including in the form of a structural adjustment loan from the World Bank and the IDB supporting the expansion of the CLAS program, in 1998 President Fujimori ultimately decided to speed the decentralization process, to the detriment of the health bureaucracy. To this date, however, the program

---

19. Apoyo S.A. 1991b, 2000. In both polls, the question reads: "In general, would you say that you trust or distrust the following institutions [name of institution]?"

continues to be revised in the hopes of improving its overall effectiveness. At present, there are at least fourteen hundred CLAS-type establishments, which represent less than 25 percent of total health facilities throughout the country (Altobelli 2002, 328).[20] This indicates the limited implementation of the reform as a consequence of continued opposition from the health bureaucracy.[21]

CONCLUSION

As emphasized in the preceding discussion, neoliberal reform induces a variety of societal responses, and these responses or lack of responses affect the prospects for the consolidation of the reform process. Put another way, and following recent contributions by Schamis (1999), Snyder (1999), and others, the politics of neoliberal restructuring, far from being a one-sided scheme crafted by insulated technocratic elites, involves an interactive process enacted between state reformers and collective actors in civil society. More important, while civil society in general may not initiate, or even embrace, market reforms through electoral choices, it becomes a critical actor as the process of reform moves onward.

Further, only by disaggregating the complex concept of market reform can we begin to discuss its impact on social interests and on implications for democratic politics. Market reforms have a highly differentiated effect on civil society. Policy initiatives, such as the tax and pension reforms, appear to have strengthened and unified elite sectors of society, particularly large-business organizations. With their abundant financial resources, sophisticated lobbies, and social ties with state actors and technocratic elites, these organizations have had some clear advantages in influencing policy making. In contrast, small-business organizations, primarily representing the informal sector, have

20. Telephone interview by the author with Laura Altobelli, a World Bank official in Lima, Janaury 13, 2003. Cortez (1998, 68) notes that "the [CLAS] does not represent a global alternative of decentralization for health services" (all translations from the Spanish are mine). Arroyo (2000, 34) also characterizes the CLAS initiative as a "partial" reform effort. As such, the CLAS initiative is probably not representative of the entire health reform process that has been taking place in Peru since the mid-1990s (see Ewig 2000).

21. The tax reform is said to be diluted because its stated reform goals were initially implemented but these goals were subsequently rolled back as a consequence of societal opposition, including corruption (see Chapter 3). In contrast, the CLAS initiative is said to be partially implemented because its stated reform goals were implemented gradually and remained in effect despite the presence of organized resistance (see Chapter 5).

turned to less sophisticated methods to raise their societal demands, such as tax revolts. Even an authoritarian government such as the Fujimori regime was forced to alter the original tax reform plan in response to the organized resistance of market vendors. When collective actors organize, however, the process of contesting or modifying decree-driven policy reforms ultimately depends on the receptiveness of state actors. In the Peruvian case, for instance, the government implemented the pension reform in a piecemeal fashion even in the absence of any strong opposition and in the presence of strong business support. The lack of a minimum-pension guarantee attests to this process. The business elite, no matter how well represented or narrowly focused on profit maximization, plays an important and reactive role but does not completely dominate the overall policy-making process.

Other policy initiatives, however, notably the poverty-alleviation reform, have not necessarily helped to recompose or strengthen civil society, particularly popular sectors. Base-level community organizations have neither contested nor sought to negotiate the direction of the reform process. Nevertheless, empirical evidence shows that the relief program has been particularly receptive to local needs in districts with greater human capital resources and more developed communities (Alcázar and Wachtenheim 2001). In contrast, program administrators have played a more critical role in remote and isolated districts by determining which projects receive funding. Thus, even where the distribution of costs and benefits of reforms creates comparatively weak incentives to contest or modify policy reforms, neoliberal reform continues to have a mixed impact across popular sectors of civil society.

Health reform has entailed an entirely different pattern involving the creation of local committees to manage primary-health-care centers as part of a broader health-decentralization effort by the national government. The losers in this instance were state actors, whose influence over health policy was diluted, while the winners were societal actors at the grassroots level.

Insofar as some sectors of society have managed to shape market reform policies in an unlikely setting such as Peru, where neoliberal reforms have been implemented by top-down executive fiat, backed by heavy-handed and authoritarian assertions of power, there are reasons to anticipate that market reforms have had similar effects elsewhere. Overall, the variable effects of reform in Peru indicate problems of generalizing about the political consequences of market reforms.

A closer look at Fujimorismo reveals the influence of a broader set of interests from actors on which elites generally relied for support. With ample military backing, as elaborated in Chapter 2, Fujimori drew on the support from three different groups, or "policy carriers" (Silva 1993, 529): technocrats, the business elite, and personal loyalists. These groups were instrumental in the implementation of economic reforms and dominated different stages of reform.

2

FUJIMORI AS MARKET MAKER

In May 1977, the military government of General Francisco Morales Bermúdez appointed Walter Piazza, a prominent business leader, as the minister of
finance. With inflation reaching unprecedented annual levels of 60 to 70 percent, Piazza announced an economic program that was designed to achieve
fiscal discipline, restore international creditworthiness, and redirect the Peruvian economy away from the economic populism and state interventionism of
the 1960s. Piazza's austerity measures proved highly unpopular, however, forcing the military government to delay economic reforms and call for democratic
elections in mid-1978. It took an additional thirteen years for the Peruvian government to adopt an economic-adjustment program that successfully tamed
inflation and restored growth. The delay imposed high social costs. By 1990,
Peruvians were experiencing a severe economic crisis, with annual inflation
reaching four digits, coupled with violent guerrilla activity and mounting civil
unrest.

This chapter provides a historical narrative of the Peruvian process of economic reform. The first section of the chapter traces major political and economic events prior to the election of Alberto Fujimori to the Peruvian
presidency in 1990. In the second section I examine the implementation of
market reforms in the post-1990 period in relation to the broader political context. The final section of the chapter contains an analysis of the process of state
reform under Fujimori, which has been pivotal to the success of market-
oriented policies currently in place. This analysis shows that while the initial
wave of policy reforms designed to achieve economic stabilization was crafted
mostly by insulated technocratic elites, the process of reconstructing the state
has been more consultative in nature. In their attempt to enhance tax collec-

tion, social security pension privatization, and social-sector reforms, state leaders have made efforts to enlist the support of several sets of actors, particularly the business sector.

STATE-LED GROWTH IN PERU, 1968–1990

Unlike those of many of the larger Latin American countries, the Peruvian economy remained relatively market friendly and noninterventionist until the early 1960s (Thorp and Bertram 1978; Sheahan 1999). Economic growth revolved heavily around direct foreign investment and the exportation of primary products, including fish meal, copper, and oil. The nationalistic and reformist military regime of General Juan Velasco Alvarado (1968–75), however, abruptly altered this pattern of development. In 1968, the military initiated a far-reaching process of economic and social change, decimating the export oligarchy through land redistribution to peasant organizations, expropriating foreign mining enclaves, and creating numerous state-owned enterprises. Like other governments across Latin America introducing import-substitution policies, the Velasco regime attempted to build an indigenous industrial base through protective tariffs and to reduce dependence on foreign investment by borrowing from private banks.

The military's interventionist policies led to a series of balance-of-payment crises. As a result, the International Monetary Fund (IMF) began pressuring the military to open the economy and to return to market-friendly economic policies. Yielding to international pressures, the military regime of General Morales Bermúdez (1975–79), which succeeded the government of General Velasco Alvarado, implemented an orthodox monetarist-style stabilization package in May 1978. This stabilization package, however, coincided with a period in which export prices rose to record levels and new oil deposits were discovered (Hamann and Paredes 1991, 69). This situation led to a balance-of-payments and fiscal bonanza, which in turn created the illusion that the stabilization package had worked (Webb 1991, 8). Consequently, the need to address the structural weaknesses of the economy was simply forgotten. The government's revenue base, for example, continued to be limited as a result of generous tax exemptions and privileges. More important, the expansive role of the state in the economy was never questioned. Shortly after the stabilization package, the military stepped aside and called for a constitutional assembly to draft a new constitution.

With the new 1979 constitution in place, Peru made a peaceful transition to democratic rule, a political process that swept across Latin America during the following decade. In the 1980s, Peruvian democracy appeared to move forward. Municipal elections, for instance, were reinstated and scheduled for every three years. In an attempt to further decentralize government processes, the 1979 constitution stipulated the creation of political regions. But the military had left civilian authorities with a growing foreign debt, rising inflation, and serious underlying economic frailties, all of which made the democratic transition difficult. Like the military, as Wise (1994, 83) points out, the democratic governments of the 1980s would "go to any extreme in order to avoid adjustment." They sought new foreign loans, printed money, and "burned up" international reserves, in a series of "evasive" strategies that in the end exacerbated the economic crisis (Webb 1991).

The democratic transition began in July 1980, when Peruvians reelected former president Fernando Belaúnde. Belaúnde, who had been deposed by the military in 1968, was the leader and founder of Popular Action (AP), a center-right political party established in 1956. Belaúnde opted for market-oriented policies, but his economic program was fraught with many inconsistencies. As Hamann and Paredes (1991, 41) indicate, "speeches [by government officials] emphasized the need to reduce inflation, liberalize price controls, and increase the openness of the economy; in practice the authorities began an expansive fiscal policy and a passive (or accommodating) monetary policy." In addition, anticipating conflicts with the military, President Belaúnde was reluctant to sell off the vast number of state companies created by the military during the 1970s. Nevertheless, the biggest inconsistency was the government's decision to discontinue the trade liberalization program because of strong pressure from organized industrialists (Pastor 1992, 113; Conaghan and Malloy 1994, 174–76). Belaúnde's commitment to market or neoliberal principles was highly instrumental rather than ideological (Conaghan, Malloy, and Abugattás 1990, 16). The president had an ambitious plan for the construction of numerous public works, such as dams and housing projects, which required a steady flow of credits from foreign lenders. Pedro-Pablo Kuczynski (1977, 27), a manager from the Central Bank during the first Belaúnde administration (1963–68), described the then president as a "builder" of public-work projects who paid no more than lip service to the fiscal constraints of public investments.

In mid-1983, however, economic conditions dramatically worsened because of a severe reoccurrence of El Niño, which devastated a significant amount of agricultural production. The deepening regional debt crisis further aggravated the economic situation as foreign commercial banks began to cut trade loans and refuse new lending. The debt crisis fueled a new set of emergency economic measures—basically another stabilization package but without structural reforms—none of which were successful in reducing inflation. GDP fell by 12 percent in 1983 and inflation reached three digits (125 percent) for the first time in the century (Figs. 1 and 2). Peruvians ultimately associated their worsening living standards with the president's "neoliberal" policies, although even in dealings with the international banking community Belaúnde's administration was anything but orthodox (Webb 1994).

The emergence of the Shining Path (Sendero Luminoso), a Maoist guerrilla group, which initiated violent incursions in the Peruvian central highlands in the early 1980s, presented Belaúnde with a second major policy dilemma. The president realized that in order to protect the lives of Peruvians, he would have to turn control of some regions over to the military, which would suspend some basic constitutional rights and liberties (Cornell and Roberts 1990). Aware of this consequence, Belaúnde was hesitant to call for a military solution to halt political violence. This situation changed once key cabinet members, including the minister of finance, Manuel Ulloa, resigned because of the lack of a counterinsurgency strategy (Webb 1994, 366). The president never gained control over the insurgency problem.

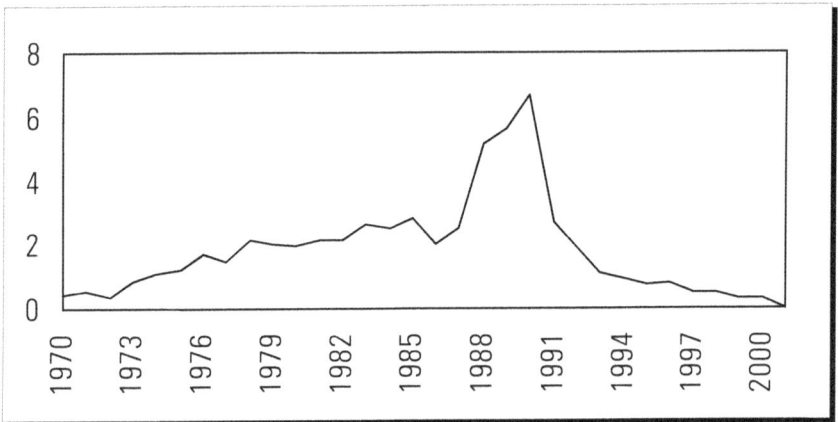

Fig. 1   Inflation, 1970–2001

SOURCE: INEI, *Compendio Estadístico* (various years)

NOTE: Annual inflation values were logged

Fig. 2   GDP growth, 1970–2001

SOURCE: INEI, *Compendio Estadístico* (various years)

In 1985, Peruvians elected Alan García, a charismatic leader who capital-ized on the failure of the Belaúnde administration. García brought new vigor to the American Popular Revolutionary Alliance (APRA), an old mass-based political party founded in 1930. García quickly reversed Belaúnde's market-oriented economic policies and launched a series of expansionary fiscal poli-cies involving greater state intervention as well as price controls to reduce inflation. García also decided to reduce foreign debt service to no more than 10 percent of export earnings, thus isolating the Peruvian economy from the international lending community. Between 1986 and early 1987, the Peruvian economy experienced a short-lived period of growth, but the economic experi-ment—dubbed "heterodox"—ultimately led to a hyperinflationary crisis, with annual inflation reaching yet another historical record in 1990 (7,649 percent). Between 1988 and 1990, GDP dropped about 25 percent (also see Figs. 1 and 2).

Political violence intensified under García, who sought a peaceful settle-ment with the Shining Path (Fig. 3). Attempting to address the presumed un-derlying causes of this violence, García advanced a set of economic policies, hoping to stimulate private investment in the areas most affected by poverty. He also charged the military with human rights violations against guerrilla activists, which created hostility in some segments of the armed forces (Mc-Clintock 1998, 143).

In response to García's economic policies and mounting civil unrest, the

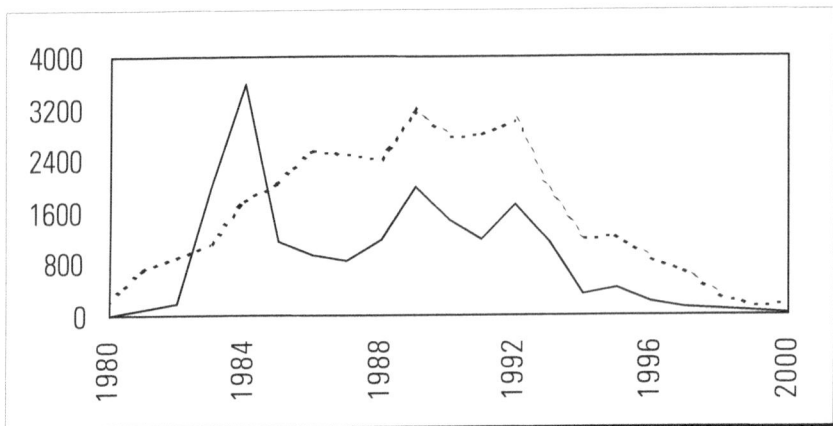

Fig. 3   Political violence, 1980–2000

`- - - - - -` Terrorist activities   ———— Number of deaths

SOURCE: INEI, *Compendio Estadístico* (various years)

business sector became increasingly antagonistic toward the government.[1] A critical turning point was the president's decision to nationalize the private banking system in mid-1987. The expropriation of banks brought greater unity to CONFIEP, the business umbrella association created in 1984 (Durand 1992). According to Durand (1999), the volatile, pendular economic policies of the 1980s spelled great uncertainty for business leaders, who for the most part took a reactive stance.

To summarize, the management of the Peruvian economy over the course of the period 1968–90 was associated with limited economic growth and mounting macroeconomic disequilibria (Kuczynski 1977; Sheahan 1999; Wise 2003). Debt payments went into arrears, the fiscal deficit rose dramatically, and inflation skyrocketed. Interestingly, these problems were associated with a steady decline of government revenues as opposed to an increase in public spending (Pastor 1992, 123). The shrinkage of government revenues is also symptomatic of a more general weakening of the Peruvian state, which gradually became fiscally incapable of providing basic services, such as police protection and social welfare. Neither Belaúnde nor García was willing to assume the political costs associated with economic reform. Thus, the protracted economic and political crises inevitably took a toll on the traditional political party system of the 1980s.

---

1. The business sector originally supported President García largely because the previous president, Belaúnde (1980–85), had left the economy in a deep recession.

Mayoral races are indicative of the widespread disintegration of the traditional political party system. During the 1980s, for example, Lima's mayoral
race had been highly contested by several political parties, including leftist
coalitions (Roberts 1996). In 1989, however, Limeños elected Ricardo Belmont,
a television producer with no political background, as mayor of the city. Belmont's election revealed that Peruvians had grown weary of politicians and
traditional political parties. Public-approval ratings for political parties were
and remain the lowest compared with those of any other civil society organization or state agency: 13 percent in September 1991, 11 percent in September
1993, 14 percent in September 1997, and 18 percent in September 2000.[2] This
trend was also reflected in the 1990 presidential election.

MARKET REFORMS UNDER FUJIMORI

In 1990, Peruvians elected Alberto Fujimori, an independent candidate and
political outsider, to the presidency.[3] In a runoff election, Fujimori defeated
novelist Mario Vargas Llosa, who had made a political alliance with two traditional parties, AP and PPC (Popular Christian Party), and was endorsed by the
business association CONFIEP. Upper- and middle-class sectors of society voted
disproportionately in favor of the writer (Cameron 1994, 141). Fujimori, in contrast, drew his electoral support largely from the poor.

Fujimori initially proposed a gradual program of economic adjustment, but
once elected turned to a classic program of neoliberal orthodoxy in accordance
with the so-called Washington consensus. As a political outsider, Fujimori had
great advantages in pushing for stabilization and structural adjustment programs, but unlike his predecessors Belaúnde and García, he did not have majority support in the Congress, which was a critical limitation early on in his
administration.

On April 5, 1992, President Fujimori closed down the Congress and purged
much of the judiciary, declaring emergency rule (see Mauceri 1995). Fujimori
justified the temporary suspension of democracy—which lasted from April to
December 1992—on the basis of congressional defiance of his economic pro-

2. Apoyo S.A. 2001. In the poll, the question reads: "In general, would you say that you trust or
distrust the following institutions [name of institution]?"

3. By documenting Fujimori's ties to Alan García before the 1990 presidential election, Planas
(2000, 296–301) questions Fujimori's credentials as a true outsider or independent.

gram.[4] While the international community condemned the presidential coup, Peruvians applauded it. Supporters of Fujimori read the autogolpe as a necessary step to break with the past and the political demagogues of the 1980s. The autogolpe led to the election of a new Congress in which Fujimori's party obtained a majority of seats. The new Congress, known as the Democratic Constitutional Congress (CCD), crafted a new constitution that, among other things, provided the legal framework for a market economy and enabled Fujimori to run for reelection. The new constitution was narrowly approved by popular referendum in late 1993.

Fujimori had managed to advance substantial market restructuring even prior to the autogolpe. According to Carlos Boloña, Fujimori's second minister of finance, the structural reforms were introduced in three great waves of presidential decrees. The first wave began in early 1991 and consisted of sixty-one presidential decrees, which encompassed policies that reduced tariffs and tariff-like barriers, liberalized exchange and labor markets, eliminated public monopolies, and stipulated the privatization of eighty public companies. The second wave began in May 1991 and lasted until November that same year. It involved 117 decrees, which enabled the executive to legislate in matters related to peacekeeping and the promotion of investment and employment. The third wave of structural reforms coincided with the timing of the presidential coup and consisted of 745 decrees. Some of these decrees involved laws to restore constitutional guarantees as well as policies affecting the commercial, public, productive, and social sectors (Boloña 1996, 186).

The autogolpe had major economic and political ramifications. Economically, it facilitated the implementation of market reforms that were initially opposed by important actors, even within the state. Otherwise stated, it provided technocrats the political space in which to consolidate the ongoing process of market restructuring. Prior to the autogolpe, for instance, the Fujimori administration drew up a list of 80 companies to be privatized, but was forced to reduce the original list to 23 because of opposition from cabinet members (Boloña 1996, 186). By the end of 1996, the government had privatized more than 130 companies.[5] Likewise, policy reforms that initially appeared to be extreme were easily carried out after the autogolpe. The third wave of presi-

---

4. As Kenney (2004, 226) writes, "The April 1992 coup was not carried out primarily to implement austerity measures, but some justified the coup as a means of keeping structural reforms from being reversed." The Peruvian Congress was also seen as obstructive in controlling political violence (Obando 1998).

5. BCRP 1996.

dential decrees, for instance, stipulated the privatization of social security pensions. Along with promoting social security pension reform, the government allowed for the operation of a private health insurance system as a counterpart to the traditional state-run public system.[6] In 1995, the government passed a new law that lifted restrictions on private ownership of land, effectively reversing the military-sponsored land reform of the 1970s.[7]

In addition to facilitating economic stabilization and adjustment, the autogolpe enabled Fujimori to reengineer the nation's democratic institutions by strengthening the power of the presidency and thus limiting institutional checks and balances. The legislative branch, for instance, which was originally set up as a bicameral institution involving 240 representatives, was reduced to a single representative chamber of 120 members. Moreover, because a single national electoral district was established for the entire unicameral Congress, the traditional party system further collapsed into a myriad of new independent movements, and the strength of regional political constituencies was seriously undermined.[8] While other Latin American presidents have also sought to strengthen executive authority in pursuit of a program of market-oriented reform (Teichman 2001), Fujimori, as Manzetti (2003, 318) put it, "made a mockery of the democratic process."

The president also asserted government control over the judiciary by politicizing the appointment of judges. Fujimori's counterinsurgency strategy is illustrative. The president dealt with the Shining Path forcefully, militarizing the counterinsurgency effort to a far greater degree than had previous administrations. Fujimori's strategy of "select repression" led to a series of human rights violations on the part of the military (Obando 1998, 406). The politicization of the judiciary, however, brought impunity to military officers charged with crimes in the fight against guerrilla groups (Cameron 1998).

While legislation via presidential decrees was customary throughout the 1980s, it was the Congress that was most altered by the autogolpe. Under Belaúnde and García, the Congress was an institution capable of contesting government policies. Furthermore, throughout the 1980s, discrepancies among members of Belaúnde and García's parties were common. Such differences

---

6. Known as health promotion entities (EPSs), the private companies offering such insurance provide health plans and compete for the enrollment of users. Regulated by Law 26790, three EPSs (Rímac International, Santa Cruz, and Novasalud) began operations in 1998.

7. BCRP 1995.

8. In the 1980s, a single national district had been used for the election of one legislative chamber—the Senate.

not only may explain the eventual derailment of market policies, particularly during Belaúnde's tenure; more important, they suggest that Congress was at least somewhat responsive to popular pressures. In contrast, under Fujimori, the Congress became increasingly muted. In fact, Fujimori was able to minimize political dissension within his own party, thus expediting congressional approval for policy initiatives drafted by the executive. This rigid discipline made the Congress more isolated and less engaged with society, allowing Fujimori's congressional majority to override any type of political opposition. As Cameron (1998, 129) notes, "The *autogolpe* created an oxymoron: a non-deliberative legislature."

The implementation of Fujimori's economic program by top-down executive fiat rapidly stopped hyperinflation and restored economic growth. In 1994, the Peruvian economy registered a record-high rate of 13 percent GDP growth. Fujimori was equally successful in controlling rampant political violence. The capture of the Shining Path's leader Abimael Guzmán in late 1992 was a turning point (see Fig. 3).[9] By early 1995, only 4 percent of the population believed that "terrorism" was the biggest problem facing the nation, that item lagging far behind unemployment, with 50 percent, and poverty, with 20 percent.[10] The president's success in restoring order was appealing to the average Peruvian citizen and the business elite, which had borne substantial losses as a result of political violence. The shared goal was the foundation of a new democracy, a "democracy with order" (Durand 1998, 274).

Given these considerations, the reelection of Fujimori in April 1995 came without surprise, and Peruvians rewarded him with a new congressional majority. As the Peruvian media would characterize it, Fujimori, the unknown university professor without a party, had defeated two of the most well known Peruvians, novelist Mario Vargas Llosa in 1990, and former United Nations secretary general Javier Perez de Cuellar in 1995.

THE PROCESS OF REFORMING THE STATE

Central to the success of market-oriented economic policies and an aggressive counterinsurgency strategy was a far-reaching reform of the state, which

9. According to the National Institute for Statistics and Information (INEI), political violence in Peru left a death toll of approximately 25,000 people. The Truth and Reconciliation Commission—an investigative committee established by the governments of Paniagua and Toledo to examine human rights violations during the two-decade-long armed conflict—gives the approximate number of deaths as 69,280. See Comisión de la Verdad y Reconciliación 2003.

10. Apoyo S.A. 1995. In the poll, the question reads: "Which major problem affecting the country do you think the next president must resolve [name of problem]?

helped restore fiscal discipline and increased the efficiency and autonomy of the state apparatus. Part of this process was carried out by the Commision for the Promotion of Private Investment (COPRI), which successfully sold numerous state enterprises (Manzetti 1999, 232–93). Complementing the privatization program, the government began a process of reconstructing the state apparatus, boosting the quality of performance of important state agencies, including the tax collection agency, SUNAT; the customs agency, the National Superintendency for Customs Administration (SUNAD); the social security bureau, the Peruvian Institute for Social Security (IPSS); and a new antipoverty program, FONCODES.[11]

This process of state reform, in comparison with "big bang" economic-stabilization measures, has been more prolonged, requiring the cooperation of a wider range of actors, both within and outside the state apparatus.[12] To push the market reform agenda forward, Fujimori enlisted the support of three important groups, or "policy carriers" (Silva 1993, 529): technocrats, who had ties with the multilateral banking community and the private business sector; the business elite organized in CONFIEP, representing primarily the export and financial sectors, often at the expense of import-competing industries; and personal loyalists, who were connected with Fujimori through personal, familial, or social ties. Among the personal loyalists, some were interested in promoting technocratic policy management (technocratic loyalists), while others were primarily concerned with advancing party politics (populist loyalists). As discussed below, each of these groups had a distinct "policy repertoire." Policy repertoires are defined as "coherent frameworks of beliefs, values, and ideas" and "include conceptions about the proper role for government and the appropriate means of government intervention" (Snyder 1999, 181). Each of these groups occupied different positions within the cabinet, where much of policy discussion took place. They dominated different phases of economic reform, and while all of them were instrumental in the Fujimori regime, the relative importance of each shifted according to the electoral calendar and the progress of the market agenda. Moreover, when differences between these groups appeared irreconcilable, Fujimori was prone to endorse the views of one group to the detriment of the others. As the chief of economic advisors Fritz Du Bois put it, "Our job was to design reform proposals . . . when certain reform pro-

---

11. With the reform that created the EPS program, the IPSS was subsequently renamed ESSALUD (Peruvian Institute for Social Insurance in Health). See note 6, above.

12. This section draws on Arce 2003b.

posals were not approved or executed, it was because we failed to persuade the president."[13]

Apart from these three "policy carriers," the military also provided a critical source of support for the Fujimori regime, yet its actual involvement in the formulation of economic policy has been marginal. Fujimori's chief liaison with the military was Vladimiro Montesinos. Montesinos's influence on the government and on Fujimori grew steadily, particularly beginning in the mid-1990s. As Bowen and Holligan (2003, 117) write: "In the same way that civilians had to be vetted by Santiago Fujimori [the president's younger brother and main advisor] before gaining an audience with the President, military top brass had to negotiate their access with Montesinos." By controlling key channels of influence, such as the judiciary and the tax and customs agencies, Montesinos would eventually undermine accountability in a political sense and effectiveness in an economic sense. Fujimori's lack of an institutionalized base of support, a lack that he utilized as a political asset to challenge entrenched vested interests during a time of crisis-ridden policy change, may have encouraged his increased reliance on Montesinos.[14]

In the final section of this chapter I present an overview of the relative importance of these policy carriers. The analysis reveals that the emphasis placed on top-down authoritarian versions of successful implementation of market reforms often overlooks sources of support, which have been critical to the advancement of reforms even within the state apparatus.

The Orthodox Phase (1990–92): Technocrats on the Rise

As in other Latin American countries, in Peru marketization has depended heavily on the expertise of technocrats, mostly trained in foreign universities, who have implemented key government decisions within the state bureaucracy and have "overseen the most significant overhaul of the state apparatus" (Mauceri 1997, 900). This technocratic group provided the ideological basis for the ongoing process of economic reform and was very influential within and outside the Finance Ministry. Key figures were Finance Minister Carlos Boloña and the executive director of COPRI, Carlos Montoya.

13. "A mi nunca me consultaron sobre el efecto político de una medida económica," *Debate*, March–April 1999, 12. Minister of Finance Jorge Baca also indicated that the president deliberately staffed his cabinet with members of these groups and continued with the same practice throughout the 1990s (interview by the author, Washington D.C., July 14, 1999). For a similar discussion, see Boloña 1993, 25.

14. I thank an anonymous reviewer for bringing up this point.

According to Gonzales de Olarte (1998), Boloña—a conservative economist in his own right—was truly the promoter of market initiatives. In fact, the Boloña tenure has been described as "the most dynamic phase" of reform.[15] As indicated above, the Boloña years coincided with the timing of the auto-golpe, which expedited the approval of a vast number of economic-reform initiatives via presidential decrees.

During the initial phase of reform, Fujimori took a strong stance in his dealings with the business sector. As Manzetti (1999, 250) pointed out, the president, as a political outsider, "appeared to owe few favors to the tradition-ally powerful in Peru, thus, 'giving him a free hand in policy-making.'" Gener-ally speaking, international investors were preferred over domestic economic groups, because the latter, according to Fujimori, were considered too small to play a major role in the economic-transformation process. Bowen (2000, 37) suggested that Fujimori and his innermost circle of advisors (or personal loyal-ists, described below) evaluated almost every single reform proposal according to "which economic interests stood to benefit from the measure." The privati-zation of the national airline, Aero Perú, was a case in point. The airline was initially sold to a domestic consortium, but Fujimori would later overturn the sale and award the airline to Mexican investors at a second auction (Manzetti 1999, 250). Such was Fujimori's capacity to set policy independently from the Peruvian business sector.

With the basic set of reforms in place, the Peruvian economy stabilized and executive priorities began to change. For the business sector and the president, Boloña had simply become too orthodox, leading to his dismissal, in early 1993, and to the subsequent appointment of a business leader as head of the Finance Ministry.[16]

The Pragmatic Phase (1993–98): The Business Elite Steps In

As the economic situation gradually improved, the president began to court business more seriously in order to broaden his base of political support. He reached out to the business elite organized in CONFIEP by appointing various business leaders to key cabinet positions (Table 3). During this phase of reform, the business sector and the government became inextricably linked. Politi-

15. "A mi nunca me consultaron sobre el efecto político de una medida económica," *Debate*, March–April 1999, 11.

16. "La salida de Boloña: Presidente busca recomponer base política," *Perú Económico*, January 1993, 1–3.

Table 3   Summary of some government positions held by business

	Business Background	Government Position
Jorge Camet	CONFIEP	minister of finance
Liliana Canale	National Exporters Society	minister of industry
Alfonso Bustamante	Peruvian Banking Association	minister of industry
Arturo Woodman	National Exporters Society	FONCODES director
Ricardo Márquez	National Industrial Society	vice president
Efraín Goldenberg	National Fishing Society	minister of finance

cally, the business elite had supported the president at a critical time: during the autogolpe. Economically, the president provided the business community with the social and economic predictability that had been lacking in Peru since the late 1970s. He not only appeared committed to the market orthodoxy, but also applauded and defended the bulk of IMF-sponsored policies. He argued that he was a "fondomonetarista," suggesting a strict adherence to the agreements signed with the IMF (Gonzales de Olarte 1998, 45).

The appointment of Jorge Camet in early 1993 as head of the ministry in charge of managing the economy was a turning point in the relationship between the organized business sector and the government. Camet, a business leader in the construction sector, headed the Finance Ministry longer than any other minister in recent history, almost six years, from early 1993 to mid-1998. Observers noted that the president and Camet got along well mostly because the latter, unlike the previous finance minister, Boloña, kept a low profile. Durand (1994a, 172) pointed out that when Camet was president of CONFIEP during 1990–91, the business umbrella organization "had a weaker, less experienced leadership." With these factors in place, Fujimori was making sure that he would monopolize the credit for economic success.

Fujimori's overture to business leaders, nonetheless, had important economic and social consequences. First, the management of the economy became increasingly favorable to both business and executive interests. Second, it created schisms within the business community. Third, it facilitated collusion and selective rent-seeking behavior, largely because of the absence of a broader framework of institutionalized consultation or dialogue.

Under Camet, the economic program took on a different slant. While its direction was still largely neoliberal, the Finance Ministry became packed with accommodating technocrats, suitable to the interests of the business sector and the president. Estela Benavides (2001, 105) and others have characterized these technocrats as "pseudoliberals" because they abused their positions in power to reward political clienteles and, in some cases, to enrich themselves at the expense of the national, public interest.[17] To put it another way, Camet's technocratic—or "kleptocratic" (Durand 2003, 421–97)—network was keen on advancing particularistic gains and rents in association with certain private businesses.[18] Furthermore, Camet worked very closely with the Peruvian Institute of Economics (IPE), CONFIEP's pro-business think tank created in 1994, to the extent that it became increasingly difficult to distinguish which sets of proposals were drawn by the IPE as opposed to the government itself.[19] As Table 4 shows, the IPE also became an effective "revolving door" mechanism for the exchange of jobs between key government institutions and the business sector.[20]

As one would expect given Camet's business background, business leaders channeled their demands directly to him (Durand 1998, 271–72). During this phase of reform, the president agreed to certain tax cuts and restructured the privatized pension system, among other things. Business had demanded some of these policy changes for quite some time. In response to the executive's electoral necessities, namely, the 1995 presidential reelection campaign, under Camet the Finance Ministry also eased certain aspects of macroeconomic policy, particularly with regard to social spending (Graham and Kane 1998).

Table 4   Summary of some government-IPE exchanges

	Prior Position	Later Position
Roberto Abusada	IPE founder	economic advisor
Jorge Baca	IPE director	minister of finance
Leoni Roca	prime minister advisor	IPE director
Fritz Du Bois	economic advisor	IPE director

17. Javier Iguíñiz described this group as "second-rate technocrats" (*técnicos de mando medio*) in part because they were "guardians of something [economic ideas] that they did not create," yet their arrogance in government appeared to demonstrate otherwise. See "Un economista indignado," *Quehacer*, January–February 2001, 6–12.

18. Examples from this network include Carlos Boloña, who appeared as a shareholder of a private-pension company after stepping down as finance minister (see Chapter 4); Roberto Abusada, who was involved in the privatization of the national airline while advising Finance Minister Jorge Camet (see Congreso de la República 2002 and Chapter 3); and Jorge Baca, who was a former manager of the Bunge and Born Corporation, subsequently became tax director of SUNAT, and later finance minister (see Chapter 3). In this chapter and beyond, these individuals are characterized as technocrats with business interests because of their widespread connections with the private business sector and their willingness to act on behalf of these interests.

19. Interview by the author with IPE's director Leoni Roca Voto Bernales, Lima, August 27, 1997. When I refer to her in her capacity as policy maker, I cite her as Leoni Roca; when naming her as author, I use Roca Voto Bernales.

20. The "revolving door" practice may involve prior or subsequent employment with a regulated industry as well as prior or subsequent service for a regulated industry. On revolving doors, see Gormley 1979; Cohen 1986; and Schamis 1999, 268.

Naturally, Fujimori's overture to business leaders was welcomed by some and rejected by others (see Castillo 1995, 1997). As in other Latin American countries, in Peru holders of more mobile factors, for example, the financial sector and export-oriented primary producers, were more pro-market than were holders of more specific or dedicated assets, for example, local manufacturing (see Frieden 1991). On repeated occasions, for instance, the president of the National Industries Society (SNI), Eduardo Farah, defended local manufacturing as opposed to extractive activities (such as mining and fishing) because the former, he argued, created jobs.[21] In response, the president of CONFIEP, Manuel Sotomayor (from the National Fishing Society), indicated that "the role for business people was to create not jobs, but wealth."[22] To technocrats in the Finance Ministry, including some business leaders, Farah was the "antichrist" of market policies incarnate, because of his repeated requests for greater protectionism in the form of a higher, more differentiated system of trade tariffs.[23]

Perhaps one of the reasons for Camet's lengthy tenure as minister of finance was that his appointment coincided with that of several presidents of CONFIEP who represented *gremios* (business associations) holding more mobile factors and who thus benefited more from market restructuring. Such were the cases of Arturo Woodman (1994–95), from the National Exporters Society (SNE); Jorge Piccaso (1996–97), from the Peruvian Banking Association (ASBANC); and Manuel Sotomayor (1998), from the National Fishing Society (SNP).[24] While ASBANC brought together the financial sector, both the SNE and the SNP represented exporters of traditional goods (primarily produced through extractive economic activities, including mining and fishing). Because these gremios were open to the new economic model, business demands on the government were inherently less hostile or conflictive, and thus the government was more inclined to accommodate them. Some observers noted that Camet had actually "handpicked" Woodman, Piccaso, and Sotomayor to lead CONFIEP.[25] In contrast, other gremios, including the Association of Exporters (ADEX), which

21. "Somos liberales, pero no tontos," *Perú Económico*, November 1996, 12.

22. "La tarde del volteretazo," *Caretas*, March 12, 1998.

23. "Marzo de candela," *Caretas*, March 5, 1998; and "Somos liberales, pero no tontos," *Perú Económico*, November 1996, 12.

24. In 1998, the SNE changed its name to COMEXPERU (Peruvian Society of Chamber of Exporters).

25. "La tarde del volteretazo," *Caretas*, March 12, 1998. Minister of Finance Baca, who succeeded Camet, indicated that the tenure of the latter coincided with an unprecedented bonanza of short-term capital inflows, which in turn helped Camet to keep business demands at bay (interview by the author, Washington, D.C., July 14, 1999).

unites exporters of nontraditional goods, and the SNI, were more critical of the government. Both gremios represented a large number of manufacturing companies, and they generally had not been able to adjust quickly to the emerging market rules.

The struggle between the "winners" and the "losers" was also reflected within CONFIEP. In fact, in March 1998, the organization faced the prospects of a breakdown when elections polarized the organization into pro-Camet and independent candidates. Trade associations such as ADEX and the SNI perceived the leadership of CONFIEP as too close to the government, leaving the umbrella association without an independent voice (see Cotler 1998, 25). In March 1999, these conflicts intensified when CONFIEP's president, Manuel Sotomayor, who happened to be a close friend of Minister Camet, sought reelection. In the end, CONFIEP's leaders acquiesced to the demands of trade associations seeking an independent voice by electing Roque Benavides, a representative of the National Mining, Petroleum, and Energy Society (SNMPE), to the presidency of CONFIEP.[26] Benavides appeared to be a more independent candidate than the incumbent Sotomayor. This schism within CONFIEP that appeared for the first time in 1998 intensified at the end of the decade. In early 2001, the SNI and ADEX, among others, effectively abandoned the business umbrella organization.[27]

Finally, the connections between government and business led to collusion and selective rent-seeking behavior. As Durand (1999, 45) points out, Fujimori's overture to business leaders did not necessarily evolve into an institutionalized form of dialogue or consultation; instead, informal channels of access to state officials dominated the government-business landscape. Appointees such as Camet and other business leaders derived particularistic benefits from government service.[28] Furthermore, at least three different prime ministers sat on the board of directors of the newly created pension companies almost immediately after leaving office (see Chapter 4). Windfall benefits included the awarding of construction and privatization contracts, the concession of generous tax abatements, and the implementation of financial rescue

---

26. "El retorno del KID," *Caretas*, January 18, 1999.

27. "Sociedad Nacional de Industrias decide retirarse de CONFIEP," *El Comercio*, March 29, 2001.

28. Camet's construction company, for instance, appears to have benefited from a large number of government contracts. In a ranking of Peru's largest firms, J. J. Contratistas Generales S.A. went from the 1,285th position in 1987 to the top 70 in 1993. During that time, Camet served for two years in the Ministry of Industry and later was appointed head of the Finance Ministry (see "Los años del tigre," *Caretas*, January 29, 1998). By 1999, J. J. Contratistas was the eighth-largest Peruvian construction company (see Webb and Fernández 1999, 903). See also Congreso de la República 2002, 125–30.

operations for banks.[29] Malfeasance practices spread from Dionisio Romero Seminario, the owner of the largest bank in the country—Credit Bank of Peru (BCP)—and arguably the most powerful and influential businessman in Peru, to the military top brass, and of course, Fujimori's family, including key populist loyalists such as finance minister Víctor Joy-Way and minister of agriculture and presidential advisor Absalón Vásquez. Some of these cases were directly tied to the "fixer" (*arreglador*) Vladimiro Montesinos.[30] Given the institutional weakness of the Peruvian judiciary, however, the task of prosecuting policy makers and top executives has been extremely difficult. In the words of Bowen and Holligan (2003, 454), "Notably—with the exception of some television channel owners—those Peruvian businessmen who had sought Montesinos's favors and conspired with him to pervert the course of justice, came off lightly."[31] I revisit the problem of corruption in the conclusion, where I address the prospects for the sustainability of market reforms.

Although the business sector continued to support Fujimori, the president's endorsement of the market orthodoxy began to wear down during his second presidential term, and considerably more so by the end of the 1990s. The president's changing views about the progress of economic reform resonated primarily among personal loyalists.

The Watered-Down Phase (1998–2000): Personal Loyalists on the Rise

Complementing the technocrats and the business elite, Fujimori nurtured an informal network of personal loyalists, most of whom were connected with the president through personal, familial, or social ties. This "kitchen cabinet" was dubbed the "populist wing" and its members "populists," because their views, according to technocrats such as Finance Minister Boloña, deviated from market principles. They were also known as the "santiaguistas" because of their association with the president's younger brother and main advisor, Santiago Fujimori. Last but not least, they were called the "socially sensitive" wing, because the majority of them ended up serving in ministries with a social slant, such as Health, Education, and Labor (Bowen 2000, 297). Personal loyalists afforded the president "the sort of loyal following within the state bureaucracy

---

29. Investigative congressional reports that trace corruption during the Fujimori regime include Diez Canseco 2002; Congreso de la República 2002, 2003. See also Bowen and Holligan 2003, 285–307; Conaghan 2002; Durand 2003, 421–97; Caretas Dossier 2001; and "Pobreza y corrupción," *Quehacer*, September–October 2003, 4–25.

30. The word "fixer" is Durand's (2003, 425).

31. See also "Chasing the Kleptocrats," *New York Times*, September 29, 2003, A22.

that is often associated with a political party" (Mauceri 1997, 907). Throughout the entire Fujimori regime, personal loyalists occupied various official as well as unofficial positions within the state bureaucracy. However, as explained below, their ideas became prevalent only in the late 1990s.

Ironically, personal loyalists failed to coalesce into a cohesive, united group, reflecting again the lack of institutionalization within Fujimorismo. They can be crudely clustered in two camps: technocratic and populist loyalists. Among the technocratic loyalists, who were also very close to the president, important actors were Manuel Estela (head of SUNAT), Beatriz Boza (head of the consumer protection agency, the National Institute for the Defense of Competition and the Protection of Intellectual Property Rights [INDECOPI]), and Alejandro Afuso (director of the targeted poverty-alleviation program FONCODES). As documented later, the tenure of technocratic loyalists was highly selective and, of course, highly dependent on the president and even Montesinos's will. Technocratic loyalists such as Estela approached government service as an opportunity to promote the public interest, and thus criticized the other group of technocrats—the "pseudoliberals"—who colluded with the private business sector to extract particularistic gains and rents.[32]

Among the populist loyalists, by contrast, important figures were Absalón Vásquez (minister of agriculture), Yong Motta (minister of health), and Víctor Joy-Way (minister of industry and subsequently minister of finance). Vásquez became "one of Fujimori's closest confidants and most unreserved admirers" (Bowen 2000, 336) and was particularly instrumental during Fujimori's third presidential bid in 2000.

Populist loyalists had a distinct "policy repertoire" very unlike that of the radical neoliberals. They were more skeptical about the alleged benefits of market policies. In what came to be regarded as Absalonómics, Absalón Vásquez openly criticized, among other things, the privatization of public utility companies because it had led to monopolistic practices and higher fees, the liberalization of the banking system because it had resulted in prohibitive interest rates for consumers, and open-trade policies that had seriously hurt the industrial and agricultural sectors.[33] In short, Absalonómics called for a bigger state presence and, through more regulations and government oversight, hoped to contain the pressure wielded by powerful business interests.

---

32. Interview by the author with Manuel Estela Benavides, Lima, November 5 and December 15, 2003. When referring to him in his role as policy maker, I use the name Manuel Estela; as author, he is cited as Estela Benavides.

33. "Absalonómics: ¿Táctica electoral o nuevo enfoque económico?" *Perú Económico*, March 2000, 6–9.

The economic restructuring process under Fujimori is replete with examples of which technocrats, business leaders, and personal loyalists from both the technocratic and populist camps vying for policy-making pull. In 1993, for instance, when populist loyalist Absalón Vásquez was minister of agriculture, he proposed preferential tax treatment for agriculture. But the then finance minister Camet rejected Vásquez's proposal, stating that sectoral policies simply contradicted the main objective of the ongoing tax reform, which was to maximize tax revenues.[34] Personal loyalists from the technocratic side were entrusted with the direction of the consumer-protection agency INDECOPI, and the president repeatedly endorsed its work. However, business leaders and technocrats with business interests objected to INDECOPI, particularly when the institution acted on behalf of the state without an explicit request from consumers.[35] As is expanded on in Chapter 3, perhaps there was no other policy forum in which technocratic loyalists' preferences were more at odds with those of business leaders and technocrats with business interests than that of the tax reform itself.

Central to the balance of power among these groups was the control of the cabinet, where much of policy discussion took place. The prime ministership became a pivotal position that could easily help sway the debate in favor of or against the market orthodoxy. According to Fritz Du Bois, the most serious threat to the continuation of reforms took place in mid-1995, when the president, following the recommendation of his brother Santiago, appointed Dante Córdoba as prime minister and minister of education.[36] But technocrats and business leaders closed ranks, forcing the resignation of the Córdoba cabinet in early 1996. Shortly after, Santiago Fujimori withdrew as the main presidential advisor. It goes without saying that the departure of Santiago Fujimori enabled Vladimiro Montesinos to increase his influence on the government.[37] However, the defeat of personal loyalists was only temporary.

Various factors contributed to the reemergence of the "populist wing" in the 1998–2000 period. On the external side, instability in international markets

34. "Agricultura propone rebajar a 5% el IGV para alimentos," *El Comercio,* November 10, 1993.
35. INDECOPI was dubbed "ghost buster." See "Los cazafantasmas, SUNAT e INDECOPI," *Presencia,* April 1996, 17.
36. "A mi nunca me consultaron sobre el efecto político de una medida económica," *Debate,* March–April 1999, 15. Like Vásquez, Córdoba attempted to set up protective measures for the agricultural sector. See "Fujimori, el multiministro," *Sí,* April 15, 1999, 8–15.
37. In the words of Bowen and Holligan (2003, 278), "Santiago's departure in April 1996 left Montesinos to govern the judiciary alone." See also "Habla Santiago," *Caretas,* October 19, 2000, and "Los sinsabores de Santiago," *Caretas,* January 18, 2001.

plunged the Peruvian economy into a deep recession. A new occurrence of El Niño in early 1998 also pounded the economy. The economic recession gradually resurrected organized political opposition to the president, which continued well into the year 2000. On the domestic front, the president prepared himself for a highly controversial second reelection. In response to these events, Vásquez suggested that one means by which to simultaneously counterbalance the rising political opposition to the president and increase Fujimori's electoral chances in the 2000 presidential race was political mobilization among lower-class sectors. As a result, the poverty-alleviation program FONCODES increasingly became a target of Vásquez's political ambitions. In mid-1998, FONCODES director Alejandro Afuso, a technocratic loyalist, was forced to resign by pressure from the populist loyalist Vásquez because the former was seen as "uncooperative" and "disobedient."[38] FONCODES was perhaps the last standing social program to overtly fall prey to Fujimori's growing electoral machine.

The impact of these events was even more dramatic in the ministry in charge of managing the economy; these events signaled the end of the technocratic-business era. In early 1999, the president appointed an old populist loyalist, Víctor Joy-Way, as the new minister of finance.[39] The new minister ousted the entire team of economic advisors, who had assisted Boloña and Camet for almost seven consecutive years. During the last two years of Fujimori's second term, the president replaced ministers of finance three times, with each minister's tenure averaging six months. Fujimori thus came full circle: in 1990 he began his first administration by improvising a set of market initiatives; he ended his second term in 2000 also improvising, this time without a clear sense of direction.

In the absence of any sign indicating possible changes to the market model, the economic recession eventually took a toll on business unity. In fact, the business-state alliance forged during the Camet years, an alliance largely dominated by traditional exporters and the financial sector, shifted in favor of local manufacturing and agriculture. Signaling tensions between business and government, in 2000 the president failed to appear at the Annual Conference of

---

38. "Presiones oficialistas causaron renuncia de ex jefe de FONCODES," *El Comercio*, September 15, 1998.

39. Camet resigned in mid-1998, but managed to entrust the direction of the ministry to a close friend, Jorge Baca. Baca's tenure lasted only five months. In the early 1990s, Joy-Way described himself as a "prudent heteredox" in direct defiance of Boloña's strict orthodoxy. See "Tiempos de Joy," *Caretas*, January 14, 1999.

Executives (CADE), the elitist yearly meeting of business executives. The president also began to court SNI president Farah, who had been a fierce critic of market economics and Fujimorismo. Farah went on to become a congressional representative in Fujimori's party. The alienated sectors of CONFIEP, such as the SNI and ADEX, appeared to join ranks with the populists led by Vásquez, who was also elected to Congress. But the new governing coalition never materialized. Three months into his third presidential term, mounting evidence of corruption and gross criminality forced Fujimori to resign from office and seek refuge in Japan.[40]

To sum up, different groups with varying resources and repertoires shaped the process of economic reform in Peru. Essentially, technocrats with business interests, who dwelled in the Finance Ministry, collided with technocratic loyalists such as Manuel Estela, who were more independent and interested in technocratic policy management; the business elite organized in CONFIEP represented primarily the economic sectors that benefited more from the new economic model; and populist loyalists prioritized political survival over economic reforms. Both the electoral calendar and the progress of the economic reforms determined the importance of these groups. Personal loyalists were always critical players throughout the entire Fujimori regime. They attempted to capture the cabinet in the mid-1990s, albeit unsuccessfully. Growing doubts about the benefits of the market model served to encourage changes in the state-business coalition from traditional exporters to industrialists. The discrepancies within the business sector ultimately led to the collapse of CONFIEP as an encompassing organization. Only in the late 1990s did the ideas from personal loyalists and industrialists, aided by an economic recession and electoral uncertainty, find a receptive audience in the executive. If anything, as discussed in greater detail in Chapter 6, by the end of decade the president ceased to pursue marketization altogether.

CONCLUSION

Whereas Belaúnde and García are often chastised for the country's poor economic performance throughout the 1980s, Fujimori is equally criticized for his undemocratic political tactics. The 1992 presidential coup stands out as the biggest single reversal of the process of democratization that has swept Latin

---

40. For a discussion of these events, see Balbi and Palmer 2001; Conaghan 2001; García Calderón 2001; and Marcus-Delgado and Tanaka 2001.

America since the early 1980s. However, in addition to a successful macro-economic-stabilization program, which defeated hyperinflation and restored economic growth, Fujimori's reconstruction of the Peruvian state has been a pivotal factor in the consolidation of the new market model (Wise 2003). Even after the abrupt collapse of the Fujimori regime in 2000, the economy appeared to be on solid ground, at least at the macro level.

With ample military support, Fujimori relied upon three different "policy carriers" to shape economic policy making, often manipulating these groups to his own advantage. Although his association with technocrats drew positive support from the business elite, Fujimori also paid attention to his cohort of personal loyalists, thus making sure that reforms retained a popular appeal. The payoff was a broad coalition of support that transcended social-class distinctions. Incidentally, technocrats were seen as part of a mostly white affluent minority, the cream of the Peruvian social crop. In contrast, personal loyalists were seen as a new rising class of mestizos, who had been traditionally excluded from active participation in the government. Being a son of Japanese immigrants, Fujimori was initially seen as the embodiment of the working-class ethic that was shared by this new class of mestizos.

The reforms central to this study unveil various instances in which conflicts between these groups were present, and the president endorsed the views of one group to the detriment of the others. These groups not only affected the pace at which policy reforms have been implemented, but also provided opportunities for societal actors to "talk back" to the state, thus reshaping policy reforms originally implemented by executive fiat. In the following chapters I examine and compare four key policy reforms that illustrate this process. Together they underline the importance of examining societal interests and the feedback effects of those interests on reform processes. Even in one of the most highly centralized and least democratic systems in Latin America, reforms generated political responses, and those responses, in turn, affected the outcome of the reforms already in place.

THE BATTLE FOR TAXES

In 1997, the Peruvian government collected an unprecedented record of more than U.S.$8 billion dollars in tax revenues. Government revenues, which had been drastically reduced by hyperinflation in the 1988–90 period, increased from 7.3 percent of GDP in 1989 to 14.3 percent in 1996.[1] This historic recovery was the outcome of a comprehensive tax reform, which simplified the tax system and reorganized the office responsible for tax collection, SUNAT. The tax reform began in early 1991 shortly after Fujimori's election and was viewed as a critical step toward increasing the government's limited revenue base and restoring fiscal discipline. The reform was thus designed to consolidate the economic-stabilization package implemented by Fujimori in August 1990, which had addressed the problem of hyperinflation, but failed to restore macroeconomic stability. As of 1991, inflation was still running at a rate of 140 percent.

The Peruvian tax reform is representative of a broader regional trend. As countries in Latin America began trade liberalization in the mid-1980s, tax reform often followed. The Fujimori administration lowered tariffs in August 1990, and tax reform began in early 1991. With widespread trade liberalization, which implied a significant reduction in tariff revenues, taxation became the centerpiece of fiscal policy under the new market model. As in Peru, tax systems across Latin America have changed considerably to fit the new paradigm. The importance of taxes on foreign trade has diminished in favor of higher taxes on consumption (IDB 1996). Some observers originally anticipated an immediate shortfall in government revenues as a result of tariff reductions, but

---

1. BCRP 1998.

such a forecast did not become a reality, mostly because there has been a significant increase in trade flows (Rey 1996). Global market forces have also shaped the design of current tax systems across Latin America. Taxes on business profits, for instance, have been harmonized with those of the United States so as not to discourage foreign investment (IDB 1996).

More fundamentally, the Peruvian tax reform provides significant insights into the complex and changing nature of state reform. The reform was initiated in the midst of a severe economic crisis and gathered momentum after the autogolpe. During this initial phase, tax reform was insulated from any form of opposition, allowing state and technocratic elites to advance important policy changes. As a political outsider, Fujimori wholeheartedly supported the reform initiative and did not hesitate to confront powerful interest groups, particularly those representing the business elite, in order to implement policy change. The initial phase of the reform was thus characterized by limited input from societal actors and heavy reliance on coercion, which extended to the use of the military to help enforce tax compliance.

As the economic situation improved and SUNAT succeeded in broadening the tax base, mostly by rigorously enforcing tax laws and controlling tax evasion, societal actors, in both the formal and informal sectors, began to contest the reform process. The strongest and most enduring source of opposition to the reform came from the organized business sector, although informal-sector actors also contested the policy change. As is suggested in Chapter 2, President Fujimori found himself in need of building a stronger rapport with the business elite. As a result, the reform process became less insulated and more open to negotiation between state officials and societal interests. Acquiescing to business demands, the government began to offer a series of tax concessions with little consideration to the costs of implementing such handouts. The first evidence of this process came in late 1996 when the government announced a broad tax amnesty and reintroduced a series of tax incentives to promote certain economic activities. While these concessions benefited business organizations, they also resulted in a gradual loss of policy efficacy, thus diluting the original reform effort. Government revenues as a percentage of GDP have stagnated since 1996 at 14 percent. State and IMF officials originally hoped for a tax collection equivalent to 18 percent of GDP by 1994 (Hurtado Miller 1990, 186).

This pattern of change conforms to the theoretical expectations outlined in Chapter 1. The costs of the tax reform were highly concentrated, whereas its benefits were widely distributed across society. This asymmetrical distribution of costs and benefits sparked organized resistance and opposition from a well-defined group—business organizations—but very little organized support. As a consequence, the political activity of societal actors served to slow down, and ultimately dilute the reform process.

However, in addition to lobbying by the business sector, which led to important tax concessions and abatements, the reform was weakened during the mid-1990s because of the influence of Vladimiro Montesinos. By controlling some of the key enforcement vehicles of the tax office, such as the Special Unit for Tax Audits (UEIT), the "fixer" Montesinos further diluted the tax reform process. Montesinos's rising influence over the SUNAT coincided with the departure of Santiago Fujimori, and as a result, technocratic loyalists who were central to the initial reform lost their final control over the tax agency and the reform.

In the first part of this chapter I compare the pre- and postreform tax scenario in Peru. Thereafter, I trace the economic and societal impact of the reform, paying particular attention to the response of societal interests in both the formal and informal sectors. The third section centers on an analysis of the feedback effects of these responses on the tax reform process. These feedback effects are further analyzed through an interrupted time-series (ITS) analysis, and the results show a gradual dilution of the reform process. In the conclusion I address comparative perspectives and summarize the findings of this chapter.

TAXATION IN PERU: AN OVERVIEW

Since the 1960s, tax collection in Peru had been under the control of the Directorate General for Taxation (DGC), a branch of the Finance Ministry. The García administration changed this arrangement in June 1988, when it created a new tax administration called SUNAT to replace the DGC.[2] In theory, responsibility for tax collection was to be separated from the ministry responsible for managing the economy and placed in the hands of an autonomous administrative unit. In practice, the change was in name only, as the new SUNAT functioned in the same way as the old DGC (Castro and Zavala 1996, 102). The weak and inconsistent authority delegated to SUNAT by President García and the hyperinflationary economic crisis of the late 1980s, among other things, prevented the reform from being fully implemented (Durand

2. Law 24829.

and Thorp 1998, 138). The reform only became effective in 1991 under the Fujimori regime, when improved tax collection became a central emphasis of government policy.

Administratively, the SUNAT, like most of the state bureaucracy, was an overstaffed agency, with tax administrators earning low wages and some employees even holding a second job in the private sector (Arias 1991, 208). By the early 1990s, the tax office had lost the ability to identify taxpayers or to conduct basic auditing operations. It had issued more than 5 million tax identification cards (Fuentes, Arias, and Durand 1996, 193), but the tax base in Peru was never close to 1 million taxpayers. Bribes and under-the-table agreements between friendly tax employees and large taxpayers were common (Durand 1997, 6). More important, tax evasion was never prosecuted, and as such, it grew into something of a "national sport" (Tanzi and Shome 1993, 810).

Further, the tax system was extremely complex. With more than sixty different taxes and a multitude of deductions and exemptions, it has been reasonably described as a "legal jungle" (Durand and Thorp 1998, 137). As Arias (1991, 226) suggests, this complexity reflects the tendency of governments to use taxation to pursue a broad range of policy goals, including decentralization, investment promotion, and income redistribution.

From 1970 to 1984, government revenues—including both tax and nontax revenues—averaged 14 percent of GDP (INEI 1992, 347). After 1985, however, government revenues began to decrease dramatically, reaching their lowest figure in 1989 at 7.3 percent of GDP (Fig. 4). Government revenues fell primarily for two reasons. The first was hyperinflation, which eroded the real value of tax revenues because of collection lags.[3] As revenues declined, the budget deficit increased substantially, which in turn exacerbated inflation. With lower revenues, basic government services, such as police protection and social welfare, collapsed. According to Webb (1991, 1), the collapse of the state ultimately led to a process of "de facto privatization" of most basic government obligations. Second, government revenues fell because of longer-term problems, notably the inefficiency of the tax office and the growing complexity of the tax system. As Arias (1991, 226) points out, it was widely understood within policy circles that "long-term macroeconomic stability would require reforms of both the structure and management of taxes."

To summarize, the Peruvian pre-reform tax scenario consisted of a weak tax administration and a complex tax system, both of which made tax collection

---

3. The opposite is true when the rate of inflation falls. This is known as the Olivera-Tanzi effect.

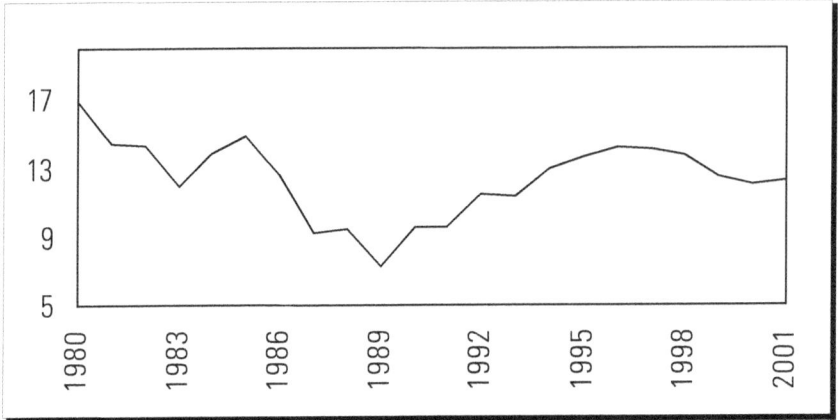

Fig. 4   Government revenues as a percentage of GDP, 1980–2001

SOURCE: Banco Central de Reserva del Perú, *Memoria* (various years)

difficult and highly inefficient. The polar opposite of this scenario would be the combination of a strong tax administration and a simple tax system, which could be considered optimal.[4] In reality, however, most tax systems do not approach the ideal combination of tax-policy simplicity and tax-office effectiveness. As Tanzi (1996, 20) notes, "Tax systems are very much like fields which, unless they are cleared from time to time, become overgrown."

THE 1991 TAX REFORM

In August 1990, faced with an acute budget deficit, Fujimori imposed a series of special contributions and emergency taxes on business property and exports. In addition, the government dramatically increased excise taxes on fuels and fees for various public services. This early "tax package," however, did not entail the reform of the tax system or the tax office, both of which were seen as critical to the consolidation of the economic-stabilization program (Arias 1991, 209).

The 1991 reform sought to make changes to both and thereby maximize government revenues. The reform began in February 1991, when technocratic

4. Other scenarios include the combination of a weak tax administration with a simple tax system or a strong tax administration with a complex tax system, all of which could yield suboptimal tax results.

loyalist Manuel Estela, a manager from the Central Reserve Bank of Peru (BCRP), was appointed tax director, and it gained momentum during the auto-golpe. In December 1992, the Fujimori regime issued a decree rationalizing existing taxes into five types: income taxes on business profits and personal incomes; a general sales tax on goods and services (a variant of the so-called value-added tax); a selective excise tax levied mainly on fuels and luxury goods; a housing and urban planning tax known as FONAVI (National Housing Fund); and a tax on corporate net worth.[5] The decree also eliminated a great number of tax exemptions and deductions. With the new tax structure, the government eliminated most of the emergency taxes and special contributions that had been in place since August 1990.

To reduce tax evasion, the rationalization of taxes also implied an important reduction in tax rates. Income taxes are an example. In the early 1980s, taxes on personal incomes had as many as thirteen different tax rates, ranging from 2 to 65 percent; and taxes on business profits had rates of 30, 40, 50, and 55 percent (Baca 2000). By the end of the 1990s, there were two tax rates for personal incomes (15 and 30 percent) and only one for business profits (30 percent).[6] On the whole, the rationalization of taxes into five types and the across-the-board reduction in tax rates alluded to the universality of tax obligations, which, as we will see, extended to the taxation of the informal sector.

With the technical assistance of the IMF, the IDB, and the Inter-American Center of Tax Administrations (CIAT), tax director Estela initiated a profound transformation of the SUNAT. The reorganization of the SUNAT had two major components: human resources and wage policy. With respect to personnel, the SUNAT employed 3,150 workers in early 1991, 66 percent of whom worked in Lima. After the introduction of a series of competency exams, SUNAT's labor force was reduced to 800 employees and recruitment was increasingly based on merit.[7] The tax office was authorized to contract personnel on a private basis, offering wages similar to those in the private sector. With the SUNAT's budget equivalent to 2 percent of the revenues collected, wages for tax admin-

5. Legislative Decree (DL) 25988. Income taxes on business profits included a minimum income tax with a rate of 2 percent of the value of net assets. In 1994, the government further simplified taxes by eliminating the tax on corporate net worth because its tax yield was insignificant.

6. In 2001, tax rates for personal incomes were modified by adding a third tier: 15, 21, and 27 percent. The tax rate for business profits was reduced to 27 percent.

7. Taliercio and Engelschalk (2001, 3) note that Fujimori did not interfere with SUNAT's recruitment process in part because he "did not face pressure from an established political party to dispense patronage." These circumstances made the Peruvian case different from many other reforms in the developing world.

istrators were raised from a monthly average of U.S.$65 in 1991 to U.S.$635 in 1992 and to U.S.$2,000 in 1998 (Baca 2000, 189). In addition, the tax office was moved to new premises, which offered computerized systems and modern communication facilities.

The SUNAT created a special unit to monitor the most significant taxpayers—known as PRICOS (major taxpayers)—who paid their taxes directly at SUNAT headquarters. In addition, the SUNAT raised an army of inspectors (*fedatarios*), formed mostly by young university recruits, who visited thousands of commercial establishments all over Peru to enforce tax compliance. Among the penalties for tax evasion, the most common were fines and the temporary closure of establishments. The SUNAT closed 5,316 businesses in 1992, 7,268 in 1994, and 10,555 in 1996.[8] Finally, the SUNAT began prosecuting tax evasion through the judicial system. The government cooperated by modifying the penal code to expedite trial proceedings for tax evaders.

The impact of the tax reform was only tangible after 1992, when inflation had receded. Tax revenues gradually increased from 9.6 percent of GDP in 1990 to 12.9 in 1994 and to 14.2 in 1996.[9] Income tax revenues increased from .6 percent of GDP in 1990 to 3.3 percent in 1999, while sales tax revenues climbed from 1.7 percent of GDP in 1990 to 5.8 percent in 1997.[10] As income and sales tax revenues increased, the government's budget became less dependent on revenues from excise taxes, particularly fuel taxes, which had been critical to sustaining the stabilization package of August 1990. With an average rate of 134 percent in late 1990, excise taxes on fuels were reduced to 93 percent in early 1992 and then to 70 percent by the end of the same year (Gómez, Urrunaga, and Bel 1997, 45). As a percentage of GDP, revenues from the excise tax decreased from 3.6 percent in 1990 to 1.9 percent in 1997.[11] Including import duties, which are not administered by SUNAT, tax collection has exceeded U.S.$8 billion dollars since 1996.

To sum up, beyond the increase in tax revenues as a result of the fall in the rate of inflation, the SUNAT maximized government revenues by introducing substantial changes in both the structure and the collection of taxes. These changes have not gone unnoticed. In fact, in a public opinion poll conducted

8. SUNAT, *Memoria de la unidad de clausura y sanción* (1996).

9. BCRP 1997. Peruvian economist Gonzales de Olarte (1998, 60), among others, argued that tax revenues were probably equivalent to 20 percent of GDP. This problem arises from an overestimated GDP. I revisit this issue in Chapter 6, where I discuss the effects of policy centralization on the sustainability of reforms.

10. BCRP 1997.

11. BCRP 1997.

in early 1998, 83 percent of Limeños believed that they currently paid more taxes compared with what they paid five years earlier.[12] In the following section I explore the response of societal actors to these policy changes.

RESPONSES TO THE TAX REFORM: BUSINESSES FIGHT BACK

To obtain larger tax yields, the restructured tax office made efforts to reach those who did not previously pay taxes—the informal sector. Peruvians were strongly in favor of the reform initiative (Table 5), yet their approval did not evolve into an organized response. Certainly, the Peruvian tax base increased considerably as a result of the inclusion of the informal sector. For instance, in April 1998 almost seven hundred thousand taxpayers filed tax returns.[13] In theory, the broadening of the tax base suggests that the costs of the reform would be more widely dispersed. In practice, as Wilson (1980, 366) argues, what matters is the perceived distribution of these costs and their incidence across different segments of society. Considerations about the fairness or unfairness of a proposed policy are also particularly relevant to political action.

The tax reform, as explained below, yielded a pattern of concentrated costs and diffused benefits. As such, it sparked little organized support, and had no identifiable winners, but strong organized resistance and opposition from well-defined groups in both the formal and informal economy. Large- and small-business associations contested the reform initiative for different reasons, using different political strategies to reshape policy.

Table 5 Preferences with respect to the taxation of the informal sector

In general, should street vendors be required to pay the general sales taxes?

		Socioeconomic Level (in percentages)		
Responses	Total	Upper	Upper Middle	Lower Middle	Lower
In Favor	84	98	95	89	71
Against	14	2	4	9	27
Uncertain/No Response	2	0	1	2	2
Number of Respondents	519	43	101	188	187

SOURCE: Apoyo 1991a.

12. Apoyo S.A. 1998a. In the poll, the question reads: "Compared to five years ago, would you say that Peruvians pay more, the same, or less taxes?"

13. SUNAT 1998. April is the month when tax returns are due.

CONFIEP's Response

The strongest reaction to the reform came from the organized business sector represented by CONFIEP. In the beginning, when the Fujimori government imposed a series of emergency taxes, business leaders rejected the "tax package," criticizing the tax measures in a series of press releases (Castillo and Quispe 1996, 96–97). With a restructured tax office, however, the business elite adopted new strategies to cope with the new tax discipline imposed by the SUNAT. The business elite demanded the elimination of taxes that particularly affected the business community as well as advocated for the more general broadening of the tax base.

CONFIEP was particularly critical of the FONAVI and the minimum income tax. First, the FONAVI was perceived to be less of a contribution than a "payroll tax," because it was paid mostly by employers (CONFIEP 1997, 63).[14] As such, it increased labor costs—making Peruvian companies less competitive in world markets—and discriminated against labor-intensive industries.[15] The FONAVI was also rarely used for its intended purpose, which involved housing projects. Former minister of finance Carlos Boloña, in fact, described the FONAVI as Fujimori's "petty cash" fund.[16] However, revenues from the FONAVI were not necessarily an insignificant amount. In 1996, they rose to almost 1 percent of GDP.[17]

Second, the minimum income tax, which had a rate of 2 percent of the value of net assets, was originally set up as an emergency tax, in August 1990. Later, however, rather than eliminating it, the government decided to make use of the tax as a mechanism to prevent the underreporting of business profits, thus indirectly promoting business efficiency and competitiveness.[18] Only companies with profits equivalent to less than 6.67 percent of their net assets were subject to the tax. By extension, companies reporting losses or facing temporary closure were taxable (Urrunaga 1994, 3).

The association repeatedly argued that both these taxes were, among other things, "antitechnical," confiscatory in nature, and inequitable.[19] Based on these grievances, business organizations affiliated with CONFIEP made policy

---

14. The FONAVI was created in 1979 by the military regime of Morales Bermúdez (Law 22591).
15. "Deben modificarse normas tributarias," *Presencia*, October 1996, 17–19.
16. Lecture given at the Universidad San Ignacio de Loyola, Lima, June 23, 1997.
17. BCRP 1996.
18. IPE 1997a, 27.
19. "Deben modificarse normas tributarias," *Presencia*, October 1996, 17–19.

demands, such as asking simultaneously that the government eliminate what the business elite interpreted as "extra tax costs" (*sobrecostos tributarios*). This unified approach, as will be explained later, was particularly effective (Castillo and Quispe 1996, 96).

The broadening of the tax base was another source of complaint for CON-FIEP.[20] This was a contentious issue because it became clear that the tax obligations of small businesses were not monitored with the same frequency as the obligations of the most significant taxpayers. In 1998, for instance, more than two hundred thousand taxpayers filed returns, yet they did not pay taxes (Table 6). This large group of evaders primarily included self-employed individuals and small businesses in the informal sector (Table 7). While the number of filing taxpayers during the 1994–98 period increased by 65 percent, the number of paying taxpayers only increased by 23 percent. This gap between filing and paying taxpayers has grown wider over time (see Table 6).

Because the number of paying taxpayers remained stagnant, the burden of the tax reform became increasingly concentrated on large and medium businesses. In November 1995, for instance, 8,450 taxpayers paid 78 percent of

Table 6   **Filing- and paying-taxpayer ratios (average per year in thousands)**

	1994	1996	1998	2000
Taxpayers Filing Tax Returns (A)	387	552	640	672
Taxpayers Paying Taxes (B)	350	425	432	418
Ratio B/A	0.90	0.77	0.68	0.62

SOURCE: SUNAT, *Nota Tributaria* (various years).

NOTE: The 1994 averages includes only June–December.

Table 7   Tax revenue concentration (March 1997)

	Large	Medium	Small	RUS/RER	Total
Registered Taxpayers	10,800	22,500	857,229	705,524	1,596,053
Filing Taxpayers	10,800	22,500	195,995	384,478	613,773
Paying Taxpayers	10,800	22,500	88,001	326,806	448,107
Revenue Collected (%)	85	10	4	1	100

SOURCE: SUNAT 1997a.

NOTE: The RUS/RER are special tax regimes for small taxpayers, including market vendors.

20. Interviews by the author with Rafael Villegas, former president of CONFIEP, Lima, November 21, 1997; and Luis Abugattás, director of the Economic and Social Studies Division of the SNI, Lima, September 3, 1997, and February 12, 1998.

the revenues collected by the SUNAT (Arias 1995, 53), and in March 1997, 10,800 taxpayers paid 85 percent (see Table 7). In other words, less than 2 percent of taxpayers filing returns accounted for about 80 percent of the revenues collected by the tax office.[21]

In a word, CONFIEP demanded fair treatment across all businesses—however small—and pressured the SUNAT to close the gap between registered and filing taxpayers as well as the gap between filing and paying taxpayers.[22] Largely confirming CONFIEP's grievances, a 1996 survey conducted by Apoyo S.A. asked businesses to point out what they considered the most urgent change regarding the government's current fiscal policy (CONFIEP 1996). While large and medium businesses suggested the gradual elimination of the minimum income tax as the most immediate policy change, small businesses proposed the strengthening of the SUNAT so that those who did not currently pay taxes would do so. The policy preference of small businesses suggests that tax evasion among small businesses provided avenues for uneven competition. More important, it indicated that the SUNAT had focused its tax collection efforts on large and medium taxpayers. Tax enforcement among small businesses, however, was and continues to be difficult to implement, given their sheer number and informal status. Along these lines, Tanzi and Shome (1993, 809) note that "a country where much of the economic activity takes place in small shops and small farms, or is conducted by single individuals, is likely to experience a lot of evasion." Last, while some SUNAT officials pointed out that it had not been economically efficient to collect revenues from the hard-to-tax informal sector, they all agree that it was necessary to broaden the tax base so as not to discourage tax compliance from larger taxpayers.[23]

Informal Sector's Response

Although the tax yield of small businesses could be regarded as economically insignificant, these businesses also objected to the reform. In July 1993, when

---

21. Most Latin American countries produce this same tax concentration pattern (IDB 1996,127).

22. Luis Abugattás, director of the Economic and Social Studies Division of the SNI, spoke of repeated requests to the SUNAT to audit small businesses, particularly those in the informal sector. The SNI prepared a study, which measured electricity consumption in marginal urban districts like San Juan de Lurigancho in Lima. The study found some households with well above average electricity consumption levels, suggesting the likely existence of small to medium informal shops. According to Abugattás, however, the SNI's petitions were ignored (interview by the author, Lima, September 3, 1997).

23. Interview by the author with José Reyes, a tax official from SUNAT's Tax Administration Institute (IAT), Lima, July 6, 1997.

the SUNAT attempted for the first time to enforce tax compliance in markets selling food products, associations of market vendors put up the most organized resistance.[24] For tax purposes, it was necessary to formalize small-market vendors in order to audit larger and wealthier intermediaries and distributors. Market vendors, however, responded by organizing a series of strikes and refusing service to the public.[25] This "tax revolt" caught SUNAT officials by surprise.

The rationale for the revolt was somewhat complex. Shortly after the first tax revolt, President Fujimori announced in the annual July 28 presidential address that the government would exempt food products from the sales tax. However, tax director Sandro Fuentes pointed out that the president had only reconfirmed what already existed.[26] In fact, in December 1992 the government had already decreed that most food products were tax exempt.[27] One of the reasons for the tax exemption was to make food products cheaper for everyone, particularly the poor.[28] In addition, the government stipulated that only small businesses with monthly sales greater than 2,700 Peruvian soles (about U.S.$1,356) were taxable.[29] This rule applied to market vendors selling products that were not considered tax exempt, such as beef, chicken, eggs, and rice.

In October 1993, market vendors organized another, albeit partial, strike.[30] The reasons for the recurrent revolts were twofold. First, market vendors selling beef, chicken, and related products argued that all food products should be declared tax exempt because they were all equally "perishable." Simply stated, these market vendors were comparing their equity with or judging it against that of the rest of market vendors with whom they had much in common. This perception of unfairness was sufficient to spark political action.[31]

Another reason for the recurrent protests was the compliance costs imposed

---

24. These associations deal primarily with local, municipal authorities. Some examples were the National Federation of Merchants in Markets and Subsidiaries (FENTRACOM) and the Federation of Street Vendors of Lima and Callao (FEDEVAL).

25. "El cierra puertas de mercados fue generalizado," *El Comercio*, July 22, 1993, A12; and "Paro de mercados dejó pérdidas por S/. 400 millones," *El Comercio*, July 23, 1993.

26. "De buena fuente," *Caretas*, August 12, 1993, 30.

27. "Gobierno eliminó exoneraciones al impuesto general a las ventas," *Gestión*, December 24, 1992.

28. Interview by the author with Roberto Abusada, economic advisor under Finance Minister Jorge Camet, Lima, July 31, 1997. Most Latin countries also exempt perishable items from the sales tax (see IDB 1996, 123–33).

29. Average exchange rate for 1993 was 1.99 soles per U.S. dollar.

30. "Paro parcial de minoristas no impidió ayer la atención en mercados y paraditas," *El Comercio*, October 15, 1993, A3.

31. In November 1993, market vendors called for another strike. See "Otro paro de mercados contra IGV," *Expreso*, November 15, 1993, A2.

by the SUNAT.[32] In fact, the tax office originally attempted to formalize a large number of market vendors by introducing special tax regimes with reduced tax rates. In the case of the sales tax, for instance, large businesses paid the regular rate, equivalent to 18 percent, while small businesses were supposed to pay a reduced rate of 5 percent. However, both large and small businesses had to file the same returns and produce the same paperwork; thus compliance costs were equal for both groups of taxpayers.

Because illiteracy is present among market vendors, it was particularly burdensome for many to comply with the required bookkeeping. Tax specialist Armando Zolezzi argued that the existing tax regime was inadequate for this population, urging SUNAT experts to do some "creative thinking."[33] Only in 1994 did the SUNAT design a more simplified tax system, known as the RUS (Special Simplified Regime), for small businesses. The RUS is a fixed monthly quota and replaces the income and sales taxes.[34] Small businesses in the RUS system, however, were not entitled to tax credits for their purchases. As a result, the SUNAT launched yet another special tax regime, known as the RER (Special Income Tax Regime). Both the RUS and the RER are indicative of the complexity involved in taxing small businesses.

While tax specialists often object to the creation of special tax regimes (Urrunaga 1995), the RUS has benefited not only market vendors, but also a large number of small businesses elsewhere. It was the concentration of market vendors in a specific location that provided them with a powerful negotiation tool in their dealings with the government. This workplace concentration enabled market vendors to overcome their dispersion by numbers and thus to organize collective resistance.

In summary, the tax reform process, which began in early 1991, sparked organized opposition in the form of lobbying and protest activity. Large businesses primarily sought to attenuate their tax burden by demanding a series of tax cuts. More important, as the tax office attempted to spread the costs of the

32. *Compliance costs* refers to the cost to the taxpayers—in terms of lost time, added stress, payments to tax accountants and lawyers, trips to the tax office, and so forth—associated with a given tax payment (Tanzi and Shome 1993, 815).

33. "El problema de los minoristas no reside en los impuestos sino en la facturación," *El Comercio*, October 14, 1993, A7.

34. At the time of this writing, the RUS applied to small businesses whose monthly gross sales or incomes were less than 18,000 Peruvian soles (about U.S.$6,000) and the fixed monthly quota ranged from 20 to 540 soles (about U.S.$7 to U.S.$180). When it was created, it applied to small businesses whose monthly gross sales or incomes were less than 12,000 Peruvian soles (about U.S.$5,400) and the fixed monthly quota ranged from 10 to 300 soles (about U.S.$5 to U.S.$136). See SUNAT 1995b.

reform by broadening the tax base, it also encountered organized resistance from small businesses, particularly associations of market vendors. These associations objected to the reform partly because of compliance costs. With the new simplified tax regimes created in 1994, opposition from small businesses gradually disappeared.[35] In addition, during the Fujimori regime the government continued with the same policy of granting tax exemptions to most food products by extending these exemptions almost every other year. By contrast, large businesses continued to exert pressure on the government to introduce further tax policy changes.

RESHAPING TAX POLICY: TECHNOCRATIC LOYALISTS MEET THEIR MATCH

The capacity of societal actors to modify the government's tax policy was limited in the beginning for various reasons. First, the pursuit of fiscal discipline seriously constrained the ability of the government to modify the existing tax policy. In this sense, President Fujimori repeatedly rejected policy proposals that could have potentially destabilized the country's fiscal health. Second, as discussed in Chapter 2, under Fujimori, potential points of access for policy negotiation or influence, including Congress, were increasingly marginalized. The emergency taxes enacted in August 1990 are illustrative. At that time, business leaders rejected the "tax package" and successfully pressured Congress to block some of these taxes (Castillo and Quispe 1996, 89–98). The permeability of the pre-autogolpe Congress, in which Fujimori's party did not have a majority of seats, created a sense of frustration, particularly among the technocrat core from the Finance Ministry (Boloña 1993, 93). In contrast, the post-autogolpe Congress functioned increasingly as a rubber stamp for executive orders. Finally, influencing tax policy was at first difficult because of the insulation of tax policy makers as well as the autonomy granted to the restructured tax office (Durand 1998, 271–72).

The tax reform indeed provided an important policy forum in which the preferences of technocratic loyalists, who were more independent and inter-

35. Former adjunct tax director Luis Alberto Arias claimed, in retrospect, that the market-vendor strikes had little to no effect on the progress of the reform (interview by the author, Lima, July 16, 1997). The tax exemptions granted to most food products, nonetheless, has limited the tax base of the sales tax. In 2003, the total cost of the existing exemptions from the sales tax approximated 1.55 percent of GDP (Zavalla 2003, 159).

ested in sound tax policy, clashed with those of business leaders and technocrats with business interests, who dwelled in the Finance Ministry. At the outset of the reform, and following the advice of Santiago Fujimori, President Fujimori entrusted the tax office to a core of technocratic loyalists. SUNAT's first three directors—Manuel Estela (1991–92), Sandro Fuentes (1992–94), and Adrían Revilla (1994–97)—came from the BCRP and were sworn in by the president himself.[36] Both Estela and Fuentes received a great deal of presidential support, thus expediting the early stages of the reform process. In contrast, tax director Revilla led the SUNAT during a period in which personal loyalist influence across the technocratic and populist camps weakened, and thus support from and communication with the executive gradually diminished (Durand and Thorp 1998, 145–46). Moreover, Revilla had not been part of the original team that revamped SUNAT. His newcomer status may have facilitated the tax changes sought by business and its technocratic clienteles, an alliance that by the mid-1990s had already established a tight grip on the Finance Ministry.

As leaders of a new institution, these directors sought to assert the autonomy of the tax office, which above all meant minimizing the influence of the Finance Ministry, particularly in questions regarding tax policy. In fact, the technocrats with business interests who dominated the Finance Ministry viewed the SUNAT merely as an administrative agency. However, without the influence of Santiago Fujimori, who withdrew from the government in the mid-1990s, the tax office was basically left standing alone, vulnerable to rising demands from business as well as continual criticism from the Finance Ministry. As Durand and Thorp (1998, 145) indicate, when Santiago Fujimori retreated from the political arena, "SUNAT lost its privileged access to the presidency." Organized businesses, as explained below, managed to modify the government's tax policy by increasing their influence in the Finance Ministry first, and from there, the restructured tax office.

These changes began to take place once the economic situation improved, a period that also brought the government and the business sector closer together. As explained in Chapter 2, a turning point in the relationship between the government and organized business was the appointment of Jorge Camet in early 1993 as minister of finance. During his tenure, as one would expect, the tax reform process became gradually more open to negotiation between state officials and CONFIEP.

---

36. By the end of the García administration, the BCRP was considered the last bastion of technical competence and expertise (Fuentes, Arias, and Durand 1996, 187).

Changes in tax policy were facilitated by the IPE—CONFIEP's pro-business think tank—which technically assisted Camet and the Finance Ministry. The think tank drafted proposals to gradually eliminate the two taxes that had been heavily criticized by the association—the FONAVI and the minimum income tax—and assisted CONFIEP leaders in formulating technical arguments about the efficiency of these two taxes.[37] During the Camet years, the Finance Ministry proved to be more receptive to business demands, which, in the case of tax policy, extended to the reintroduction of tax incentives to promote certain economic activities. Roberto Abusada—IPE's founder and an economic advisor to Camet—indicated that even though tax exemptions implied a loss of revenue in the short term, such losses were significantly less when compared to the potential gains for the economy in the long term as a result of greater investments.[38] However, the loss of revenue resulting from these tax breaks, as discussed below, was substantial, and in some cases, the price tag of these breaks almost matched the income received by the state through the sale of state-owned enterprises. To state it simply, these generous, long-term tax breaks meant that some state-owned enterprises were in fact transferred to private agents very cheaply (Durand 2003, 451–58).[39] In all, under Camet, the IPE, CONFIEP, and the Finance Ministry became virtually intertwined. CONFIEP thus directed its demands to the Finance Ministry via Camet (Durand 1998, 271).

Camet's Finance Ministry became increasingly critical of tax director Revilla because of Revilla's objections to a proposed tax amnesty.[40] In September 1996, under pressure from Camet, the president sanctioned the amnesty as law.[41] The amnesty created a serious administrative burden for the SUNAT. There were 90,908 applications, which had to be handled on a case-by-case basis.[42] Shortly afterward, in January 1997, tax director Revilla resigned.[43] As

37. Interview by the author with IPE's director Leoni Roca, Lima, August 27, 1997.

38. Interview by the author, Lima, July 31, 1997. In Chapter 2, Abusada is characterized as a technocrat with business interests in part because he was involved in the privatization of the national airline (Aero Perú), while serving as an economic advisor to Camet. For further discussion on Abusada's business background and Aero Perú, see Diez Canseco (2002, 123–65), and Congreso de la República (2002).

39. See also Humberto Campodónico, "Rentabilidad en el sector eléctrico: Las ganancias de las empresas privatizadas," *Actualidad Económica* 198 (July 1999): 12–15.

40. Interview by the author with tax director Adrián Revilla, Lima, August 21, 1997.

41. DL 848.

42. SUNAT 1997b.

43. In July 1995, the tax office had also weakened with the forced resignation of prominent technocratic loyalist Luis Alberto Arias, SUNAT's adjuct tax director, who had served since 1991 under tax director Manuel Estela. See "Jefe de la SUNAT tiene concepción distinta de lo que es una administración tributaria," *El Comercio*, July 16, 1995, E2. A graduate from the London School of

Taliercio and Engelschalk (2001, 3) write, the conflicts between the tax office and the Finance Ministry over technically based tax policy "came to light [only] when . . . Fujimori's interest in the SUNAT waned."

Subsequently, following again the recommendations of Camet, the president appointed a more business-friendly tax director, Jorge Baca, to replace Revilla. Like Abusada, Jorge Baca came from the IPE.[44] It was Camet, not President Fujimori, who administered Baca's oath of office, perhaps another sign that executive priorities had already changed. Under tax director Baca, the Finance Ministry and CONFIEP gained final control of the SUNAT, thus defeating the efforts of the former tax directors to place the agency in a position of relative autonomy.

The subordination of the SUNAT to the Finance Ministry represented a victory for the business elite, because as a result the government finally decided to lower the two taxes that had been heavily contested by CONFIEP. In November 1996, FONAVI's rate was reduced from 9 to 7 percent, then in August 1997, it was reduced to 5 percent, and in September 1998, FONAVI was eliminated.[45] In November 1996, the minimum income tax was cut from 2 to 1.5 percent, then in May 1997 to .5 percent, and finally in November 1998 to .2 percent.[46]

The government also reversed its initial refusal to consider sectoral demands. In 1993, for instance, Minister of Agriculture Absalón Vásquez petitioned for a preferential sales tax of 5 percent applicable to food products that were not considered tax exempt. But Finance Minister Camet rejected Vásquez's proposal, stating that sectoral policies simply contradicted the main objective of the reform, which was to maximize tax revenues.[47] By 1996, the government had introduced a series of tax exemptions and incentives in order to promote economic activities such as construction, agroindustry, education, and tourism. As Durand (1997, 27) notes, these policy changes "indicated that the government was more open to business demands."

Economics, Arias was regarded as the "brain" of the SUNAT (interview by the author with tax director Sandro Fuentes, Lima, July 31, 1997).

44. Baca, a former manager of the Bunge and Born Corporation, directed the IPE from 1996 until early in 1997. In Chapter 2, he is characterized as a technocrat with business interests.

45. DL 870, Law 26851, and Law 26969.

46. DL 881, Law 26777, and Law 26999. Tax director Baca indicated that the government agreed to cut these two taxes because the current tax collection had exceeded the estimated collection (interview by the author, Washington, D.C., July 14, 1999). In early 1995, the taxes collected had also surpassed the estimated collection for that period. At that time, Fujimori agreed to a public-sector wage increase, which materialized a few months prior to his 1995 presidential reelection (interview by the author with tax official Laura Calderón, Lima, September 2, 1997).

47. "Agricultura propone rebajar a 5% el IGV para alimentos," *El Comercio*, November 10, 1993.

In mid-1998, Jaime Ibérico, former dean of the Association of Accountants, replaced tax director Jorge Baca. Under Ibérico, the SUNAT began a period of flexible tax enforcement and across-the-board reduction of tax penalties. The overall objective of the new set of policies was to give taxpayers "better treatment." According to Ibérico, the reduction of tax penalties was not necessarily to make the SUNAT more flexible, but rather, it was a matter of executing the law.[48] Iberico's remarks implied that the SUNAT had marginal input with regard to tax policy, and the autonomy that the founding directors Estela and Fuentes envisioned for the tax office was lost. In conclusion, the reappearance of tax incentives to promote certain economic activities as well as the reduction of tax penalties represented yet another important victory for the business elite. These changes ultimately weakened the SUNAT's ongoing tax effort.

COPING WITH DEFICITS AND THE LIMITS OF TAX REFORM

After the mid-1990s, the increase in tax collection seen in the years following the initial reform stalled, and by the late 1990s, discussions of the danger of deficits were once again at the center of the policy debate. Tax revenues fell primarily for two reasons. First, in 1998 an economic recession caused by external shocks and a reoccurrence of El Niño made it particularly difficult to sustain previous levels of tax collection. Second, a series of tax cuts and exemptions, amnesties, and loopholes, particularly in the income tax, began to take place in 1996 (see Appendix, this chapter). Figure 5 shows that tax revenues increased more than GDP during the 1993–96 period. In 1994, for instance, the economy grew at 13 percent and tax revenues increased almost twice as much. By contrast, during the 1997–98 period tax revenues fell below GDP. In 1998, the economy grew by .7 percent, and taxes dropped by almost 4 percent by the end of the same year.

With less revenue at hand, the government began improvising a series of tax measures. To CONFIEP's dismay, in September 1998 the government imposed an "extraordinary solidarity tax" (IES).[49] The new tax had the same regulations and administrative procedures as the old FONAVI. It was basically the FONAVI in disguise. In 1994, the government had plotted a similar scheme. It eliminated the minimum income tax only to have it replaced with an "extraordinary tax on net assets" (IEAN). Despite the name change, in dealings with

48. SUNAT 1998b.
49. Law 26969.

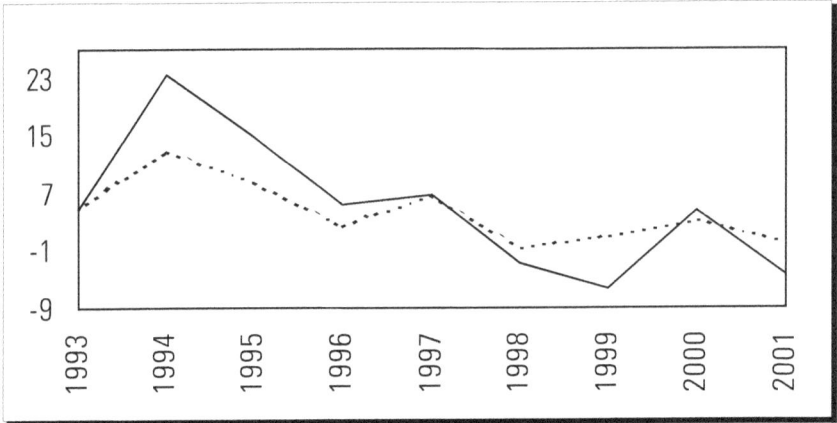

Fig. 5   GDP growth and tax revenue change, 1993–2001
------- GDP growth   ——— Tax revenue change
SOURCE: INEI, *Compendio estadístico* (various years)

the government the business elite has always referred it to as the minimum income tax. Business leaders were displeased with the IES and demanded a real tax cut and no more name changes.[50] In response, the government agreed to eliminate both the IEAN and the IES. In 2000, the government repealed the IEAN. But the budget deficit, which in that year rose to 3.2 percent of GDP, put the elimination of the IES on hold. The government then began to issue bonds to close the fiscal gap. Following the abrupt collapse of the Fujimori regime, businesses continued lobbying for the elimination of the IES, and in late 2001 the government of Alejandro Toledo reduced its rate from 5 to 2 percent.[51] The elimination of the IEAN and the reduction of the IES would complicate the fiscal health of the national treasury well after Fujimori left office.[52] In 2003, the total cost of the existing tax concessions across the income and sales taxes approximated 1.91 percent of GDP (Zavalla 2003, 159).[53]

Moreover, a special decree issued by the Finance Ministry that allowed for

50. "Optan por la austeridad fiscal para no crear nuevo impuesto," *El Comercio*, September 17, 1999.

51. BCRP 2002. The IES was reduced to 1.7 percent beginning in January 1, 2004.

52. BCRP 2000. See also "Presupuesto tiene un déficit de dos mil millones de dólares," *El Comercio*, September 19, 1999; and "Exoneraciones tributarias ascienden a nada menos que S/. 2,400 millones," *El Comercio*, January 19, 2001.

53. Durand (2003, 451) indicates that in 2000 these concessions were approximately 1.34 percent of GDP. See also Kurt Bermeo, "El costo del beneficio tributario," *Actualidad Económica* 215 (March 2001): 24–25.

the double depreciation of assets is arguably one of the most controversial deductions gained by large corporations, which, as one would expect, were mainly from the PRICOS, described above. Privatized state-owned electric companies were a case in point. Under this scheme, when these state-owned companies were bought, large corporations were allowed to reduce their income tax liabilities by depreciating their assets. And when these same corporations merged or consolidated with other companies, they were allowed to depreciate their assets once again. The origins of this income tax loophole date back to late 1994, but it was further perfected in 1996, leading in that year to a flurry of mergers and acquisitions (Congreso de la República 2003; Durand 2003, 454). Although the Finance Ministry initially issued the decree as a temporary measure, as is generally the case with such decrees, it was renewed every year thereafter, and, of course, without SUNAT's participation. According to SUNAT (2002a), 339 million Peruvian soles (about U.S.$100 million) were lost as a consequence of this income tax loophole.[54]

In addition to the reform process being weakened by technocrats who abused their position in power to reward business clienteles, it faltered because of Vladimiro Montesinos. Much of the information leading to this conclusion has come to light only since the fall of Fujimori's government, when fighting corruption became a central state goal. Montesinos indeed exploited the SUNAT to intimidate political opposition to Fujimori and to protect his own cronies, including those in the military, some business leaders, and even media executives (see Conaghan 2002). As Bowen and Holligan (2003, 293) put it, "Opponents of the government and dissenting businessmen soon began to notice they were facing disproportionately lengthy investigations that seemed to be based more on their politics than their book-keeping." In addition, to conceal much of the rampant corruption and individual fortunes being made, during Baca's tenure the SUNAT created a restricted tax registry.[55] This registry effectively blocked from future audits the tax records of individuals included in that special registry. Various government officials and their relatives, even from oppositional forces, were included in this registry for no other reason than to provide an air of legitimacy to Montesinos's elaborate scheme.

Once considered to be among the most efficient and trustworthy state insti-

---

54. This amount is based on a selected sample of 375 large corporations that took advantage of the loophole provided originally by Law 26283 and D.S. 120–94-EF. See SUNAT 2002a.

55. This registry was known as "Friendly Tax Identification Number" (RUC Sensible). As of this writing, Baca was under house arrest in Argentina, where he had been working as a consultant for the IMF.

tutions, with public approval ratings comparable only to those of the Catholic church—an "island of efficiency" according to Durand and Thorp (1998, 148)—by the late 1990s the SUNAT was beginning to lose the confidence of Peruvians.[56] In September 1995, for instance, trust in the restructured tax office reached its highest level of approval at 71 percent. By September 1997, SUNAT's approval rating dropped to 49 percent, and by September 2001, trust in the tax office fell even further to 42 percent, an overall rating that was lower than the one corresponding to the pre-reform years.[57] Montesinos was probably much to blame for this lost in trust, since many of the tax audits being conducted made it difficult to distinguish "which of the investigations were genuine and which purely politically motivated" (Bowen and Holligan 2003, 293). In a public opinion poll conducted in early 1998, 56 percent of Limeños believed that the SUNAT was being systematically used to harass political opposition to Fujimori.[58]

Finally, as the 2000 presidential elections drew near, the tax system began to experience the ups and downs of the political cycle. In fact, in mid-1999 the government granted rice a preferential sales-tax rate of 5 percent. The policy change came after repeated requests from agricultural producers. President of CONFIEP Roque Benavides opposed the policy initiative, indicating that such preferential treatment should be extended to all economic sectors and not just rice producers.[59] As noted earlier, former minister of agriculture Absalón Vásquez had made a similar request in late 1993, but at that time the Finance Ministry was able to successfully block his petition. Because the SUNAT was never consulted about the 5 percent initiative, former adjunct tax director Luis

56. Another institutional setback for SUNAT occurred in early 1999, when President Fujimori informed the media of a significant loss in government revenues resulting from phony gold-exporting companies, which had been cashing in on a special tax benefit called a drawback. The lack of proper tax audits even allowed for some of these companies to import gold into Peru only to export it again with the sole purpose of collecting the tax benefit. See "Empresas exportaban barras de níquel y plomo bañadas en oro," *El Comercio*, April 22, 1999.

57. In March 1991, SUNAT's approval rating was 44 percent. This is the only existing pre-reform figure. The data were taken from Apoyo S.A., *Informe de opinión* (various years). In these polls, the question reads: "In general, would you say that you trust or distrust the following institutions [name of institution]?"

58. *Imasen Confidencial*, January 1998. In the poll, the question reads: "Do you believe that the SUNAT is being used to pressure individuals or businesses that are against the government?" See also "Peruvians Are Growing Weary—and Wary—of 'El Chino,'" *Wall Street Journal*, October 29, 1999, A19.

59. "CONFIEP en contra de reducir IGV a arroceros," *Gestión*, July 30, 1999.

Alberto Arias indicated that the tax office had completely lost its capacity to define tax policy.[60]

COMPARATIVE PERSPECTIVES

The bulk of the literature on tax reform mainly tries to explain why these reforms take place (Durand 1994b; Mahon 2004), rather than exploring post-implementation issues that are likely to affect the direction of reforms in the longer term. Much of the success of tax reforms depends on the sustainability of reform efforts beyond the initial economic crisis that triggered these changes. Argentina, for instance, launched an important tax reform at the beginning of the Menem government (1989–99). According to Bergman (2003, 603), the reform was the most successful of previous reform attempts because "for the first time [it] aggressively tackled the administrative aspect of tax collection." By simplifying tax returns, strengthening tax penalties, computerizing tax information, and monitoring major taxpayers, among other things, the reforms led to impressive results in the beginning. However, over time tax evasion in the country returned to the historic pattern, in part because "taxpayers reali[z]ed that enforcement lacked real teeth" (604). As in Peru, executive priorities in Argentina changed, and the reform "slipped back to normality" when the fiscal and economic situation improved (604).

Pastor and Wise (1999, 40) note that tax revenues in Argentina continue to be low by international standards, and they further indicate that "policy makers have relied too heavily on value-added taxes, which are easy to collect but regressive." Incidentally, Argentina's VAT rate exceeds 20 percent (IDB 1996, 130), suggesting that efforts to strengthen the country's tax administration continues to be patchy at best. Peru approximates the Argentine pattern: the government of Toledo raised the VAT rate from 18 to 19 percent in 2003 to meet fiscal needs.[61]

The creation of semiautonomous tax offices with meaningful financial and administrative independence is another aspect affecting the sustainability of tax reforms. This autonomy, as Taliercio (2004) notes, does have a positive impact along various dimensions of tax administrative capacity, such as com-

60. "SUNAT ha perdido capacidad de decisión para definir política tributaria," *Gestión*, August 3, 1999.
61. Law 28033.

petence, effectiveness, and fairness. However, the conflicts over the much desired autonomy between finance ministries and tax offices are not unique to
the Peruvian case. In countries such as Venezuela, Bolivia, and Mexico, tax
offices that were initially conceived as semiautonomous agencies eventually
were captured by their respective finance ministries. Taliercio (2001) suggests
that these conflicts are primarily institutional, given that finance ministries
have much to lose by granting bureaucratic autonomy to tax agencies, including control over personnel, finances, and tax policy. In the Peruvian case,
however, these conflicts went beyond simple institutional turf wars. There
were in fact two different groups of technocrats who were central to the Fujimori regime, each framing the tax reform differently. Technocrats with business interests, who dominated the Finance Ministry and later SUNAT, treated
the tax office as if it were their own backyard. In contrast, technocratic loyalists,
such as Estela and Fuentes, were more independent and interested in technically based tax policy as opposed to rewarding business clienteles.

Finally, as Durand and Thorp (1998), Taliercio (2001), and others have recognized, the long-term success of tax reforms depends on the broader institutional context, in particular the modernization of institutions, such as the
judiciary and the police. Ironically, Santiago Fujimori advised his brother, the
president, not to seek reelection in 1995 in part because the difficulties of the
work ahead required a "carver, not a stonecutter."[62] As the story goes, other
interests took priority, and institutions such as the judiciary and the police
were toppled by Vladimiro Montesinos.

CONCLUSION

In September 2000, Peru captured the international spotlight when a video-
tape showed Vladimiro Montesinos, President Fujimori's chief political advisor, bribing congressman Alberto Kouri. Kouri was one among the many so-
called turncoats who received money from obscure sources in exchange for
switching political loyalties, and thus helping to construct a new pro-Fujimori
congressional majority. The tape marked the beginning of the end of Fujimori's unprecedented ten-year presidential saga. But for most observers, his
troubles with the law, or more accurately with the absence of it, dated to a few
years back. In 1997, a group of brave tax officials deliberately leaked informa-

---

62. See "Los sinsabores de Santigo," *Caretas*, January 18, 2001.

tion about Montesinos's personal income to the press. According to the reports, Fujimori's spymaster had earned more than 1.6 million Peruvian soles in 1995 (Bowen and Holligan 2003, 319).[63] The reports contradicted official accounts—including from the president himself—that had indicated that Montesinos had been working for the government without compensation.

The fact that a few SUNAT auditors provided this information to the press tells us something important about the most recent wave of market-oriented economic reforms undertaken during the Fujimori years. On the one hand, it suggests that the government's policy goal of creating a new, more autonomous, meritocracy-based state tax agency was generally successful. The efforts to modernize the state thus fostered an important espirit de corps. Various scholars have documented this process of state reinvention—dubbed "institution building"—and the tax office SUNAT is but one example of this important process of state transformation. Seen in this light, the beginning of Fujimori's troubles originated from an institution that he himself helped to create during his first administration. The Fujimori regime thus became a victim of its own success. On the other hand, the culture of modernity within these new state agencies suggest that one could be cautiously optimistic about the prospects for the sustainability of economic reform. Even when Montesinos's agents had infiltrated the SUNAT, many of the politically motivated tax probes were only partially executed. According to Sandro Fuentes, it appeared that SUNAT workers had developed a "silent culture of resistance."[64] If anything, the founding team that revamped the SUNAT were well informed of the changes being made inside the institution, and soon after the fall of the Fujimori regime, the Paniagua government moved quickly to clean the tax office of corruption.

Equally important, the 1991 tax reform helped the Peruvian government close the fiscal gap and defeat hyperinflation. In this capacity, the reform became the centerpiece of the economic-stabilization package implemented in August 1990. The reform was successful because the government maximized the collection of taxes by simplifying the tax system and reorganizing the tax office, SUNAT.

In addition to contributing to our understanding of the politics of tax re-

63. See "La SUNAT no investigó ingresos sospechosos," *El Comercio*, November 25, 2000; and "Acusan a 12 funcionarios de coludirse con ex asesor," *El Comercio*, March 1, 2001. In 1999, information about a bank account with U.S.$2.5 million under Montesinos's name was also leaked to the press (see Bowen and Holligan 2003, 290).

64. Interview by the author, Lima, October 31, 2003. Along these lines, Taliercio and Engelschalk (2001, 3) note, "More than 97 percent of agency staff were hired according to meritocratic procedures; the rest were appointed by SUNAT's superintendent." This type of recruitment indeed

form, the Peruvian experience offers a number of more general conclusions that can be drawn. First, it is important to examine the political consequences of market projects beyond their initial top-down implementation by insulated technocratic elites. Through time the reform process yielded a pattern of highly concentrated costs and widely distributed benefits. As a consequence, the reform sparked more organized resistance and opposition, but little organized support. The strongest and most enduring resistance to the reform came from the organized business sector, which is represented by CONFIEP. This organization vigorously lobbied for tax cuts and flexible tax enforcement, and beginning in 1996, the government gradually acquiesced to business demands. Overall the tax reform process brought greater unity to the organized business sector. As Castillo and Quispe (1996, 98) indicate, it appears somewhat contradictory that while business begins to embrace the new market model, they also reject one of the very foundations that makes it viable—that is, tax reform.

Second, even in Peru, with one of the most highly centralized and least democratic systems in Latin America, societal actors are able to reshape policies that were originally designed by insulated technocrats and implemented by presidential decree. In fact, business leaders were able to obtain a series of tax concessions by exploiting their organized coherence and personal links with the Finance Ministry.

Third, the Peruvian experience shows that the capacity of political outsiders to implement policy reforms may have been somewhat overstated. Outsiders such as Fujimori are able to introduce important policy changes, but their capacity to sustain these efforts is limited. This is particularly the case when reform policies, such as taxation, fail to spark an organized base of support. As a consequence, state officials are left standing alone, having to confront the organized resistance of important societal actors. The government is thus forced to make compromises in order to sustain the reform effort. In this vein, Peru's one-time maverick, reform-minded political outsider, President Fujimori, like most politicians, breached the autonomy of the tax office, reintroduced generous tax exemptions, and granted preferential tax rates and tax cuts, all of which simultaneously undermined the restructured SUNAT and the reform process itself. By weakening the tax office and by making the tax system more complex, the government clearly diluted the efficacy of the initial reform. It is likely, then, that the Peruvian tax system may need another "occa-

---

set the Peruvian tax reform apart from many other cases of reform in the developing world. See also "La SUNAT estará en buenas manos," *Semana Económica,* July 31, 2001, 20.

sional pruning or cleaning" in the future (Tanzi 1996, 20). But if societal demands can dilute some reforms, as in the case of the tax reform, they can also deepen other market projects, particularly those that provide concentrated benefits. In Chapter 4, I examine the privatization of social security pensions as one such example.

APPENDIX

To assess the impact of the post-1996 tax policy changes on revenue collection, I perform an interrupted time-series (ITS) analysis. This technique is particularly useful in studying the effects of new public policies or of new laws (Lewis-Beck 1986). The ITS analysis can help determine whether the occurrence of a particular event (for example, the 1996 tax amnesty or the 1996 loopholes in the income tax) changes the behavior of a variable (such as tax collection) over time. The baseline ITS model used in this chapter is as follows:

$$Y_t = b_0 + b_1X_{1t} + b_2X_{2t} + b_3X_{3t} + e_t$$

where Y_t = N time-series observations on the dependent variable; X_{1t} = a counting variable for time from 1 to N (hereafter trend); X_{2t} = a dichotomous dummy variable scored 0 for those observations before the event and 1 for those observations after the event (hereafter dilution); X_{3t} = a counting variable for time scored 0 for observations before the event and 1, 2, 3 . . . for observations after the event (hereafter postdilution).

The dilution dummy variable—which broadly represents the set of tax changes that began to take place in 1996—is coded 0 for observations before 1995 and 1 for observation January 1996 and after. The postdilution variable is coded 0 for observations before 1995 and 1 (at January 1996), 2 (at February 1996), . . . 48 (at December 1999). Encompassing the same amount of periods both before and after the event, the data consist of monthly tax revenues over an eight-year period (1992–99), creating an "n" of 96. Monthly GDP is used as a control variable. A dummy variable for the month of April—which is the month when tax payments are due—is added to correct for potential biases associated with underspecification. Finally, to correct for autocorrelation, the

ITS analysis includes a lagged dependent variable on the right-hand side of the equation.[65]

Table 8 shows the results of the statistical analysis. With respect to the trend of tax collection (slope change), tax revenues increased at the rate of .85 percent a month prior to 1996. Then, after 1996 the rate decreased .91 percentage points. In other words, the estimated monthly rate of tax collection decrease after 1996 is .06 ($b_1 + b_3$). Therefore, in the long run, the Peruvian tax reform is associated with a downward trend in tax collection. The tax policy changes

Table 8   Postreform tax politics, 1992–99

Independent Variable	Tax Revenues
Intercept (b_0)	4.118***
	(.840)
Trend (b_1)	.008***
	(.001)
Dilution (b_2)	.024
	(.029)
Postdilution (b_3)	−.009***
	(.001)
GDP	.104*
	(.063)
April	.180***
	(.025)
Tax revenues $_{t-1}$	.195**
	(.083)
Adjusted R^2	.89
N	96
Durbin's h	.16

NOTE: Standard errors are in parenthesis.
  *$p < .10$.
 **$p < .05$.
***$p < .01$ (two-tailed tests).

65. The data consist of revenues collected directly by the tax administration, such as income, sales, and excise taxes. Tax figures were taken from *Perú: Compendio estadístico económico financiero*, published by the INEI (various years). The GDP figures were taken from Webb and Fernández, *Perú en números* (various years). Tax and GDP figures were logged to achieve distributional normality. Moreover, because the dependant variable is logged, a percentage-change interpretation of the coefficients can be made. The Durbin's h statistic (.16, p = .37) indicates that the serial correlation has been removed. The results do not change significantly using the Prais-Winsten method, which removes the OLS lagged dependent variable.

that began in 1996, however, were not necessarily followed by a short-run increase or decrease in the level of tax collection as indicated by the nonsignificant intercept change, b_2. The analysis also reveals that tax revenues depend on output. More specifically, a 1 percent increase in GDP increases tax collection by about .10 percent. Predictably, tax revenues are particularly high in the month when tax filing is due, April.

THE PRIVATIZATION OF PENSIONS

Since 1990, states across Latin America have introduced reforms privatizing social security. The Peruvian reform process began in December 1992, when the Fujimori government decreed the creation of a private pension system of social security. The new system was set up to supplement the conventional pay-as-you-go public regime with a capitalization system based on individual retirement accounts managed by private companies called pension fund administrators (AFPs). The AFPs were to be regulated by a new state agency called the Superintendency of Pension Fund Administrators (SAFP). The reform sought to protect workers from the bankruptcy of the public pension system by allowing them to choose their own pension fund managers. The reform also offered potential gains for the economy as a whole in the form of increased national savings and investment.

Like the process of tax reform (see Chapter 3), the pension reform was subject to continued negotiations between societal actors and state officials. In contrast to the tax reform, however, the pension reform sparked both organized support and some opposition—primarily from the social security state bureaucracy—even before the reform came into effect. The complete state of disarray of the social security system at the outset of the reform, as expanded on below, severely weakened the viewpoint of the state bureaucracy, and following the autogolpe their opposition diminished considerably. Organized support, in contrast, became stronger, establishing a basis for the deepening of the reform. The pension reform indeed generated benefits to a well-defined group (the pension industry), while spreading the costs in the form of monthly contributions over a large number of formal-sector workers. The costs arising from these pension contributions, however, were insufficient to induce formal, unionized workers to exercise further political influence.

The dual pension system initially established by the social security reform provided strong incentives for workers to stay in the public system, which limited the prospects for the AFP industry. As a consequence, societal actors with a stake in the new pension system, mostly investors from the banking and insurance sectors, chartered a new business organization called the Association of Pension Fund Administrators (AAFP), which has successfully lobbied for the consolidation of the private pension scheme. In July 1995, the government passed legislation eliminating most of the advantages encouraging workers to stay in the public system. The process of social security privatization is thus consistent with the theoretical expectations outlined in Chapter 1, inasmuch as a pattern of concentrated benefits (on the part of the pension companies) compared to relatively dispersed costs (on the part of workers in the formal sector) led societal actors to exert pressure on the government to deepen the course of the reform process.

The dynamic of the pension privatization is theoretically interesting and important in that it contradicts the notion that market reforms are politically problematic because when they impose concentrated costs to well-organized groups while dispersing benefits across society (see Hellman 1998; Teichman 2001, 210–11). The experience of pension privatization in Peru suggests otherwise: benefits can be concentrated, costs can be diffused, and winners may be better organized than losers, thus helping to consolidate or even deepen the reform project.

The first part of this chapter provides background information on the social security system prior to the Fujimori administration. In the second part I trace the implementation of the pension reform and compare the public and private pension schemes prior to July 1995. In the third section I analyze the consolidation of the private pension system by exploring the lobbying efforts of the AFP industry. The conclusion addresses comparative issues and summarizes the contributions from the Peruvian case.[1]

SOCIAL (IN)SECURITY IN PERU: AN OVERVIEW

At the end of the García administration in July 1990, the national health-care and pension systems were both in need of serious reform. Both were on the

---

1. This chapter draws on Arce 2001.

verge of bankruptcy, significantly contributing to the fiscal woes of the Peruvian state. The health-care system was funded directly by the state. Social security, however, was operated on the basis of a conventional pay-as-you-go pension system, in which pension funds do not accumulate and active workers finance the benefits of retirees. The system was all but depleted in real terms because of negative real investment yields, a significant state debt, high administrative costs, and substantial evasion and delay of payments (Mesa-Lago 1996, 108–9).

The Peruvian Institute for Social Security (IPSS), the state agency created in 1980 to manage the health-care and pension systems, had become one of the most inefficient and corrupt government institutions (Ausejo 1995; Petrera 1993; Reményi 1993). Overstaffed with more than 45,000 employees, the IPSS had about 993 political appointments, or *puestos de confianza* (Ausejo 1995, 139–40). The overstaffing of the IPSS was attributable primarily to the García administration, since the social security bureau had only employed 25,000 workers before his 1985 election. This situation led to a widespread belief that the social security system had broken down and could not be fixed. According to an opinion poll conducted by Apoyo S.A. in March 1989, only 17 percent of Limeños had confidence in the IPSS.[2]

Unlike the more comprehensive Chilean social security reform (Büchi 1996; Barrientos 2000), the initial privatization proposal of the Fujimori government allowed for private initiative only with respect to pensions, leaving health care entirely public until early in 1997.[3] On the whole, this was indicative of the gradual pace of social security reform, which was at variance with that of the tax reform (see Chapter 3), and showed that Peruvian state officials were not fully convinced of the merits of privatization. The president of the IPSS, Luis Castañeda Lossio, noted that "in [the] health [sector], private insurance, competition, and market principles simply do not work" (quoted in Ortiz et al. 1999, 39). Put another way, the IPSS's social mandate with respect to pensions and health care "was never put into question" despite the agency's deteriorated image (Cruz-Saco 1998, 169). Perhaps more important, pension reform encountered some organized political opposition primarily from the social security state bureaucracy, forcing state officials to proceed with caution.

There were at least three important societal groups affected by the reform:

2. In the poll, the question reads: "In general, would you say that you trust or distrust the following institutions [name of institution]?"

3. In November 1991, the government decreed the creation of a private health-insurance system to compete with the IPSS (DL 718), but the decree was never enforced.

the social security state bureaucracy, which primarily feared job losses; formal-sector workers, most of whom were actually eager to abandon the state-run pension system because of its notorious bankruptcy and inefficiency; and pensioners, who demanded better earnings regardless of the type of pension system—whether private or public—in place. As expected, these groups failed to form a broader coalition strong enough to prevent the reform from taking place. Further, the chaotic state of the social security system at the time of the reform, described below, undermined the credibility of societal actors who opposed the pension reform initiative.

The strongest opposition to reforming the IPSS came from the social security state bureaucracy, whose members were organized in unions and associations. Examples were the Workers Central Union (CUT) and the Medical Association of the Peruvian Institute for Social Security (AMSSOP), both of which were run by adherents to APRA and other leftist groups (Roggero 1993, 48–49). The primary concern of the CUT and AMSSOP was job losses (Ausejo 1995, 139). At the outset of the reform, unions demanded wage indexing according to inflation as well as unpaid salaries, because the García administration had issued paychecks without funds (139). Later these organizations managed to link the reform of the IPSS to their opposition to the broader pension-privatization effort. Unions argued that pension privatization could potentially leave the IPSS without funds, as most workers would probably opt to transfer to the new private pension system. In reality, the IPSS had been reporting net losses since 1988 (Verdera 1997, 27–28). From the perspective of the unions, however, pension privatization was unnecessary, because the IPSS could be repaired (Ortiz et al. 1999, 40).

In the opinion of the public, however, the union organizations opposing privatization were heavily discredited. Peruvians were displeased with the IPSS because of extended strikes by health workers. Hospitals were widely known for lacking medical supplies, including basic medicines. Newspapers carried stories of patients bringing their own food and sheets to hospitals. As Deputy Mario Roggero (1993, 48) noted, "I used to imagine the national soccer stadium filled with IPSS workers (forty-five thousand total). The IPSS was indeed a dismal spectacle. At any time during the day, one could find administrators eating sandwiches and tamales, secretaries doing crossword puzzles, and runners taking naps."

Ausejo (1995, 139) pointed out that unions had managed to secure a fixed quota of the IPSS's budget (30 percent) to be spent on salaries. These funds were obviously allocated independent of workers' productivity. This situation created moral outrage. IPSS workers were economically better off than pensioners, who in 1991 received an average of U.S.$68 per month—equivalent to about one-fifth of a monthly living wage.[4] This meager pension was a fixed sum that reflected neither the numbers of years worked nor the funds collected by the IPSS. In contrast, a group of selected state employees had better retirement plans as a result of a special pension regime that adjusted their earnings to current wages. To this date, the reform has not affected the privileges of this group.[5]

Although statistical information is not reliable, the total number of affiliates in the IPSS before the pension reform was introduced in 1993 was approximately 2.5 million, about one-third of the Peruvian labor force (Cruz-Saco 1998, 168). At that time, there were also 303,554 pensioners.[6] In essence, the beneficiaries of the IPSS were loosely organized formal-sector workers. By contrast, rural workers and the self-employed (the informal sector), who make up the remaining two-thirds of the labor force in Peru, were not participants in the social security system.

Only a few politicians, mostly from the APRA and other leftist groups, sympathized with the unions and catered to their constituencies. The opposition of these politicians to the pension reform, however, was in part ideological. Simply stated, the conventional state-run system was based on principles of solidarity among workers; the private pension system emphasizes principles of individual effort and responsibility. Other politicians, such as Deputy Xavier Barrón (PPC), did not support the pension reform, because it did not address the problems of current retired workers. In the eyes of Barrón, these problems primarily had to do with low pensions.[7] Without a doubt the pension reform did not affect the rights of retired workers (or the lack of such rights). Yet unions managed to escalate the estimates of the impact of pension reform, and state actors responded accordingly.

The opposition of these unions, however, gradually dissipated as the government authorized a profound reorganization of the IPSS. More important, after the April 1992 autogolpe, points of access between organized labor and Congress were simply eliminated. As a result, unions continued to object to

---

4. IPE 1997b, 28.

5. "Vive la cédula viva," *Perú Económico,* May 1997, 4–5.

6. IPE 1997b, 26.

7. Interview by the author with Deputy Xavier Barrón, Lima, August 20, 1997. Barrón is known as "the advocate of the elderly" (*el defensor de los viejitos*).

the reform, but their concerns could not be channeled through the national legislature.

The reorganization of the IPSS began in August 1990, when President Fujimori appointed Luis Castañeda Lossio as head of the institution. Castañeda had worked for various mayors of Lima, such as Eduardo Orrego (1980–83), Jorge Del Castillo (1983–86), and Alfonso Barrantes (1986–89), earning a reputation as an individual "capable of solving old problems" (Ausejo 1995, 134). At the outset, Castañeda made plans to remove excess personnel. The government offered social security workers severance pay ranging from 12 to 24 months for voluntary retirement. Then it began administering competence exams, leading to a further reduction of personnel. About twenty thousand employees were dismissed in a two-year period (Ortiz et al. 1999, 43). In the end, most of the employees who left the IPSS were the ones who had been hired between 1989 and 1990, a period in which politicization of the IPSS had skyrocketed (Ausejo 1995, 140). In addition, under Castañeda, public hospitals were assigned a budget, and administrators had to justify expenditures on a weekly basis, prioritizing the purchase of medicines and food for patients first.

With fewer personnel and better allocation of resources, IPSS's services improved dramatically. The waiting period for prostrate surgery, for instance, was reduced from two years to three weeks. Under Castañeda, the average number of surgeries performed by doctors was increased from twenty-four to one hundred per year (143). According to polls conducted among Limeños by Apoyo S.A., approval of the IPSS increased from 23 percent in March 1991 to 51 percent in September 1993 and later to 76 percent in September 1995. In September 1998, the IPSS was ranked third among national institutions, with ratings of 60 percent, superseded only by the Catholic church and Lima's municipal government, headed by Alberto Andrade.[8] With pension privatization, the administration of the national pension system was removed from the auspices of the IPSS and entrusted to a new state agency called the Pensions Normalization Office (ONP). The IPSS (currently ESSALUD) became solely responsible for managing the public health-care system.[9]

---

8. Apoyo S.A. 1998c. In these polls, the question reads: "In general, would you say that you trust or distrust the following institutions [name of institution]?" Castañeda left the IPSS in early 1996. He subsequently created a new political movement called National Solidarity (Solidaridad Nacional) and was an unsuccessful contender in the 2000 presidential election. In November 2002, affiliated with a different political party called National Unity (Unidad Nacional), Castañeda became mayor of Lima.

9. For a discussion of recent health reforms, see Arroyo 2002.

THE INITIATION OF THE PENSION REFORM

Mario Roggero, a deputy of the Democratic Front (FREDEMO), was the original promoter of the pension reform initiative. FREDEMO was the political coalition that supported the candidacy of Vargas Llosa in the presidential elections of 1990. In his congressional campaign, Roggero proposed a private pension system similar to the Chilean model, but with some important variants. The new private system he envisioned was not designed to eliminate the state-run IPSS; it was meant to compete with it. In Roggero's words, he wanted to "democratize social security and not privatize it" (Ortiz et al. 1999, 40). In addition, workers in the private pension system could return to the IPSS if they so desired. Roggero sought congressional approval for the reform, but political parties, such as APRA and other leftist groups, which controlled the pre-autogolpe Congress, blocked the reform proposal (Ortiz et al. 1999, 37).

After Roggero's plan failed, technocrats with business interests led by Minister of Finance Carlos Boloña took charge of the reform initiative. Technocrats, however, had a more ambitious reform plan. They argued that enrollment in the private pension system should be mandatory and irreversible for all new entrants in the labor force. They also planned to increase the contribution rate of the state-run pension system in order to make the private pension system cheaper, and thus more attractive (Ortiz et al. 1999, 42). These measures were seen as vital to guaranteeing prospects for the new private pension system. They were also consistent with the preferences of investors from the banking and insurance sectors, who had a "latent" interest in the reform process.

In short, technocrats with business interests hoped to move the reform process closer to the Chilean model, in which private initiative completely replaced state participation with respect to social security pensions (Büchi 1996). As in Chile, technocrats expected to liquidate the state-run pension system. In so doing, the government could stem "growing fiscal losses over the medium run" (Nelson 1999, 13). The government would have to issue compensation bonds (also known as *bonos de reconocimiento*) to workers who decided to transfer to an AFP in order to offset the contributions made to the state-run system. Peruvian investors, in turn, expected concessions from the government similar to those that had taken place in Chile. Chilean pension companies, for instance, were given special advantages in the bidding process for the privatization of state-owned enterprises, which ultimately strengthened the investment portfolio of the AFPs. In addition, they expected the government to guarantee a minimum pension to workers whose contributions in the private system were insufficient for paying the minimum-pension level at retirement. The minimum-pension guarantee is basically a subsidy from the government to the private sector.[10] Yet Boloña (1998) objected to the minimum pension because it created a "moral hazard" problem; it gave pension companies "an incentive to invest haphazardly—to place [funds] in highly risky investments in hopes of huge returns."[11]

However, neither Roggero nor Boloña could persuade President Fujimori to launch the reform. Thus Boloña brought to Lima the mastermind of pension reform, Chile's former minister of labor José Piñera. As Boloña (1998) pointed out, "At the time of the reform, the president of Peru was very concerned. He was not convinced that we should privatize the pension system. So we brought José to talk to him, to discuss what privatization had done for Chile. And, of course, José was able to convince him that privatization was in Peru's best interest. The reform might not have been signed into law without José's assistance."

However, various authors have suggested that President Fujimori was not fully committed to the pension reform. According to Graham (1998, 115), this was a result of the initial political opposition by public-sector unions. Cruz-Saco (1998, 169) suggests that the president implemented the pension reform in a gradual, piecemeal fashion because he hoped to retain his popular appeal. As such, the president "did not challenge the working classes' prejudices against the private pension scheme" (169). Mesa-Lago (1997, 514) argues that the president was constrained by constitutional impediments that protected the rights of workers. Fujimori's concern for constitutional rights, however, is questionable at best, given the autogolpe and its aftermath (see Cameron 1998). Finally, Ortiz et al. (1999, 38) argue that the president was concerned that the pension reform would allow bank and insurance investors to dominate financial markets.

The president's distrust of big businesses and banks, an outlook that coincided with the "policy repertoire" of populist loyalists described in Chapter 2, largely defined the government's attitude toward the pension reform in its early

---

10. For a discussion of the distributional effects of the minimum-pension guarantee, see James 1998.

11. This was probably one of few instances in which technocrats in the Finance Ministry, such as Boloña, disagreed with the private pension industry. *Moral hazard* refers to the presence of incentives for individuals to act in ways that incur costs that they do not have to bear. The minimum-pension guarantee may also encourage workers to contribute only for the minimum time period required to be eligible to receive such a guarantee. In other words, it also creates a moral hazard problem on the part of pensioners. For a discussion, see Aiyer 1997.

stages. Hence, state officials led by Fujimori were hesitant to abolish the public pension system, which they viewed as a continuing alternative to the private scheme. They thus exempted themselves from any obligation to promote the new pension system, resulting in considerable public confusion. As indicated in Table 9, with the exception of individuals with higher incomes, the lack of knowledge regarding the new pension system was overwhelming.

In interviews, chief executive officers (CEOs) of the AFPs said that even though the government had initiated the privatization process, it did little to promote it.[12] José Piñera, for instance, had played an active role in promoting the Chilean reform, personally appearing in various TV spots designed to get across simple messages, such as that workers were the ultimate owners of their pensions (Graham 1998, 55). Peruvian AFPs were counting on Minister of Finance Carlos Boloña. However, Fujimori dismissed Boloña in early 1993, well before any AFP began operation. In the end, the business elite was left standing alone, having to sell the idea of a private pension system to the government and, most important, to the public.

Between 1991 and 1992, the government enacted two sets of pension reform laws, both of which reflected in one way or another the president's "political bias."[13] In November 1991, Legislative Decree (DL) 724 authorized the functioning of a supplementary private pension system. The decree was issued by the Finance Ministry with special powers granted by the pre-autogolpe Con-

Table 9   Knowledge of the Peruvian AFPs

Do you know what the AFPs are?

		Socioeconomic Level (in percentages)			
Responses	Total	Upper	Upper-Middle	Lower-Middle	Lower
Yes	39	73	58	44	24
No	57	23	40	53	72
Uncertain/No Response	4	4	2	3	4
Number of Respondents	530	66	121	209	134

SOURCE: Apoyo 1993.

12. Interviews by the author with Ramón Barúa, CEO of AFP Horizonte, Lima, May 27, 1997; Guillermo Zarak, CEO of AFP Unión, Lima, July 22, 1997; Mariano Felipe Paz-Soldán, CEO of AFP Profuturo, Lima, July 8, 1997; and Jorge Ramos, investment and finance manager of AFP Integra, Lima, August 25, 1997.

13. The term is taken from Murillo 2002. The notion of "political bias" refers to the choices available to politicians regarding how to privatize, while recognizing external and domestic pressures to do so.

gress. With lower contributions for the insured and more liberal entitlement conditions, DL 724 provided strong advantages for workers to stay in the public pension system. More important, DL 724 prohibited banks and insurance firms from participating in the new pension system, a stipulation written at the request of Fujimori himself (Roggero 1993, 110; Ortiz et al. 1999, 39). The private pension system was scheduled to begin operations in July 1992. However, DL 724 never became effective. The autogolpe paved the way for a new decree that abolished DL 724.

In December 1992, the government sanctioned a new private pension system law (Law 25897) via decree. Similar to DL 724, Law 25897 continued to provide advantages encouraging workers to stay in the state-run system. However, an important difference was that Law 25897 enabled shareholders of banks and insurance firms to participate in the new pension scheme. While the private pension system was not entirely business friendly, it set the reform process in motion. As we will see, it was the organized support of investors that got the reform off the ground.

THE PENSION SYSTEM PRIOR TO JULY 1995

Attracting various financial investors from the United States, Chile, and Peru, in June 1993 the first AFPs opened their doors to the public. There were originally eight AFPs. However, between 1994 and 1999, four of these merged, leaving the private pension system with a total of four AFPs: Integra, Horizonte, Unión Vida, and Profuturo. This process of consolidation was very similar to that in the Chilean case.

At 9 percent, contributions for the insured were significantly lower in the public scheme, one third of which was paid for by workers, compared to 15 percent in the private scheme, all of which was paid by workers (see Table 10). Moreover, the public system offered more liberal entitlement conditions with respect to retirement age: sixty for males and fifty-five for females in contrast to sixty-five and sixty, respectively, in the private system. In addition, workers who transferred to an AFP had to pay a 1 percent solidarity contribution from their monthly salaries to the national pension system. Finally, the private pension scheme did not provide a minimum-pension guarantee to its affiliates and even allowed workers to affiliate back to the state-run system if they so desired.

Even though the government decreed a 13 percent wage raise for those workers who transferred to an AFP, the raise did not take away the incentives to

Table 10   Deductions as a percentage of a monthly salary

	Employer	Employee
Before July 1995		
Private Pension System	0	15
—Pension	0	10
—Solidarity Contribution	0	1
—Insurance and Commissions	0	4
National Pension System		
—Pension	6	3
After August 1995		
Private Pension System	0	11
—Pension	0	8
—Solidarity Contribution	0	0
—Insurance and Commissions	0	3
National Pension System		
—Pension	0	11
After January 1997		
Private Pension System	0	13
—Pension	0	10*
—Solidarity Contribution	0	0
—Insurance and Commissions	0	3
National Pension System		
—Pension	0	13

SOURCE: Banco Central de Reserva del Perú, *Memoria 1995*.

*Contribution rate was not raised as mandated by Law 26504.

stay in the public pension system (Vega-Centeno and Reményi 1996, 321–22). In the end, the biases against the private scheme put the AFPs in jeopardy. Affiliation rates, which during the first six months that the AFPs were in operation averaged one hundred thousand workers per month, decreased to forty thousand during the first half of 1994 and then to eleven thousand during the second half of that same year.[14] During the first quarter of 1995, affiliation rates dropped further, to three thousand workers per month (Fig. 6). As a result, the AFPs increased their marketing expenses, hoping to secure a greater market share to cover their costs. Some AFPs took on debt in order to cover cash imbalances. Others reduced their sales force and even closed many branches (AFP Horizonte 1996). Two AFPs merged during 1994. AFP Nueva Vida and AFP Horizonte took over AFP Providencia and AFP Megafondo, respectively, thus reducing the original number of AFPs from eight to six.[15]

14. IPE 1997b, 51.
15. In 1996, AFP Profuturo merged with AFP El Roble.

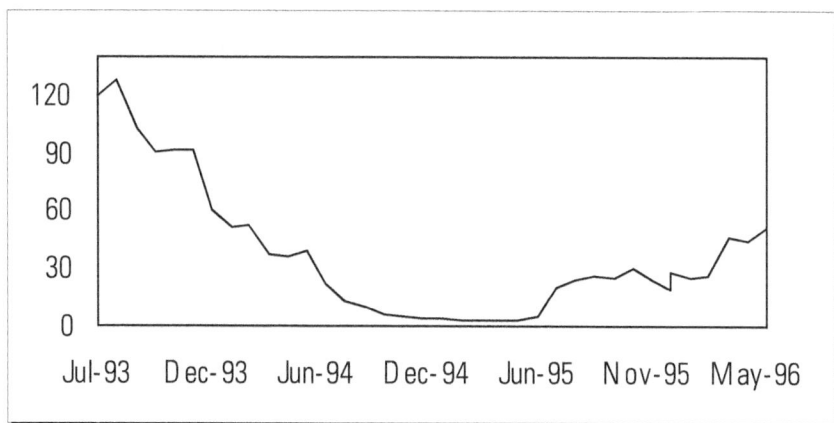

Fig. 6   AFPs' monthly affiliation, July 1993–June 1996 (thousands)
SOURCE: Superintendencia de Administradoras Privadas de Fondos de Pensiones

According to Verdera (1995), workers perceived the AFPs as an expensive alternative. Because they feared they would lose the health-care benefits they had accrued in the national pension system, workers also did not enroll in the AFPs (AFP Horizonte 1996). Most important, as the government did little to promote the new pension system and had delayed the emission of compensation bonds, workers did not trust the AFPs.

In an interview, J. Alberto León, general counsel for the Association of AFPs (AAFP), suggested that politicians capitalized on the idea that the pension-privatization reform would only benefit the wealthy, particularly bankers. Unions, he argued, although weakened by the economic crisis, latched onto that idea, and public employees were particularly reluctant to switch to the private pension system.[16] By contrast, almost five months before the AFPs began to operate, an opinion poll conducted by Apoyo S.A. in January 1993 suggested that the private pension system was already an attractive option for individuals with higher incomes (Table 11).

The public also began to wonder who the real beneficiaries of the privatization process were when the former minister of finance Carlos Boloña, who was particularly instrumental in advancing the pension reform, appeared as a shareholder of AFP Horizonte.[17] AFP Horizonte initially aired the former minis-

16. Interview by the author, Lima, July 22, 1997.
17. Even though Congress began an investigation, no charges were brought against the former minister.

Table 11   Enrollment preference toward the private pension system

If you had the opportunity to enroll in the private pension system, would you?

		Socioeconomic Level (in percentages)			
Responses	Total	Upper	Upper-Middle	Lower-Middle	Lower
Yes	16	42	23	21	7
No	15	21	21	15	11
Doesn't Know*	61	27	42	56	76
Uncertain/No Response	8	10	14	8	6
Number of Respondents	530	66	121	209	134

SOURCE: Apoyo 1993.

*Respondents who do not know what the AFPs are.

ter in various television commercials. In an interview, the CEO of AFP Horizonte, Ramón Barúa, indicated that since Boloña was perceived as an economic policy hardliner, particularly among the poor, the marketing campaign with Boloña brought more harm than good to AFP Horizonte.[18] Ironically, even though the former minister is no longer a shareholder of AFP Horizonte, Peruvians continue to characterize it as Boloña's AFP.

THE CONSOLIDATION OF THE PENSION REFORM

In striking contrast to the tax reform (see Chapter 3), the pension reform sparked organized support from a well-defined group even before the pension reform law came into effect. At that time, Peruvian investors invited various Chilean specialists to Lima to discuss the merits of the reform, the visitors including José Piñera and the superintendent of the Chilean AFPs Julio Bustamante. However, because the perception of the AFPs was somewhat hostile and the president did little to counterattack the opposition to the reform, business leaders kept a "low profile" (Ortiz et al. 1999, 41). Consistent with what Wilson (1980, 366) describes, the anticipation of benefits (business profits) was sufficient to trigger collective action on the part of Peruvian investors.

In fact, Peruvian investors did not have to look far to realize the potential profitability of the private-pension companies. Chilean AFPs were a case in point. In 1990, the Chilean AFP system reported operating profits equivalent to

18. Interview by the author, Lima, May 27, 1997.

more than 15.6 billion pesos (Büchi 1996, 81). It was also no coincidence that the two largest Chilean AFPs, AFP Provida and AFP Santa María, provided technical assistance to AFP Horizonte and AFP Integra, respectively, the latter pair eventually becoming the two Peruvian AFPs with the largest market share.[19] Consequently, Peruvian investors anticipated results similar to those that had taken place in Chile provided the government eliminated the flaws created by the December 1992 pension law. In 1994, the real rate of return (adjusted for inflation) of the Peruvian AFP system was 8.6 percent.[20] This positive outcome provided an additional incentive to continue with the reform.

As opposition to the reform diminished following the reorganization of the IPSS, and given the absence of institutionalized channels to exert political pressure—a consequence of the autogolpe—the political system was slanted to favor business interests. Private-pension companies anticipated profits that were substantially bigger, more rapid, and visible. In contrast, the costs of the reform were spread out in the form of monthly contributions over a large number of formal-sector workers. The costs arising from these pension contributions were insufficient to induce unionized workers to exercise further political influence. In accordance with the theoretical expectations outlined in Chapter 1, this pattern of concentrated benefits and diffused costs led to the creation of a new stakeholder, an association of AFPs (AAFP), which has advanced the prospects for the consolidation of the reform process.

The AAFP was created in September 1993 and was quickly incorporated into the ranks of CONFIEP. At the outset of the reform, however, common business interests were temporarily set aside because each AFP competed fiercely to secure a market share. As in Chile, the first eight to ten months of the reform were decisive for each pension company attempting to establish a market niche. This situation changed once affiliation rates continue to decrease (see Fig. 6).

With the private pension system at the brink of crisis, the AAFP and the government began negotiations to reform the existing dual pension system. The AAFP became an effective lobby of friends and acquaintances who had close ties with and easy access to state officials. Business leaders who ran the AFPs were board directors of many of the leading financial institutions in Peru. As such, they were well acquainted with Jorge Camet, a business leader in the construction sector, who served as president of CONFIEP and later replaced

---

19. By December 1998, AFP Provida owned about 16 percent of the shares of AFP Horizonte.
20. BCRP 1994.

Carlos Boloña as minister of finance (see Chapter 2). As in the case of tax reform, changes in the pension reform law materialized only after business-government relations became more cooperative and stable, that is, during Camet's tenure as minister of finance.

General counsel for the AAFP J. Alberto León indicated that the association raised its concerns directly to Camet as opposed to the SAFP, the state agency in charge of overseeing the new pension system.[21] Moreover, former cabinet members who served under President Fujimori assisted by mediating on behalf of the pension reform. Such were the cases of Alfonso de los Heros Pérez, former prime minister and chair of directors of AFP Nueva Vida; Alfonso Bustamante y Bustamante, former minister of labor and board director of AFP Profuturo; and Efraín Goldenberg Schreiber, former prime minister and board director of AFP Horizonte.[22]

The president of the AAFP, Jaime Cáceres Sayán, was particularly outspoken and began an intense campaign to promote the new pension system, giving public lectures and addressing the media in general on many occasions.[23] Cáceres noted that even though the government did set up a dual pension system, the public scheme was not a viable "choice," because it was bankrupt.[24]

In interviews, CEOs of the AFPs indicated their dissatisfaction with the performance of the SAFP, alleging a regulatory bias.[25] CEOs agreed that the SAFP did little to promote the reform. General Counsel J. Alberto León pointed out that Peruvians knew the AAFP president Jaime Cáceres Sayán better than they knew the superintendent of the SAFP, Augusto Mouchard Ramírez, who was rarely seen in public.[26] In contrast, Deputy Superintendent Enrique Díaz Ortega was somewhat more active, yet never as much as the AFPs had hoped. Appointed by Santiago Fujimori, Deputy Superintendent Díaz described his job as conservative, as he sought to protect the investments made by the AFPs.[27] The appointment of a technocratic loyalist such as Díaz to the SAFP was another indication of Fujimori's initial antibusiness stance, described above.

The AAFP's most immediate objective was to pressure the government to

---

21. Interview by the author, Lima, May 27, 1997.

22. Interview by the author with Alfonso de los Heros Pérez, Lima, August 28, 1997. Efraín Goldenberg would later become finance minister under Fujimori, replacing Víctor Joy-Way.

23. The first president of the AAFP was Juan Antonio Aguirre Roca. Roca was president of CONFIEP during the 1992–93 period (replacing Jorge Camet) and was chair of directors of AFP Horizonte. In 1995, Jaime Cáceres Sayán, chair of directors of AFP Integra, replaced Aguirre Roca.

24. Lecture given at the Universidad de Lima, Lima, May 28, 1997.

25. See note 12, above.

26. Interview by the author, Lima, May 27, 1997.

27. Interview by the author, Lima, May 9, 1997.

eliminate the obstacles that were hindering the prospects for the AFP industry. As explained below, the AAFP managed to make the private pension system more attractive, with lower contribution rates than those of the public pension system. This arrangement was precisely the way Minister of Finance Carlos Boloña envisioned the reform from the start.

In July 1995, the pension system was altered in accordance with the AAFP's demands. Law 26504 made contribution rates equal for both systems, averaging 11 percent. The contribution rate in the public scheme was raised from 9 to 11 percent and paid entirely by workers. In the private system, the contribution rate was temporarily lowered from 10 to 8 percent, and the government abolished the 1 percent solidarity contribution to the national pension system. Insurance sales and commissions earned by AFPs were exempted from the sales tax, reducing their overall cost from an average of 4 to an average of 3 percent (see Table 10). In January 1997, another amendment increased the contribution rate in the public scheme from 11 to 13 percent, further reducing the incentives for workers to remain in the public pension system. The government, however, did not raise the contribution rate for the private scheme as had been originally stipulated. To continue to attract new affiliates, the AAFP convinced state officials to maintain the contribution rate at 8 percent until December 31, 2001. These changes in contribution rates were not difficult to execute, because the new legislation gave the Finance Ministry the sole authority to modify pension rates in coordination with the SAFP. In other words, the pension reform process had little, if any, congressional oversight, and it thus became centralized within the executive branch, with which the business community was already building strong connections.

Law 26504 made entitlement conditions equal: the age of sixty-five for females and males in both systems. The legislation also gave new workers a grace period of ten days to notify their employers of whether they wished to be enrolled in the national pension system. If workers did not communicate such a preference within the ten-day period, they were enrolled by default into the AFP of the employer's choice. More important, the government set a deadline (June 1, 1996) for workers enrolled in the AFP system to return to the state-run pension. Only 3,141 workers (representing .16 percent of those enrolled in the AFP system) returned to the state-run pension system.[28]

In essence, the new legislation revitalized the private pension system, making it particularly attractive to new entrants in the labor force. In 1998, for

28. SAFP 1998.

example, about 72 percent of workers who enrolled in the AFPs were younger than forty years old.[29] With lower contribution rates, AFPs were no longer seen as an expensive alternative. As a result, affiliation rates began to increase and the pension reform gathered new momentum. Affiliation rates, which during the first quarter of 1995 averaged 3,000 workers a month, increased to 25,000 workers during the second half of that same year.[30] In the second half of 1996, affiliation rates further increased to 41,000 workers a month. By the end of December 1998, there were 1,980,420 workers affiliated in the private pension system, representing approximately 24 percent of the Peruvian labor force, which in 1998 was estimated to be close to 8 million people.[31] In contrast, the number of affiliates in the public pension system decreased from 3.4 million in 1990 to 938,259 in 1996.[32]

Law 26504 had an immediate impact on the performance of AFPs. AFP Integra was profitable as early as 1996, and by December 1997, three AFPs reported profits. In 1997, net profits of the Peruvian AFP system were equivalent to 15.3 million soles (about U.S.$5.7 million), and the AFPs achieved their highest real rate of return (adjusted for inflation), averaging 11.1 percent.[33] In 1998, net profits were equal to 34.2 million soles (about U.S.$11.6 million), and the value of the Peruvian pension fund amounted to U.S.$1.7 billion, which was equivalent to 3 percent of GDP.[34]

Perhaps the anecdote told by J. Alberto León, general counsel of the AAFP, best summarizes the government's response to the demands of the AAFP:

> It became customary for business associations that are members of CONFIEP to invite the minister of finance, Jorge Camet, to informal meetings to air out business complaints and demands. In one such meeting, AAFP president Jaime Cáceres Sayán and I were wondering what we should say. After various representatives had their turn to address the minister, Jaime Cáceres only congratulated and thanked the minister for all the support given to the pension reform process,

29. SAFP 1998.

30. IPE 1997b, 51.

31. One of the limitations of the pension reform is that more than 60 percent of the Peruvian labor force is either self-employed or works in agriculture. This creates inherent limitations for the potential enrollment into either pension scheme, public or private.

32. IPE 1997b, 23.

33. BCRP 1997.

34. SAFP 1998. By 2001, the value of the pension fund had reached 7 percent of GDP. See BCRP 2001.

thus changing the entire tone of the meeting. After that, participants in the meeting began to suggest that we were the spoiled or privileged ones.[35]

Finally, despite the improvement experienced after the new legislation came into effect, the AAFP continued to pressure the government over some pending issues. One example was the lack of a minimum-pension guarantee for affiliates in the private pension system. The Fujimori regime delayed the implementation of the minimum-pension guarantee as mandated by Law 26504, largely because of disagreements with the AAFP over its financing. While the business sector insisted that the government was financially responsible for the minimum pension, government officials remained unconvinced.[36] According to the private pension industry, the minimum-pension guarantee was the only remaining incentive that could prompt a significant number of workers, particularly those more than forty years old, to shift to an AFP.[37] In addition, the AFPs sought to diversify risks by investing a percentage of pension funds under management abroad, yet the government rejected the request, largely for nationalistic reasons.[38] Perhaps the most controversial issue revolves around the financing of the SAFP. In Peru, the SAFP is financed by the AFPs themselves through a percentage of assets under management. Business leaders have requested an end to this type of financing, but such petitions have been ignored. In sum, Peruvian business leaders continue to view Chile as their model, and they are likely to continue lobbying for these pending issues.[39]

COMPARATIVE PERSPECTIVES

The increasing role of the business sector both during the initiation and, particularly, after the implementation of pension reforms is hardly unique to

35. Interview by the author, Lima, May 27, 1997.
36. "La ley de las AFP cuenta con mecanismos adecuados para proteger fondo de pensiones," *El Comercio*, November 19,1998.
37. "Pensión mínima para afiliados a las AFP debe resolverse este año," *El Comercio*, July 14, 1998; and "Pensión Mínima Elevará Traslado A Las AFP," *El Comercio*, August 24, 2001. The government of Alejandro Toledo established a minimum pension for the AFP industry in late 2001. See "Establecerían Pensión Mímima De S/. 415 Para Los Jubilados," *El Comercio*, November 29, 2001.
38. "Anularán reglamento que permite la inversión en el extranjero de AFPs," *El Comercio*, August 9, 1999.
39. In the post-Fujimori period, the AFP industry was widely criticized by Congress for the contributions charged to workers, which were thought to be excessive. Beginning in 2001, the AFP industry agreed to gradually reduce the rate of these contributions. For further details, see "Esperando al pleno: AFP aceptaron reducir las comisiones de administración del fondo," *Semana Económica*, February 11, 2001, 15.

Peru. In fact, other cases of social security reform support the general argument that organized business, namely the AFP industry, can be a decisive player in the outcome of pension reforms. In Argentina, similar to the Peruvian case, the pension-privatization process was expedited by a dominant chief executive; declining labor influence; and most important, strong business support (Kay 1999, 412).[40] Thus one might expect not only the passage of the reform bill, but also some attempts by business to block initiatives that could hinder the prospects of the newly privatized social security system. In fact, to ease political opposition against the reform, the Menem administration (1989–99) promised organized labor government-guaranteed returns for the Banco de la Nación, the state-owned pension plan. However, members of the Argentine financial sector strongly opposed the initiative because, they argued, it provided a competitive advantage to the state-owned pension plan. Acquiescing to business demands, Menem would later decree the elimination of the government-guaranteed returns for the state-owned pension plan (Torre and Gerchunoff 1999, 27).

Social security reform in Brazil during the Cardoso administration (1995–2002) offers an interesting test case about the relative importance of the business sector in bringing about pension privatization. Similar to what happened in pre-autogolpe Peru, technocrats at the Ministry of Finance in Brazil, following recommendations from the World Bank, attempted a wholesale privatization of the state-run public pension system. Opposition to the reform originated from inside the state apparatus, the social security state bureaucracy in particular, as well as from unions and patronage-hungry political parties (Weyland 1996; Kay 1999). But neither Fujimori prior to the autogolpe nor Cardoso were able to secure congressional backing for their respective pension reform bills. Yet the organization of business and the role it played during the privatization process was a key distinction between both countries. In fact, compared to that of Peru or Chile, business organization in Brazil is regarded as weak and fragmented (Weyland 1998).[41] Also, whereas members of the Peruvian financial sector remained active and fully engaged in the privatization program, their Brazilian counterparts, as Kay (1999, 412) pointed out, "expended little effort in promoting policy reform and left the impetus to their representatives in the ministries of finance and planning." Throughout the 1990s, as is documented in this chapter, the highly organized AFP industry in Peru continued

---

40. Like Peru's, the Argentine pension bill was implemented by an executive decree.
41. Clearly, the Brazilian business sector is also more diversified (see Kingstone 1999).

to lobby for a pension bill to its liking. In contrast, the organizational fragmentation of businesses in Brazil would seriously "exacerbate collective action problems inside the private sector and weaken business pressure for social insurance reform" (Weyland 1996, 61). *Ceteris parabus* differences in the strength of business influence led to differences in pension reform outcomes. Only in late 1998 did the Cardoso administration manage to secure approval for a modest pension reform bill, affecting the existing public social security system at the margins. The reform has been described as a "reform of nothing" (quoted in Kingstone 1999, 216).[42]

CONCLUSION

Much of the recent literature on pension reform has treated the business response to privatization only in passing, and it is largely seen as disorganized and passive (Brooks 2002; Madrid 2002). It is perhaps assumed that in the era of financial globalization, private capital wields silent clout, and therefore, it does not need to organize and act collectively on behalf of its interests, given the power afforded to it by the market (see Haggard, Maxfield, and Schneider 1997, 41). Certainly, the lobbying efforts of the Peruvian AFP industry reveal otherwise.

The Peruvian pension reform indeed created a new "stakeholder," an association of AFPs that has successfully lobbied for the deepening and consolidation of the pension reform. The original dual pension system created in 1992 provided strong advantages for workers to stay in the public pension system. By mid-1995, however, the business elite had convinced the government to pass legislation that equalized the two pension systems. By 1997, the balance had shifted even further in favor of the private scheme. With lower contribution rates, the AFPs had become far more attractive than the conventional public pension system.

The successive shifts in the privatization program emphasize the importance of looking beyond the initial alignment of interests surrounding market reform initiatives to explore their political consequences. Through time the pension reform created a well-defined group of concentrated beneficiaries who

---

42. The inability to implement pension reform in Brazil has been attributed mostly to the country's constitutional structure, which disperses power and creates multiple veto points (Kay 1999). For a critique of the constitutional-structure argument, see Weyland 1996, 61–63.

pushed for the deepening of the reform process at the expense of costs that were widely distributed among workers in the formal sector.

Pension reform, unlike top-down economic-stabilization packages, as demonstrated in this chapter, has been largely the result of an interactive process involving state officials and social interests. As in the process of tax reform (see Chapter 3), the business elite has been able to dominate the dialogue between state and civil society through organizational coherence as well as by exploiting personal links with the Finance Ministry to obtain a series of important concessions and policy changes. In the case of pension privatization, however, these policy changes have deepened, rather than hampered, the reform process.

Overall the tax and pension reforms illustrate how societal responses affect the prospects for the consolidation of market reforms. Leaving economic reforms that tapped directly into business's pockets, in Chapter 5 I compare social-sector reforms in poverty alleviation and health decentralization. Unlike in the previous cases, state, not societal, actors determined their final outcome. In the case of poverty alleviation, there was not significant political activity, and the reform followed the vicissitudes and electoral needs of executive authority. In the case of health reform, the decentralization initiative pitted grassroots committees against the centralized health bureaucracy, and the government played the role of arbiter.

5

SOCIAL-SECTOR REFORMS

The poststabilization period of the 1990s in Latin America has been characterized by an increasing interest in poverty relief from international lending institutions and politicians alike. With the assistance of the World Bank and the IDB, a number of Latin American governments have implemented demand-driven antipoverty programs, hoping to mitigate the costs of economic-stabilization measures and simultaneously make market reforms sustainable (Graham 1994; Lustig 1995; Tendler 2000). The Peruvian program began in August 1991, when the Fujimori government created a new state agency called FONCODES. FONCODES simulated the demand-driven mechanism of other poverty-alleviation programs in Latin America, such as Bolivia's Emergency Social Fund, whereby base-level community organizations request and execute only the projects they think will suit their local needs.

In striking contrast to the processes of tax and pension reforms (see Chapters 3 and 4), there was a failure on the part of FONCODES to spark an organized response from societal actors. In fact, even though the program successfully directed funds to the poorest Peruvian districts, most base-level community organizations that participated in the program were project specific; that is, they did not engage in a sequence of repeated projects. The absence of enduring organizations suggests that the impact of FONCODES on societal actors was mostly direct, immediate, short term, and highly contingent on a constant flow of relief funds. Given the absence of an organized response, either in favor of or in opposition to the program, state officials were able to utilize FONCODES mostly to their own advantage, molding the program according to the electoral needs of the executive authority. In fact, state officials determined, among other things, the pace and timing of the distribution of relief funds and even which districts were eligible to participate in the program. In other words, the dialogue between the government and societal actors participating in FON-CODES was largely dominated by state officials. This outcome is consistent with the central theoretical expectations outlined in Chapter 1, inasmuch as both the costs and benefits of the program were widely distributed across society.

The major exception to this pattern involves the administration of primary-health-care centers and posts by local communities as a result of a partial decentralization effort by the national government. The decentralization initiative was called the Shared Administration Program (PAC), and the grassroots organizations that collaborated in the management of these centers were known as Local Committees for Health Administration (CLAS). The decentralization process, which sought to improve the quality of primary-health-care services, began in May 1994, and unlike the FONCODES program, it led to more permanent types of grassroots organizing. Some of these health centers and posts were actually rebuilt or rehabilitated by FONCODES, and base-level organizations that previously participated in the construction of these centers have subsequently become responsible for their daily management. In other words, while the execution of FONCODES's projects has been driven by top-down initiatives and has yielded very little in terms of collective action, the administration of these projects through the CLAS initiative has sparked enduring grassroots organizing and, consequently, more local participation and policy feedback, albeit indirectly.

In the first part of this chapter I trace the implementation of FONCODES and reexamine the political and electoral effects of targeted poverty assistance. In the Appendix, I use a cross-sectional time-series model that takes into account the results of the 2000 presidential election. In the second part, I explore the various mechanisms used by state officials to manipulate the distribution of relief funds. In the third section I examine the societal impact of FONCODES by comparing two districts in which the greatest number of projects were executed throughout the 1991–97 period: the district of Acoria in Huancavelica, which is located in the central Peruvian highlands south of Lima; and the district of La Encañada in Cajamarca, situated in the most northern part of Peru that neighbors Ecuador. To the extent that demand-driven antipoverty programs have a positive impact on the organization of civil society at the grassroots level and create new bases for democratic politics, these effects should be visible in these two "most likely" districts, given the density and continuity of projects. Subsequently, I contrast the empirical findings from these two districts with the CLAS experience, which like FONCODES called for active community participation and yet led to more enduring grassroots organizing. In the last section, I address the sustainability of these social-sector reforms.

FONCODES IN COMPARATIVE PERSPECTIVE

Traditionally, poverty relief in Latin America was carried out through subsidies and price controls, which were biased in favor of urban and middle-class sectors of society. Such policies were ineffective from the standpoint of poverty reduction, since they did not always reach the poorest of the poor. Subsidies and price controls, however, were rewarding to politicians who campaigned mostly in urban settings. The challenge, then, has been to implement poverty-relief programs that target the poorest sectors of the population and also satisfy the short-term political interests of state actors. The newer, demand-driven antipoverty programs can meet both objectives. As emphasized by studies on the electoral impact of demand-driven antipoverty programs (Arce 1996; Schady 2000), such programs can simultaneously deliver basic state benefits to citizens in the poorest and most remote areas and reward politicians with votes. In this manner, demand-driven antipoverty programs can serve to enhance the political sustainability of economic-adjustment policies (Graham 1994).

While technical objectives to alleviate poverty and political objectives to obtain electoral support may coincide, the experience of the Latin American demand-driven antipoverty programs, including Peru's FONCODES, suggests that the fundamental tension between these objectives remains unsettled. At one extreme is Mexico's PRONASOL (National Solidarity Program), which began operations in 1989 under the auspices of the Salinas administration (1988–94). PRONASOL, as Cornelius, Craig, and Fox (1994, 14) suggest, was the quintessential "presidentialist" program. It was financed entirely by the Mexican government and never functioned as an autonomous relief fund. While PRONASOL incorporated the demand-driven dimension of the new antipoverty programs, it did not represent an effort to increase the efficacy of the state bureaucracy, which is one of the central themes of this book. In fact, Dresser (1991) described the program as a "political safety net," which helped rebuild the electoral constituency of the Mexican Institutionalized Revolutionary Party (PRI). Molinar and Weldon (1994) have shown that PRONASOL's allocation criteria are better understood in terms of electoral objectives rather than of poverty indices.

In contrast to Mexico's PRONASOL, most demand-driven poverty-alleviation programs function on the basis of "matching funds": national governments must procure revenues equal to the amount loaned by international lending institutions (World Bank 1996). The newer, demand-driven poverty-alleviation programs go through frequent, independent audits to assess their efficacy in targeting the poor. In addition, these newer programs have been able to achieve a high degree of autonomy by recruiting private-sector managers, who in most cases have no salary limitations. Bolivia's Emergency Social Fund is a case in point (Graham 1994, 54–82).

Peru's FONCODES represents a mixed case of "new" and "old" ways of helping the poor. While both the World Bank and the Peruvian local media praised the effectiveness of FONCODES in redistributing state resources to the poorest areas (Francke 1997; Sagasti 1997; World Bank 1999), state officials devised various mechanisms to assert their political control over the program.[1] Examples were the appointment of "accommodating" directors who were particularly receptive to government requests; centralized spending in the form of special projects, a boom-and-bust spending cycle that followed the presidential electoral calendar; and finally, centralized policy changes without any input from a broader cross section of society in determining eligibility for participation in the program.

State actors were able to utilize FONCODES to their advantage largely because they did not encounter organized support or resistance from the societal actors who participated in or bore the cost of FONCODES. While FONCODES initially targeted what appeared to be a well-defined group, or nucleo, to bring about the execution of small-scale projects, these groups did not remain organized beyond the completion of these projects. In fact, most base-level community organizations that participated in the program tended to be project specific; that is, they did not engage in a sequence of repeated projects. On average, these organizations lasted approximately four months, which amounts to the period required for the execution of the projects. In other words, the absence of enduring organizations beyond the start of the program suggests that the benefits accruing from the completion of projects were insufficient to induce further societal organization, indicating also that across time the benefits of the projects would be widely dispersed. Similarly, while FONCODES was set up as a separate state agency outside the traditional line ministries, it did not monopolize the universe of social-assistance programs funded by the cen-

1. See also "Las obras de FONCODES," *Perú Económico*, May 1997, 23–24.

tral government. Conflicts between FONCODES and the Ministry of the Presidency, which directed a number of other social-sector programs, in fact were quite common. Thus the creation of FONCODES did not impose visible costs on an easily identifiable sector of the public bureaucracy.[2] Thus the costs of the program would be widely dispersed and borne by society at large in the form of privatization revenues or by international donors, most notably the World Bank and the IDB. In accordance with the central theoretical expectations outlined in Chapter 1, this pattern of unidentifiable winners and losers has yielded very little in terms of collective action or policy feedback. Thus state officials were able to assert their political control over FONCODES, molding the program according to the vicissitudes and electoral needs of the executive authority.

The Initiation of FONCODES

FONCODES was set up in August 1991 to finance small social and economic infrastructure projects requested by base-level community organizations. These projects include nutrition and family-planning programs, rotating credit schemes, and projects for the construction or rehabilitation of health posts, schools, water and sanitation systems, rural roads, electrification systems, and small-scale irrigation works. Since mid-1991, FONCODES has invested more than U.S.$1.5 billion in more than forty thousand small projects nationwide, reaching practically all the Peruvian districts classified as poor (IDB 2002, 1). By the end of 1995, the average project size was U.S.$30,000 (World Bank 1996).

In the beginning, funding for FONCODES came mainly from the Peruvian government and thus was limited. In fact, between 1991 and 1993, the only external support for FONCODES was a 1992 institutional development grant from the IDB. This situation changed in December 1993, when the World Bank approved the first loan to FONCODES equivalent to U.S.$100 million, which became effective after March 1994 (World Bank 1996). The World Bank loan was complemented by parallel financing from the IDB (U.S.$100 million) and the Peruvian government (U.S.$200 million). These funds would be spent over a period of three years, from 1994 to 1996.

In 1996, the Peruvian government negotiated a new set of loans: U.S.$150

2. To be sure, the only criticism of FONCODES came from politicians who were opposed to Fujimori, but these criticisms did not evolve into any type of organized resistance. Moreover, as noted in Chapter 2, because of the disarticulation of political institutions following the autogolpe, these criticisms could no longer be effectively channeled through the national legislature.

million from the World Bank and U.S.$150 million from the IDB. The Peruvian government complemented these funds with central financing in the amount of U.S.$130 million (World Bank 1996). The funds would be spent over a period of three years, from 1997 to 1999. With additional funding from a European donor consortium, FONCODES spent more than U.S.$900 million in the 1991–99 period.[3]

During the initial phase of the program, FONCODES was relatively unsuccessful in meeting its announced objectives. No statistically significant correlations exist between poverty indicators and relief expenditures for the 1991–93 period (Arce 1996, 100; Ascarza 1994, 83). The situation began to change in 1994, when external financing and technical assistance from both the World Bank and the IDB became available. Also, FONCODES was able to construct a new, better "poverty map" using the 1993 national census data. The previous national census dated from 1981, and it was all but obsolete given the magnitude of the economic crisis and internal migration during the 1980s. Consequently, beginning in 1994 FONCODES funds began to flow disproportionately toward the poorest regions (Arce 1996; Schady 2000).

Relatedly, extant research has pointed to the fact that Fujimori's electoral support had considerably weakened in these poor regions, as shown in the 1993 referendum results. The erosion of Fujimori's electoral base thus provided a political incentive to target spending in the poorest regions (Roberts and Arce 1998; Graham and Kane 1998). Accordingly, the greatest electoral boost for the 1995 reelection of Fujimori came from the areas that secured the greatest FONCODES spending, both at the department level (Arce 1996; Roberts and Arce 1998) and the provincial level (Schady 2000; see Appendix, this chapter).[4] In fact, free from many of the restrictions, paperwork, and inefficiencies of the traditional public-sector bureaucracy, FONCODES became the vehicle of an effective vote-buying strategy. Even President Fujimori publicly acknowledged the electoral benefits resulting from FONCODES projects.[5] In the following sec-

3. At the time of this writing, the government of Alejandro Toledo negotiated a new loan from the IDB in the amount of U.S.$150 million. Moreover, in 2002 FONCODES was transferred to the Ministry of Women and Social Development (MIMDES) because the Ministry of the Presidency, which previously had supervised the program, had ceased to exist. See FONCODES 2002.

4. Peru's territory is divided into 24 departments, 194 provinces, and 1,828 districts. According to FONCODES (2003), among these districts 189 are considered extremely poor (5 percent of the population), 735 are very poor (19 percent of the population), 664 are poor (25 percent of the population), 211 are average (42 percent of the population), and 29 are acceptable (10 percent of the population).

5. "Fujimori reconoce que obras de FONCODES tienen efecto político," *El Comercio*, October 18, 1999. Schady (2000, 303) noted that FONCODES funding decisions were made on the basis of both technical and political criteria.

tion I will explore the various mechanisms used by state officials to manipulate the distribution of relief funds.

THE POLITICAL MANIPULATION OF FONCODES

Conflicts Between Populist and Technocratic Loyalists over FONCODES

During the Fujimori regime, FONCODES had six different directors, alternating between populist loyalists and technocratic managers, one of them from the private business sector. These appointments capture the president's ambivalence concerning the true nature of the objectives pursued by FONCODES. Populist loyalists such as directors Luz Salgado, Manuel Vara, and Miguel Ventura, as discussed below, were usually appointed before important elections. In contrast, private-sector managers such as director Arturo Woodman, and technocratic loyalists, among them directors Manuel Estela (former director of SUNAT) and Alejandro Afuso, were appointed soon after elections.

As Graham (1994, 108) notes, the program got off to a slow start because of conflicting interests between the executive and international lending institutions. At the onset of the program, President Fujimori entrusted its direction to one of his party colleagues, congressional representative Luz Salgado. Lending institutions were wary of the appointment of a political loyalist and insisted on the designation of a manager from the private business sector. Almost a year later, in June 1992, President Fujimori nominated Arturo Woodman, a manager from the SNE, as director of the fund.[6] Woodman resigned in January 1994 because of conflicts with the Ministry of the Presidency over the political manipulation of projects (Roberts 1995, 105).

Technocratic loyalist Manuel Estela replaced Woodman, but only for a short time, from February to August 1994. Like Woodman, Estela resigned as a result of conflicts with the executive over the expeditiousness of project funding (Schady 2000, 294). In September 1994, Manuel Vara, a personal friend and then advisor to President Fujimori, replaced Estela. Populist loyalist Vara directed FONCODES during the April 1995 reelection campaign of President Fujimori.[7] Following Fujimori's reelection, in June 1995 Alejandro Afuso, a technocrat who had been working at the World Bank, was appointed director

6. Woodman later became president of CONFIEP (see Chapter 2).
7. Confirming his populist loyalist credentials, Vara Ochoa was later appointed director of the National Food Assistance Program (PRONAA), a program that is widely perceived as clientelistic.

of the fund. Like Woodman, Afuso was forced to resign in August 1998 because of conflicts with the Ministry of the Presidency. Finally, in September 1998 Miguel Ventura, a close friend of populist loyalist Absalón Vásquez, replaced Afuso as director. Vásquez became Fujimori's right-hand man (see Chapter 2) and helped organize two different pro-Fujimori electoral coalitions: Let's Go, Neighbors (VV) for the municipal elections of November 1998 and Perú 2000 for the 2000 presidential elections. He was successful in steering FONCODES to meet these electoral objectives.[8]

Coinciding with the resignation of technocratic loyalist Estela and the appointment of populist loyalist Vara, in September 1994 monthly approval for projects increased substantially (Fig. 7).[9] In fact, as Schady (2000, 303) writes, when Vara was appointed director of FONCODES, there was "a backlog of thousands of project proposals which could be funded at opportune times." However, between July and August of 1995, the period immediately following the reelection of Fujimori, the number of projects funded declined sharply compared with those funded prior to the 1995 presidential election.

It was only under Director Alejandro Afuso (June 1995–August 1998) that

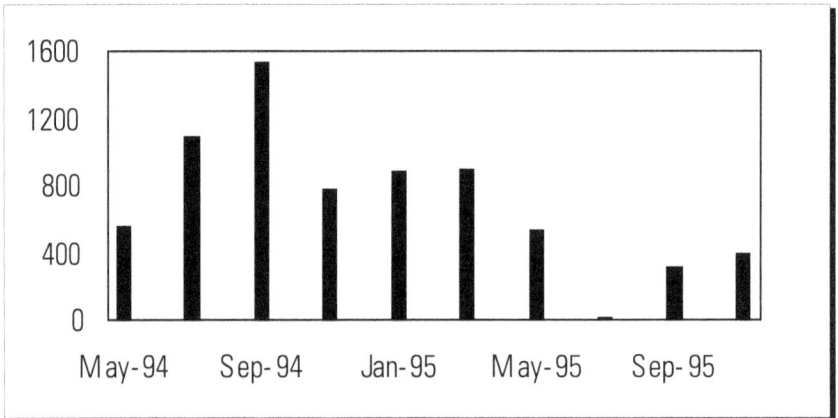

Fig. 7   Monthly approval of projects, May 1994–December 1995

SOURCE: FONCODES, *Notas mensuales* (various years)

8. Vásquez was also the lead congressional candidate of Perú 2000 during the 2000 presidential election. See "La grey del embudo," *Caretas*, February 11, 2000. Planas (2000, 296–301) documents Vásquez's ties to APRA and Fujimori prior to the 1990 presidential election.

9. For the 1994–95 period, FONCODES published bimonthly approval for projects. For the 1996–97 period, FONCODES published approval for projects on a trimester basis. Therefore, monthly data after 1995 are not easily comparable.

the program began to redirect substantially greater funds to the districts categorized as "extremely poor" (Table 12). Moreover, whereas in the 1992–95 period average per capita spending across "very poor" and "poor" districts was roughly about the same, in 1996–97 average per capita spending in "very poor" districts was two to three times greater than the amount spent in "poor" districts.[10] However, while the bulk of FONCODES projects were demand-driven and targeted, the government further expanded spending as early as 1994 via centrally designed special projects. Funding for these special projects continued throughout Afuso's tenure, and they increased even more in preparation for the 2000 presidential election (INEI 2001, 312).

The Funding of Special Projects

Special projects respond to governmental rather than local demand. These projects include the manufacturing of shovels for farmers, boat launches for isolated jungle communities, school shoes, knapsacks, and furniture, along with the provision of school breakfasts (World Bank 1996, 7). The political catch is in the distribution of these commodities, which are delivered to peo-

Table 12   Average per capita spending according to district poverty levels, 1991–2002 (U.S. dollars)

Poverty Levels	Extremely Poor	Very Poor	Poor	Average	Acceptable
1991	9.91	0.16	0.00	0.00	0.00
1992	13.00	4.97	6.69	2.16	0.65
1993	37.19	8.87	8.19	4.11	0.85
1994	22.41	9.59	7.18	2.51	0.50
1995	26.19	6.96	5.96	1.75	0.40
1996	59.24	10.00	5.33	0.42	0.04
1997	96.86	16.14	6.42	0.28	0.08
1998	21.30	17.47	14.15	0.48	0.11
1999	62.17	17.26	10.03	0.69	0.09
2000	33.25	1.26	2.59	0.47	0.00
2001	10.42	7.78	2.38	0.16	0.11
2002	6.89	5.65	3.64	0.41	0.02

Source: FONCODES.

Note: Average per capita spending is total spending divided by the total population living in these districts across poverty levels. Figures in U.S. dollars.

10. Similar average per capita spending across "very poor" and "poor" districts gives credence to Graham's (1994) argument that one of the limitations of antipoverty programs is that demand-driven projects do not always come from the poorest sectors of the population.

ple in both rural and marginal urban areas solely according to the president's discretion.

According to FONCODES officials, special projects were politically palatable because of their impact on employment.[11] Various microenterprises participated in the manufacturing of the these commodities (Table 13). Some FONCODES officials believed that these projects provided the only income available to thousands of blue-collar workers who had been laid off because of privatizations. In contrast, most demand-driven projects required some form of unpaid community participation. Only skilled workers were remunerated, yet their employment was temporary, averaging four months. Their jobs ended with the culmination of the projects.

The expansion of special projects, however, was financially dependent on the capacity of the state to secure a steady flow of tax revenues. In contrast to demand-driven projects, special projects did not have the financial backing of international lending institutions (World Bank 1996, 7). In the words of Livia Benavides, a World Bank official in Lima, "The Bank did not spend a single dollar on special projects because they were unsustainable and highly political."[12]

Funding for both demand-driven and special projects varied according to the electoral calendar. As noted previously, the approval of demand-driven projects was temporarily suspended after the April 1995 reelection of Fujimori. FONCODES funded 530 demand-driven projects between May and June 1995, but only 13 projects between July and August that year (see Fig. 7). Overall,

Table 13   Summary of special projects, 1991–96

	Quantity Manufactured	Participating Microenterprises
School Supplies		
Clothing	2,000,000	1,127
Footwear	3,250,000	779
Sports Footwear	1,000,000	19
Furniture	500,000	1,324
Agricultural Tools		
Shovels	1,000,000	249
Sandals	107,500	18

SOURCE: FONCODES.

11. Interview by the author with FONCODES director of public relations Cecilia Olaechea, Lima, May 7, 1997.

12. Interview by the author, Lima, February 6, 1998.

the number of demand-driven projects funded in 1995 decreased by 32 percent relative to the projects funded during 1994 (INEI 2001, 312). The 2000 electoral cycle led to a similar pattern of diminishing funding for projects following the elections. In 2000, FONCODES financed 389 demand-driven projects nationwide, and overall investment declined by about 70 percent compared with funding for 1999.[13] This boom-and-bust spending cycle surrounding presidential elections is indicative of the political control over the program. The allocation of funds for special projects, however, did not change much, in part because of their perceived greater political impact.[14]

Funding Small Projects in Rural Districts

Another aspect underlining government control over FONCODES was a policy change that excluded from project funding districts categorized as urban. Since the beginning of the program until mid-1995, FONCODES had been financing a wide range of projects mostly on a "first come, first served" basis. All things held equal, such a criterion meant that districts where there was abundant human capital, such as civil engineers able to design a project's profile, had greater chances in petitioning a project for funding. The proximity of a district with respect to a regional office of FONCODES also shaped the demand for projects. More precisely, because the work carried out by the members of a community who direct a project is entirely voluntary, the farther a district is from a regional office of FONCODES, the more difficult it is to elicit autonomous participation on the part of community members. As most FONCODES officials certify, the distances between remote rural districts and regional offices demand at least a full-day trip.[15] Thus, the allocation of relief funds between 1991 and 1995 was skewed in favor of urban and marginal urban districts, which had the advantage of proximity to FONCODES's regional offices.

13. This information as well as the figures reported in Tables 12 and 14 were calculated using a dataset provided by FONCODES.

14. FONCODES does not publish disaggregated spending data for special projects. Most printed information reveals output such as quantity of school breakfasts produced and beneficiaries involved. Schady (2000, 292) noted that "there is no information on the allocation formulas or the actual distribution of the special projects." Since the mid-1990s, investment in special projects has approached U.S.$400 million (see note 13, above).

15. These observations are based on extensive interviews by the author with Víctor Sevilla, former director of FONCODES in Piura, and subsequently director of FONCODES in Ayacucho; Augusto Moscoso, director of FONCODES in Huancavelica; Walter Cachay, director of FONCODES in Cajamarca; Sergio Rios, director of FONCODES in Lima; and various FONCODES supervisors in the aforementioned cities. The interviews were conducted between March and April 1998.

Throughout the 1992–95 period, districts categorized as "average" had the greatest average number of projects financed (Table 14). Most, if not all, "average" districts are located in marginal urban areas. In metropolitan Lima, for instance, San Juan de Lurigancho, Villa El Salvador, Ate, San Juan de Miraflores, and Villa Maria del Triunfo were among the top twenty districts with the greatest number of projects financed. During this period, San Juan de Lurigancho, the largest Peruvian district, with a population close to six hundred thousand people, had completed 111 projects. This pattern changed after 1995. San Juan de Lurigancho had only three projects funded in 1996 and only one in 1997.[16]

Under Afuso's tenure, FONCODES made an important policy change regarding the areas commonly assisted by the program. FONCODES decided to finance only projects from rural districts; urban and marginal urban districts such as those found in metropolitan Lima were no longer eligible to request funds. FONCODES shifted to remote rural districts because government officials within the Ministry of the Presidency believed there were plenty of government institutions, private associations, and nongovernmental organizations (NGOs) committed to poverty relief in urban districts.[17] For the 1996–97 period, unknown districts from the "very poor" and "extremely poor" categories had the greatest

Table 14   Average number of projects approved according to district poverty levels, 1991–2002

Poverty Levels	Extremely Poor	Very Poor	Poor	Average	Acceptable
1991	0.05	0.06	0.00	0.00	0.00
1992	0.92	1.49	1.81	3.40	1.55
1993	3.10	2.60	2.99	6.67	2.17
1994	2.02	2.46	2.41	4.06	1.03
1995	1.86	1.63	1.68	2.49	0.76
1996	5.39	2.75	1.72	0.82	0.10
1997	6.54	4.35	2.18	0.56	0.14
1998	6.15	4.31	2.80	1.00	0.21
1999	6.47	4.55	3.08	1.18	0.14
2000	0.28	0.23	0.21	0.13	0.00
2001	1.63	1.22	0.59	0.26	0.31
2002	0.94	0.93	0.78	0.51.	0.03

SOURCE: FONCODES.

NOTE: Average number of projects is the total number of projects approved divided by the total number of districts according to poverty levels.

16. See note 13, above.

17. Interview by the author with Máximo Matos, an advisor to the Ministry of the Presidency, Lima, February 4, 1998.

average number of projects financed (see Table 14). The districts of Acoria in Huancavelica and La Encañada in Cajamarca are two examples.

FONCODES officials revealed different opinions regarding the viability of the post-1995 rural-districts-only policy, suggesting that the "real poor" do not necessarily live in rural districts.[18] The policy change, however, similar to the implementation of special projects, shows that what was originally conceived as a "hands off" safety net was continually molded according to the interests of state actors. It is telling that the policy shift toward funding projects only in rural districts passed without notice or political debate.

THE SOCIETAL IMPACT OF SOCIAL POLICIES

The FONCODES Experience

To execute a project, communities would gather in an assembly and select a nucleo made up of four individuals, who become responsible for the daily conduct of the project on a voluntary basis. Two different surveys conducted by Apoyo S.A., one of the beneficiaries of the projects and the other of the members of the nucleos themselves, revealed that most nucleos were project specific, that is, they did not engage in a sequence of repeated projects (Table 15).[19] What is more, only one out of four nucleos remained organized after the completion of an initial project, suggesting that the impact of FONCODES on societal actors had been mostly direct, immediate, short term, and highly contingent on a constant flow of relief funds. The nature of these nucleos was in fact strictly project oriented and very localized, dissolving after the completion of projects. These nucleos were merely relief-aid recipients and did not make broader political claims on the state.

Consistent with the data in Table 15, the societal impact of FONCODES in the districts of Acoria and La Encañada, where the program financed a significant number of projects, has been limited.[20] Interviews with community represen-

---

18. Interview by the author with Ezio Varese, supervisor of FONCODES in Lima, Lima, March 13, 1998.

19. These surveys are also known as *evaluaciones ex-post*. The first two surveys do not provide information with respect to the survival of nucleos and were not conducted by Apoyo S.A.

20. Tanaka (2001) conducted a parallel study on local participation associated with social policies, including FONCODES's nucleos. Districts in the departments of Ayacucho, Cuzco, San Martín, and Lima were part of the sample. Tanaka also poses difficulties in generalizing about the effects of social policies given the complexity and variety of Peruvian districts.

Table 15   Survival of nucleos

Has the nucleo in charge of the administration of the project continued working on other projects?

Responses of Nucleo Members

	Yes (%)	No (%)	No Response (%)	N
Third survey	28	68	4	293
Fourth survey	26	67	7	395

Responses of Beneficiaries

	Yes (%)	No (%)	No Response (%)	N
Third survey	19	50	31	1463
Fourth survey	17	60	23	895

SOURCE: FONCODES.

NOTE: The third survey was conducted in September 1995 and involved 300 projects funded in 1994. The fourth survey was conducted between March and June 1997 and involved 350 projects funded between 1994 and 1996. Apoyo S.A. conducted both surveys.

tatives and local officials in both districts revealed that the only active organizations associated with FONCODES were nucleos directing ongoing projects. In addition, there was no evidence suggesting horizontal ties between nucleos.[21] In many ways, the absence of enduring organizations contradicts the conventional wisdom regarding the impact of targeted antipoverty programs, which suggests that demand-driven safety nets may help build up civil society or popular participation.

Both Acoria and La Encañada are considered rural and very poor by FONCODES's standards as well as alternative government sources. The predominantly rural district of Acoria in Huancavelica, located in the central highlands of Peru, has had the greatest number of projects executed throughout the 1991–97 period. During this period, Acoria's inhabitants petitioned for a total of 279 projects, of which 153 were funded. Total per capita disbursement in Acoria was U.S.$151 for the 1991–97 period. The district of La Encañada in Cajamarca, situated in the northern part of Peru, has also had a significant number of projects financed. It ranks twenty-fifth among districts according to the number of projects executed throughout the 1991–97 period.[22] During this

21. Although it represented more the exception than the norm, in Huancavelica FONCODES officials reported instances in which communities physically destroyed one another's projects because they expected the government to fund projects simultaneously (interview by the author with Augusto Moscoso, director of FONCODES in Huancavelica, Huancavelica, March 30, 1998).

22. Districts that preceded La Encañada were either categorized as "urban," and as such they had a limited number of projects for the 1996–97 period, or they were inaccessible because of the severe occurrence of El Niño that took place early in 1998.

period, La Encañada residents requested a total of 144 projects, of which 82 received funding. In La Encañada, total per capita spending was U.S.$104 for the 1991–97 period. The population of both districts is dispersed throughout numerous villages and small towns. Some villages had no more than forty families, the minimum number required by FONCODES in order for it to fund a project.[23]

The partisan loyalties that were generated by FONCODES in these districts suggest a contingent, highly instrumental type of political support. This finding is consistent with the transformation of partisan identities in Peru throughout the 1980s and much of the 1990s, which have steered away from traditional political parties and in favor of a vast number of independent political movements (see Parodi and Twanama 1993). District mayors of Acoria and La Encañada as well as provincial mayors of Huancavelica and Cajamarca fit into this category. More important, these malleable political loyalties had more to do with securing tangible material benefits than with supporting democratic rule itself. As aptly quoted in García Calderón (2001, 57), "[T]he big daily concern of most poor people [in Peru] is not whether their mayor, congressman, or president was fairly elected, but rather how to fill their plate and find a job."

In Acoria, many people reacted to FONCODES with skepticism. With resources at hand to carry on projects, various FONCODES officials pointed out that it was difficult to prompt the participation of community members. Such a finding seemed unusual for villages that had already executed a FONCODES type of project. According to FONCODES officials, those difficulties were not the result of a lack of community organization, but rather distrust of a government willing to provide basic state benefits to remote and forgotten districts. FONCODES officials repeatedly pointed out that many communities were hesitant to participate because of their frustration with politicians who in the past had failed to carry out their electoral promises. FONCODES was not immune from such response. In fact, whenever FONCODES held up the approval of projects because of technical stipulations, they unintentionally dissuaded the eventual participation of base-level organizations. In Yananaco, a small town in Acoria, I asked community leaders to list the projects that their community needed the most. Although they could readily list several, Yananaco leaders had neither petitioned funds from FONCODES nor seemed willing to do so. A community

23. The populations in both Acoria and La Encañada, where in-depth field research was carried out during 1998, exceed twenty-two thousand people. In addition, a third of the population of each district lives in extreme poverty and very few households enjoy basic services, such as electricity and potable water.

leader stated, "Why should we insist? We tried before and did not get anything."[24]

However, the reluctance to participate in projects can also suggest a more complex response signaling short-term calculations of material self-interest on the part of community members. This alternative interpretation implies that it is not necessarily the case that communities fail to participate in projects because of their past frustrations with politicians or their lack of knowledge of the way FONCODES works. Some communities may indeed understand the politics surrounding social-assistance programs quite well and have already learned to take advantage of the way the government, and particularly FONCODES, operates. In Huiñaccpampa, another small town in Acoria, a community leader stated: "There is no need for us to request projects. Elections are near and that means that FONCODES will pay us a visit."[25] Contrary to the attitude of Yananaco residents, the confidence of those in Huiñaccpampa was striking. Residents of Anta in Acoria had a similar view. Villagers believed that the probabilities of having a project funded were greater when the initiative was taken by FONCODES as opposed to one taken by community members.

The information obtained from interviews in Huiñaccpampa implies that even FONCODES's demand-driven projects have less to do with the grassroots participation than with the interests of the program administrators. The department of Madre de Dios is a case in point. According to Graham and Kane (1998, 98), the more active a constituency in the political arena, the more successful the implementation of demand-driven programs such as those of FONCODES. However, as the authors (98) also note, Madre de Dios received the highest 1993–94 per capita FONCODES disbursement, yet they had the most significant increase in voter abstention, rising from 20 percent in 1990 to 47 percent in 1995. Could it be that relief expenditures in Madre de Dios did not reflect autonomous demand for projects?

The evidence from interviews in Huancavelica suggests that the answer to this question may be yes. When Augusto Moscoso was appointed head of FONCODES in Huancavelica in late 1997, he had about forty projects ready to execute. That number of projects was insignificant relative to the large budget assigned to Huancavelica. According to Moscoso, he "held a meeting and told supervisors to go out and bring in more projects."[26] Certainly, the implementation of the post-1995 rural-districts-only policy led to a sharp increase in the

---

24. Interview by the author, Huancavelica, March 31, 1998.
25. Interview by the author, Huancavelica, March 31, 1998.
26. Interview by the author, Huancavelica, April 2, 1998.

number of projects requested by "extremely poor" and "poor" districts, all the while reflecting state promotion rather than local, bottom-up demand for projects.

I probed leaders of Huiñaccpampa and Anta for their responses regarding the hypothetical scenario that FONCODES failed to fund any of the projects promoted by their officials. A resident of Anta responded, "We would feel very disappointed with the government; only time would tell what we would do next."[27] Such a response suggests again that political support for President Fujimori was highly contingent on a constant flow of material benefits.

Interviews carried out in Chainapampa, another small town in Acoria, corroborate this finding. A community leader stated, "We support the government as long as the government supports us."[28] In Chainapampa, FONCODES has rebuilt the elementary school and provided potable water. Chainapampa residents took those two projects as a sign of continuous relief assistance from the government.

Finally, La Encañada in Cajamarca differed from Acoria in Huancavelica in various respects. Even though both departments have comparable poverty indicators, Cajamarca has some relative advantages over Huancavelica. Among other things, it has a better transportation infrastructure, which in turn provides access to Trujillo, a major city and market; a university offering precisely the specialization required to design and oversee FONCODES projects; and important gold mining and tourism activities. Cajamarca also has had the greatest number of projects both demanded and approved throughout the 1992–97 period. The social-assistance budget for Cajamarca was significantly larger than that of any other department because of a special relief program sponsored by the European Union called INKA-RENOM.[29] FONCODES assisted in the approval of projects but did not oversee their execution. This created a situation in which various nongovernmental organizations interested in executing small projects competed with FONCODES's nucleos. Unlike those of Huancavelica, Cajamarca residents could easily appeal to alternative relief sources, such as INKA-RENOM, should FONCODES turn them down.

At the community level, La Encañada in Cajamarca reflected greater grass-roots participation in the demand for projects than did Acoria in Huancavel-

---

27. Interview by the author, Huancavelica, March 31, 1998.
28. Interview by the author, Huancavelica, March 31, 1998.
29. The INKA-RENOM program covered the INKA region, which includes the departments of Cuzco, Apurímac, and Madre de Dios, and the RENOM region, which includes the department of Cajamarca's north oriental region of the Marañón.

ica.[30] Human resources, for instance, were abundant. It is telling that the demand for FONCODES jobs outstripped the supply. In Huancavelica, it was quite the opposite, as personnel were frequently recruited from Lima. Walter Cachay, the director of FONCODES in Cajamarca, indicated that "the number of projects ready to be executed generally exceeded their budget allocation."[31] In other words, there was no need for the state to promote projects.

The political legacy of FONCODES in La Encañada is best captured by the testimony from a community leader in Polloc. When I asked about the community's response to FONCODES, he replied: "We do not let ourselves be surprised, we know that politicians visit us more frequently during elections. And the word *reelection* is very popular nowadays; but in the 1990s, the ones [politicians] who talk a lot are in trouble."[32]

The remarks of the Polloc leader suggest that the careers of politicians who lack concrete benefits to distribute are not promising. To summarize, the evidence from both Acoria and La Encañada supports recent literature, which has emphasized the fluid, instrumental character of lower-class political behavior in Peru (Cameron 1994; Roberts and Arce 1998). If anything, political support generated by FONCODES is largely determined by short-term calculations of material self-interest.

The CLAS Experience

The fact that FONCODES's nucleos did not remain organized after the completion of projects, however, does not necessarily suggest the complete disarticulation of the Peruvian social fabric.[33] Both urban and rural districts have a rich web of grassroots organizations, such as neighborhood associations (*juntas vecinales*) and community assemblies (*asambleas comunales*), which precede FONCODES. Leaders of these organizations have often been involved in the selection of nucleos or have become presidents of the nucleos themselves. Even in marginal urban districts such as San Juan de Lurigancho, where FON-

---

30. Cajamarca is known for its strong communal organizations, called self-defense committees in the countryside (*rondas campesinas*). For a discussion, see Pérez 1996.

31. Interview by the author, Cajamarca, April 16, 1998.

32. Interview by the author, Cajamarca, April 17, 1998.

33. Studying the shortcomings and deficiencies of urban popular movements, Schönwälder (2002, 195) writes: "The real problem seems to lie not in the dissolution of the social fabric as such, but in the lack of suitable allies that could play the role of intermediaries between civil society and the state, especially *political parties*" (italics mine). For a discussion of collective activism by women during neoliberal adjustment in Peru, see Hays-Mitchell 2002.

CODES suddenly canceled operations, FONCODES's withdrawal did not have any effect on the work of these associations.[34] Being mostly community service oriented, these organizations are the primary intermediaries between local authorities and citizens at large.

An important exception to the absence of enduring organizations associated with FONCODES has been the creation of local committees to manage primary-health-care centers and posts—most of which were actually built or rehabilitated by the targeted relief program. These base-level community organizations are also known as CLAS, and similar to FONCODES's nucleos, CLAS members work on a voluntary basis.[35] Each CLAS has seven members: six are community representatives, and the seventh is the primary-health-care professional, usually the chief physician.

These local committees have legal and financial responsibility for the administration of health posts and centers. They receive public resources to pay for existing health personnel; monies are deposited in a commercial checking account controlled directly by CLAS members. These local committees generate their own revenues, which come from fees paid for medications and services. CLAS members decide on amounts of fees for services as well as determine exonerations from fees. These revenues, however, are not sent back to the government but instead are retained for use in the local facilities—primarily to improve the existing health services, or to contract additional personnel or hours on a private basis. CLAS members have direct control over the hiring and firing of contracted health personnel.

A few words are in order on the nature and implementation of the CLAS initiative. The CLAS program began in early 1994 as part of a partial health-decentralization effort by the national government (Cortez 1998, 68; Arroyo 2000, 34).[36] Moreover, as pointed out in Chapter 2, the initiative was originally launched as a pilot program, and state actors central to the reform kept a very "low profile" as they sought to expand the reform quietly over time (Ortiz et al. 1999, 22–23).

34. This observation is based on various visits and interviews by the author with local representatives in San Juan de Lurigancho late in 1997.

35. There are numerous studies that have assessed the local participation effects triggered by the CLAS initiative. For instance, Cortez (1998) provides information on twelve CLAS establishments distributed across the departments of La Libertad, Lima, and Junín. Studying four CLAS establishments, Ewig (2001) carried out her investigation in the departments of Ayacucho and Lima. Altobelli (2002) presents information on sixty-one CLAS establishments distributed nationwide. Accordingly, this section draws heavily on these studies as well as on Ortiz et al. 1999.

36. As noted in Chapter 1, the CLAS initiative is probably not representative of the entire health reform process that has been taking place in Peru since the mid-1990s (see Ewig 2000).

Equally important, the reform took place during a time when the IPSS, the state agency in charge of managing the national health-care system, had already gone through a substantial reorganization process, which, in turn, helped improve its overall performance. As seen in Chapter 4, approval of the IPSS increased from a dismal 17 percent in March 1989 to 51 percent in September 1993, and later to 60 percent in September 1994.[37] To be sure, the timing of the CLAS reform signaled a striking difference from the period in which technocrats began privatizing the national pension system. In other words, the improved public perception of the postcrisis IPSS led indirectly to greater credence for social actors who opposed the CLAS initiative.[38]

The reform indeed sparked strong and better-organized societal opposition from various sources. Regional health authorities opposed the CLAS because it reduced their bureaucratic control over substantial financial resources. Public-sector health workers—grouped in the Federation of Health Ministry Workers (FTMS)—objected to the reform because private contracts eroded their monopoly over public-sector employment. Finally, medical associations and guilds opposed the reform because of its potential to "privatize financial administration" in the health centers (Ewig 2001, 159). Health decentralization has thus created concentrated, visible losses for a well-defined group—the health bureaucracy.

The CLAS program did foster incentives for local committees to remain organized in part because the administration of health posts is permanent. The opposite was true in the case of FONCODES, in which incentives to remain organized ended with the completion of projects, averaging four months. Stated otherwise, the CLAS initiative, unlike FONCODES, provided benefits that mobilized a well-defined societal group, which survived beyond the initial start of the program. Moreover, the CLAS initiative, unlike FONCODES, threatened the centralized allocation of a fixed pool of resources traditionally managed by the health bureaucracy. Therefore, the health-decentralization process created concentrated beneficiaries or "stakeholders" on the part of these local committees, leading to a classic interest-group conflict that pitted health administra-

37. Apoyo S.A. 1991b, 2000. In the polls, the question reads: "In general, would you say that you trust or distrust the following institutions [name of institution]?"

38. At the cabinet level, the Ministry of Health staffed officials who embraced the market orthodoxy and sought to extend it into the health area, such as Ministers Jaime Freundt-Throne and Marino Costa Bauer, and those who adopted a more centrist, statist approach toward health policy, such as Minister Eduardo Yong Motta (interview by the author with Juan Arroyo Laguna, professor of public health at the Universidad Peruana Cayetano Heredia, Lima, August 8, 2002). In Chapter 2, Minister Yong is characterized as a populist loyalist. A significant expansion of the CLAS program took place under Minister Yong.

tors against grassroots organizations. As a consequence, the decentralization initiative placed the government in the role of arbiter. This outcome is consistent with the central theoretical expectations of this book inasmuch as the benefits and costs of the decentralization program were both concentrated on specific, easily identifiable societal groups. Largely in response to pressures from international lending institutions in the form of a structural adjustment loan from the World Bank and the IDB supporting the expansion of the CLAS program, in 1998 President Fujimori ultimately decided to speed the decentralization process, to the detriment of the health bureaucracy. At the time of this writing, there are approximately fourteen hundred CLAS-type establishments, which represent approximately 24 percent of total health facilities throughout the country (Altobelli 2002, 328). To date, the program continues to be revised in the hopes of improving its overall effectiveness.[39] This indicates the limited implementation of the reform as a consequence of continued opposition from the health bureaucracy.

Ewig (2001, 256–304) describes the CLAS program as unique, in that community members participate in the actual administration of health posts through the local committees. The author notes that the CLAS program has served to empower the members of these local committees by allowing them to make a number of important decisions, "including the hiring and firing of personnel, fiscal management, decisions regarding improvements in center services and the approval of a local health plan." Essentially, the decision-making authority and leadership opportunities provided by the CLAS program have increased the voice of community members, thus permitting them to demand better-quality health services. In addition, and beyond the increased capabilities gained by the members of the local committees, Ewig found that as many as 30 percent of community members participate in health-center-related activities sponsored by CLAS. Involvement in such CLAS-sponsored activities include attending informative talks, participating in health campaigns, and receiving instruction to become health promoters.

These local committees that have emerged as a consequence of the CLAS program, and to a lesser extent under FONCODES, approximate the notion of "associative networks" and represent new and substantially different structures of popular representation (Chalmers, Martin, and Piester 1997). They also conform with Yashar's (1999) idea of "neoliberal citizenship regimes," in that

---

39. Telephone interview by the author with Laura Altobelli, a World Bank official in Lima, Janaury 13, 2003. One proposal sought to create "networks" of CLAS establishments, which would reduce the absolute number of CLAS centers reported here.

political participation has become more localized and autonomous. In the words of Altobelli and Pancorvo (2000), "CLAS alone does not represent community participation in health. Rather, CLAS is a facilitator of community participation." These local committees did not lead to widespread citizen mobilization, but instead provided an important pool of localized, organized support that enabled state actors to get the reform off the ground.[40] All told, marketization, in particular some decentralization initiatives, does create new forms of societal recomposition.

THE SUSTAINABILITY OF SOCIAL POLICIES

One striking aspect of the projects sponsored by FONCODES that surfaced in my visits to Acoria and La Encañada was their state of disrepair. What is more, when I asked about the poor maintenance of these projects, community members overwhelmingly expressed a lack of ownership.[41] Along these lines, Alcázar and Wachtenheim (2001, 27) found that compared to all of the projects funded by FONCODES, water and sanitation projects were the most successful, in large part because these projects "are characterized by a clear emphasis on community training." In other words, the best projects in the long term were the ones that required some form of continuous local participation. In many ways, the CLAS experience has sought to remedy these shortcomings by giving community members direct control over the quality of health services that they receive. More important, because the CLAS committees incorporate at least one health-care professional—in this case, the chief physician—the fate of the health centers and posts does not depend solely on the participation of community members; rather, a type of shared administration or co-management takes place. It is the synergy of local participation (in the hands of CLAS members) and government supervision (in the hands of the chief physician) that appears to yield the most successful social outcome (see Paredes and Taylor 2002).

Aside from the lack-of-ownership problem affecting the sustainability of FONCODES projects, the fate of the program itself was in jeopardy at the end of

---

40. "Associative networks," however, do not necessarily aggregate interests across society as, for instance, political parties do, but rather are more problem-oriented and centered around specific purposes. The ways in which these associative networks could be incorporated into formal, institutionalized channels of representation is surely an endeavor worthy of study.

41. On the performance of demand-driven antipoverty programs, see Tendler 2000.

the Fujimori regime. As noted in Chapter 2, the economic recession of the late 1990s resurrected political opposition to Fujimori. In response to this, populist loyalist and presidential advisor Absalón Vásquez suggested that one way to counterbalance the rising political organization against the president was through political mobilization among lower-class sectors. These efforts were targeted at increasing Fujimori's electoral chances, in particular his highly controversial second presidential reelection. But the president had openly avoided and discouraged this type of partisan grassroots mobilization (Roberts 1996; Mauceri 1997). In fact, rather than establishing an institutionalized base of support, Fujimori created four "disposable parties":[42] Change '90 (C90) for the presidential campaign of 1990, New Majority (NM) for the constitutional assembly of 1992 and the presidential reelection campaign of 1995, Let's Go, Neighbors (VV) for the municipal elections of November 1998, and Perú 2000 for the presidential campaign of 2000.[43] In the end, Vásquez successfully persuaded the president to go along with the idea, which implied, among other things, the manipulation of government relief programs. As such, FONCODES increasingly became a target of Vásquez's political ambitions. In mid-1998, FONCODES director Alejandro Afuso, a technocratic loyalist, was forced to resign by pressure from the populist loyalist Vásquez, the former seen as "uncooperative" and "disobedient."[44] Along with Afuso, five regional directors were dismissed for similar reasons, including Huancavelica's Augusto Moscoso.[45]

42. "Disposable parties" is borrowed from Levitsky (1999, 81). As noted in Chapter 2, Fujimori's lack of an institutionalized base of support may have encouraged his increased reliance on Vladimiro Montesinos.

43. Unlike the previous political organizations, the VV movement (or "party") created great confusion. While populist loyalist Absalón Vásquez and the Ministry of the Presidency were instrumental in chartering the organization, leaders representing the VV movement denied their connections with the government. See "Congresistas de oposición demandan se investigue uso de recursos del FONCODES," *El Comercio*, July 14, 1998.

44. "Presiones oficialistas causaron renuncia de ex jefe de FONCODES," *El Comercio*, September 15, 1998.

45. "Despiden a funcionarios que no quisieron colaborar con campaña electoral," *El Comercio*, September 14, 1998. In the November 1998 municipal elections, the VV movement won in 6 out of 24 departmental capitals and in 71 out of 194 provinces. In Lima, the VV movement won in 16 out of 42 districts (Apoyo S.A. 1998b). None of these 16 districts in Lima, however, were eligible for FONCODES funding, because they had been classified as "average." In fact, during 1997 there were only five projects funded in all these districts. In contrast, during 1997 Acoria and La Encañada had fifty-four projects funded, and both districts elected mayors from the political organization VV. Yet it is difficult to assess whether the victory of the VV movement in these districts represented a solid pro-Fujimori coalition. The mayor of La Encañada Manuel Vazques, for instance, was elected as an independent in the municipal elections of 1996, and then he was reelected in 1998 as a member of the VV organization.

FONCODES was perhaps the last standing social program to overtly fall prey to Fujimori's growing electoral machine.

When interviewed, Afuso acknowledged that conflicts between FONCODES and the Ministry of the Presidency were common, but it was always the president who resolved the differences.[46] Yet Fujimori decided to forsake Afuso precisely when the World Bank officially ended its commitment to FONCODES. The Peruvian government and the Bank had previously agreed that "FONCODES would maintain an Executive Director and Line Managers with experience and qualifications satisfactory to the Bank" (World Bank 1996, 29). As the agreement expired, FONCODES was freed from the Bank's constraints, making it particularly fitting to the electoral needs of President Fujimori. In the absence of controls and external audits imposed by lending institutions, FONCODES easily followed the path of Mexico's PRONASOL and became increasingly more clientelistic and less technical.

CONCLUSION

Research on the poverty-alleviation program suggests that in Peru the fundamental tension between technical objectives to alleviate poverty and political objectives to obtain electoral support remains unresolved. To date the experience of FONCODES shows that the balance between political and technical objectives tends to wax and wane with the electoral cycle, with political objectives predominating around election periods.[47] In this vein, President Fujimori exploited every available opportunity to assert his control over FONCODES. This outcome conforms to the theoretical expectations outlined in Chapter 1. The costs and benefits of the poverty-alleviation program were widely distributed across society. This symmetrical distribution of costs and benefits has not led to an organized response from societal actors and has thus yielded very little policy feedback.

Both the poverty-alleviation program FONCODES and the CLAS initiative

46. Interview by the author, Lima, October 14, 1997.

47. This tension has continued beyond the Fujimori regime. Whereas the Paniagua government appointed Pedro Francke, an official from Peru's Central Bank, as director of FONCODES, Toledo appointed a political loyalist, Alejandro Narváez. FONCODES's funding also declined considerably following the collapse of the Fujimori regime. The depletion of privatization revenues and dwindling tax revenues severely constrained the continued expasion of FONCODES that occurred in the 1990s. More precisely, whereas in the 1992–99 period the average spending per year was U.S.$180 million, in the 2000–2002 period it was U.S.$69 million. This information was calculated using a dataset provided by FONCODES.

sought to bring basic government services closer to the population, the poor in particular. Both programs also called for active community involvement at the grassroots level. Only the CLAS initiative, however, had the desired empowerment and local accountability effects, which is often voiced by social observers and in the academic literature (Graham 1994). The CLAS initiative gave community members not only a degree of autonomy in the management of health facilities, but also a measure of supervision in the hands of the chief physician. In the words of Graham (1998, 110), "the record of the CLAS also reflects the strong community organizational capacity that exists throughout Peru and contributes to the potential effectiveness of the approach."

It is also important to note that FONCODES's gains in improved targeting, which began in 1996 when "extremely poor" districts began to receive a larger portion of available funding, have been accompanied with losses in the autonomous bottom-up demand for projects. In other words, state actors have increased the efficacy of FONCODES's targeting by making it less demand-driven. Isolated departments such as Huancavelica have been particularly vulnerable. Political support for Fujimori, nonetheless, was highly contingent on a constant flow of material benefits. If anything, community leaders in remote and marginal areas seemed to be very aware of the politics surrounding relief programs such as FONCODES.

On the whole, the policy shifts surrounding the targeted poverty-alleviation program were neither negotiated nor contested. Instead, FONCODES was shaped by a policy compromise between the government and international lending institutions. The World Bank achieved structural adjustment reforms with a human face, and President Fujimori obtained the electoral support needed to pursue market-oriented projects. However, the partial implementation of the CLAS initiative, resulting from continued opposition from the health bureaucracy, serves as a reminder of the limits on improving the delivery of basic social services, despite the collective activism and organizational capacity of the poor.

APPENDIX

In Table 16 existing research on the electoral impact of FONCODES is expanded on to encompass the 2000 presidential election. The dependent variable "Fujimori vote" is the percentage of votes received by Fujimori in the following five elections: the 1990 presidential election, the 1992 constitutional assembly

Table 16   Determinants of Fujimori's vote, 1990–2000

Independent Variable	Fujimori Vote
Fujimori vote$_{t-1}$	$-.22$***
	(.05)
GDP growth	21.69***
	(10.093)
Political violence	3.97***
	(.81)
FONCODES spending	1.03***
	(.33)
Constant	60.66***
	(4.00)
Adjusted R^2	.32
Wald chi^2	79.06***
N	96

NOTE: Entries are unstandardized regression coefficients; robust standard errors are in parenthesis.

***$p < .01$.

election, the 1993 constitutional referendum, the 1995 presidential election, and the 2000 presidential election.[48] The independent variables are growth in gross domestic product, growth in the number of "subversive actions," which could be broadly characterized as "political violence," and FONCODES per capita spending among the population living in extreme poverty. All observations are at the department level.[49] To estimate the impact of these independent variables on Fujimori's vote, I use a cross-sectional time-series GEE model. The analysis includes a lagged dependent variable on the right-hand side of the equation to correct for autocorrelation.[50]

Similar to conclusions drawn by Weyland (2000, 491), the results indicate

48. The "Fujimori vote" for the 1990 and 2000 presidential elections is for the first-round electoral contest. The electoral votes cast in the first rounds, rather than the runoffs, are interpreted as clear-cut support for Fujimori. There was no runoff election in the 1995 presidential election. The "Fujimori vote" for the 1992 constitutional assembly election corresponds to the votes received by Fujimori's New Majority (NM) party; and for the 1993 constitutional assembly, the votes in favor of the new constitution.

49. Data for "subversive actions" and FONCODES spending were taken from *Perú: Compendio estadístico económico financiero* and *Perú: Compendio estadístico socio-demográfico*, both published by the INEI (various years). The GDP figures were taken from Webb and Fernández, *Perú en números* (various years). FONCODES spending figures were logged to achieve distributional normality.

50. The results do not change significantly using OLS with panel-corrected standard errors.

that increases in guerrilla activity led to increases in votes for Fujimori. Otherwise stated, the growth of guerrilla activity did not necessarily undermine Fujimori's electoral chances, because during those years voters were "likely to see [political] violence as rationalizing a hard-line stance" (Arce 2003a, 577). Economic growth and FONCODES per capita spending were also positively associated with Fujimori's vote (see Roberts and Arce 1998, 236; Weyland 1998, 558). The negative coefficient of Fujimori vote$_{t-1}$ could be indicative of the volatility of the Peruvian electorate. In the early 1990s, for instance, Fujimori drew his political support largely from the poor. By the mid-1990s, upper- and middle-class sectors of society supported Fujimori. In the late 1990s, however, the Peruvian electorate became as polarized as it had been in the early 1990s. Overall, the results presented below provide clear-cut evidence that Fujimori benefited politically by exploiting FONCODES.

POSTNEOLIBERALISM POLITICS

The societal impact of market-oriented economic reforms is highly variable and highly dependent on the initial distribution of gains and losses. That is the central finding of this book. In the Peruvian experience, some policy reforms have created incentives to form new societal organizations and engage in collective action, while other reforms have generated limited organizational responses. Concentrated gains, as in the pension reform, and concentrated losses, as in the tax reform, have yielded strong organized support and opposition, respectively. Concentrated gains and losses, which approximates the case of health decentralization, pitted grassroots organizations that generally endorsed the reform initiative against health administrators who resisted it. With dispersed gains and losses, as in the poverty-alleviation program, state reformers, rather than collective actors in civil society, have manipulated the reform process to their own advantage.

Clearly, as Schamis (1999) and other scholars have suggested, the impact of marketization is not politically neutral. Market projects tend to benefit some groups and some interests over others. The gains and losses resulting from market restructuring have typically been more concentrated at the elite level as opposed to the middle or lower classes, ultimately facilitating collective action at the expense of society at large. This differentiated pattern of political response has helped to strengthen elite sectors of society, notably the Peruvian business community, whose political leverage has increased vis-à-vis other societal actors. Peruvian business leaders have been able to "talk back" effectively to the state by exploiting their organizational coherence as well as social ties with state reformers. These interactions have diluted reforms regarded unfavorably by the business community, while accelerating and deepening reforms seen as favorable to business interests. Hence business leaders have been able to modify policies that were originally implemented by decree and with limited societal input, dominating to their own advantage the dialogue between state officials and civil society at large.

But the globalized, neoliberal variant of capitalism has spawned new forms of interest intermediation, albeit more localized and pluralistic than previous corporatist arrangements (Yashar 1999; Chalmers, Martin, and Piester 1997). Administrative and political decentralization to subnational units is one of the main forces contributing to new forms of societal recomposition. In the Peruvian case, the health reform process led to the creation of local committees at the grassroots level to manage health centers as part of a partial decentralization effort by the national government. The targeted relief fund FONCODES rebuilt or rehabilitated a large number of these centers, and base-level organizations that had previously participated in the construction of these health facilities have since been placed in charge of their daily management. The rapid expansion of the CLAS program is highly suggestive with respect to the capacity of decentralization initiatives to trigger new structures of popular representation.

Another example of important collective resistance was the series of strikes organized by market vendors, primarily representing the informal sector, to protest against the government's taxation efforts (see Chapter 3). By exploiting their workplace concentration, associations of market vendors managed to overcome the collective-action problems associated with their dispersion in terms of numbers. Market vendors continue to be taxed, yet in a different way from what was originally projected by state reformers. Their success in altering the original tax reform speaks to the potential for reform initiatives to generate new bases for societal organization in opposition to market reform.

An initial glance at the four sets of policies central to this book would probably place the health-decentralization and tax-reform processes as exceptions to the broader pattern of structural dominance and unequal access to the policy-making process by powerful business interests. However, the cluster of failed reform policies, such as the voucher-based education program, described below, and other important privatizations that were stalled because of labor opposition, suggests that traditional labor organizations continue to matter even in Peru, where the disorganizing effects of marketization appear to have been the strongest. Otherwise stated, Peruvian labor unions, which traditionally have not been particularly strong and which have not developed ties with political parties as in other countries, such as Argentina or Mexico, have not been entirely locked out of the political game.[1] Furthermore, as expanded below, in the wake of the collapse of the Fujimori regime, the country has experienced a wave of localized protests against the continuation of neoliberal reforms and, in certain cases, their lingering effects (Ballón 2002).[2] The violent, popular uprising against the privatization of the electric companies in the region of Arequipa is a case in point.[3] These social mobilizations appear to have increased as a consequence of the regime change, in part because of the perceived political opportunity to "talk back" to the state.

By examining the effects of market reforms on societal interests, and the feedback effects of those interests on reform processes, this study goes beyond most recent work on the politics of economic reform. The bulk of existing literature focuses almost exclusively on state structure and autonomy, not social interests; specific sectors or industries, not broad neoliberal reform initiatives; and policies typical of the first stages of economic reform, especially related to macroeconomic stability, not those characteristic of later stages of neoliberal restructuring, including attempts to revamp state institutions to sustain economic governance. In a sense, and complementary to Snyder's (1999) "one sector [industry], many places [states]" strategy, my approach compares many policies across different sectors and levels of organization in society. The advantage of this approach is that, by holding national institutions and macroeconomic conditions constant, it highlights how variation in political responses results in contrasting policy outcomes.

The following section extends the framework advanced in this book to other policy reforms. Immediately after, I reexamine the distinctive societal impact of neoliberal reform, paying particular attention to the increasing importance of business in the market era. In the the last section I analyze the prospects for the sustainability of market reform projects with a focus on state reform and suggest how democratic institutions can contribute to the deepening of economic reforms throughout Latin America.

1. Aside from education, and despite business support, organized labor successfully blocked various privatizations. Examples include the aborted privatizations of the state-owned oil, water, and hydroelectricity-generating companies. See "¿O es que le sobra la plata?" *Perú Económico*, April 1999; and Manzetti 1999, 262.

2. See also "¿El que no llora no mama?" *Caretas*, December 5, 2002.

3. See "Arequipa's Anger, Peru's Problem," *Economist*, June 22, 2002, 33–34; and José Luis Vargas Gutiérrez, "¡Erupcionó Arequipa¡" *Quehacer*, May–June 2002, 72–77.

EXTENDING THE FRAMEWORK: THE CASES OF EDUCATION AND TRADE REFORMS

As is written in Chapter 1, if a policy creates concentrated costs for a well-defined societal group and concentrated benefits for another well-defined societal group, it will lead to organized conflict, as each group has an incentive to mobilize and take political action. Moreover, there will not be significant political activity when policies have widely distributed costs and benefits. Finally, if a policy creates concentrated costs (benefits) to a specific, easily identifiable societal group and dispersed benefits (costs) across the general public, taking action to reduce those costs (obtain those benefits) will trigger little opposition. To distinguish these policies, one must consider whether a policy that provides benefits to one societal group generates opposition by another societal group, and whether a policy that imposes costs to one societal group generates support from another societal group.[4]

Two other reform cases, education—a counterfactual—and trade, illustrate the generalizability of the framework advanced here.[5] In 1992, following the autogolpe, the Fujimori government sought to decentralize administration of the schools as well as introduce a voucher-based subsidizing system for both public and private schools. While the education reform was actually decreed, it was never implemented. Mobilized in the Sole Union of Workers of Peruvian Education (SUTEP), unionized teachers were successful in indefinitely stalling these reform plans. In fact, according to some observers, the education reform plan almost cost Fujmori approval of the 1993 constitution, which, among other things, provided the legal framework for a market economy and enabled the president to run for reelection.[6] Similar to the CLAS initiative (see Chapter 5), the education reform threatened the centralized allocation of a fixed pool of resources traditionally managed by the public-sector education bureaucracy. The education reform thus created concentrated, visible losses to a well-defined group—unionized teachers.

A staple of "second-generation" reforms, the education reform, particularly the decentralization component, would have unleashed a similar interest-group conflict between education administrators who opposed it (concentrated

---

4. This section draws on Baron (1994, 34–35). See also Chapter 1, note 8.
5. For a discussion on counterfactuals, see Fearon 1991.
6. For further discussion, see Graham 1998, 100–105; and Ortiz et al. 1999.

losers) and grassroots organizations that may have potentially endorsed it (concentrated beneficiaries). Moreover, it is likely that the decentralization reform—which stipulated local administration of schools through local committees also in charge of personnel decisions—would have had empowering and participation effects at the grassroots level, similar to the CLAS experience described in Chapter 5.[7]

In the case of trade liberalization, which can be broadly portrayed as a process involving concentrated losers (for example, organized industrialists) and dispersed, unidentifiable winners (for instance, society at large), the Fujimori government had made substantial progress toward a uniform, flat tariff structure.[8] Predictably, the policy efforts to impose such a tariff structure sparked strong opposition from organized industrialists and thus created strong incentives to lobby. Certainly, trade liberalization has not been kind to industrialists, given that they have had greater difficulties in bearing the costs of a liberalized economy vis-à-vis other sectors. Throughout the entire Fujimori regime, industrialists openly criticized the economic program as being particularly skewed to favor the financial and traditional export sectors. They also had demanded, albeit unsuccessfully, a higher, more differentiated system of trade tariffs (see Chapter 2). Although there is some evidence indicating that the Fujimori government became more receptive to industrialists' requests in the late 1990s, the executive had previously rejected these requests for protectionism. Only in 2001 would the transitional government of Valentín Paniagua terminate Fujimori's policy efforts to impose a flat tariff structure by introducing greater tariff dispersion, and thus greater protectionism.[9] To keep business pressures at bay, Fujimori made changes in the tariff structure a constitutional prerogative exclusive to the executive. Paniagua took advantage of the same type of policy centralization, but with an entirely different purpose. To be sure,

7. As noted previously, the education reform provides another important example of collective action in civil society during market restructuring. For a review of recent reforms on education under Paniagua, see Nicolás Lynch, "La educación sobre el tapete," *Perú Económico*, July 2003 17–18; and "El pensamiento arcaico en la educación peruana," *Perú Económico*, October 2003, 14–16.

8. Tariff dispersion declined from thirty-nine levels in the early 1990s to two (12 and 20 percent) by the end of 1998. For further discussion, see Abusada et al. 2000; and Boloña 2002, 114–16. Typically, trade liberalization is not considered a "second generation" type of reform. The framework of costs and benefits, nonetheless, remains a useful conceptual tool with which to analyze the politics of trade opening.

9. The new tariff system was proposed by Emilio Navarro, who in the past served as president of the SNI and under Panigua became minister of the presidency. See "Política arancelaria cambia radicalmente tras diez años," *El Comercio*, April 27, 2001. For similar tariff changes that took place in Chile during the Pinochet regime, see Edwards and Lederman 1998.

the differences within the business community over trade tariffs proved difficult to reconcile, and they ultimately led to the collapse of CONFIEP as the sole
peak association representing business. In retrospect, the continuation of the
market model, in particular the policy efforts to impose a uniform, flat tariff
structure, shattered business unity.[10] These state-society interactions are central
to the study of the politics of economic reform.

ORGANIZED BUSINESS AND THE STATE IN THE MARKET ERA

While market reforms have helped advance the interests of the business sector,
at the same time, the Peruvian state has become increasingly more dependent
on business interests. A telling example is the successive shifts in the pension-
privatization process (see Chapter 4). Introducing a variant of what Murillo
(2002) has identified as a "political bias," Fujimori actually went as far as to
prohibit banks and insurance firms from participating in the privatization program, only to cave in to business demands later on. The implications of this
change are far reaching, inasmuch as the Peruvian state under President Fujimori, at least in the early years, demonstrated a far greater capacity for relatively autonomous decision-making than did other states in Latin America.

As noted in Chapter 2, in the early 1990s, during the implementation of the
fiscal-austerity and economic-adjustment program, technocrats dominated the
policy debate. During the orthodox phase (1990–92), Fujimori dealt with business from a position of strength and did not hesitate to confront the traditionally powerful in Peru. Early reforms were largely state imposed, but generally
supported by business. Through time, however, as the economic situation improved, business-government relations became gradually more cooperative
and stable. Both business and government were ultimately interested in economic recovery. During this period, which I referred to earlier as the pragmatic phase of 1993–98, business effectively exploited the policy-making
process, and the government became more responsive to business demands.
The core of technocrats with business interests, who dominated the Finance
Ministry, were particularly instrumental in steering policy, largely through tai-
lor-made laws (*leyes sastre*), to favor certain economic sectors.

In all, market change, contrary to the common characterization of marketization as a revolution from above, represents an interactive process involving

---

10. "Sociedad Nacional de Industrias decidió retirarse de la CONFIEP," *Gestión*, March 29, 2001.

shifting state-capitalist coalitions (Silva 1996). Business organizations in Peru and other parts of Latin America have been more proactive and agenda setting than previously theorized. In Peru, this pattern is reflected in the series of policy proposals advanced by CONFIEP in cooperation with the government. During the peak of the pragmatic phase, as documented in Chapter 2, it became virtually impossible to differentiate which sets of policy proposals were drawn by the business sector as opposed to government itself. Various associates of CONFIEP's think tank—the IPE—began to work closely with government. Moreover, by appointing business leaders to pivotal positions in the state, governments across Latin America have made efforts to enlist the support of the business sector (Silva and Durand 1998; Schneider 1998). In the Peruvian context, and to name but one example, a business leader in the construction sector—Jorge Camet—headed the Finance Ministry longer than any other minister in the recent history of that country, almost six years, from early 1993 to mid-1998. The increasing dialogue and interaction between organized business and government in the market era can no longer be ignored. As Schneider (1998, 101–2) aptly noted, "[I]n the wake of neoliberal reform, the opposite of state-led development is not market-led development but rather business-led development."

Future research, however, should specify the conditions under which close relations between business and government are likely to be conducive to development in the sense of Evan's (1995) "embedded autonomy," as opposed to merely secretive collusive "revolving door" relationships between corporate and executive posts. Embedded autonomy speaks to the close ties between government bureaucrats and businesses in which the former retain the ability to formulate and act on preferences autonomously.[11] Thus far, studies have suggested that encompassing or peak business associations can maximize cooperation between government and business better than sectoral associations or individual firms. Encompassing associations can ameliorate distributional conflicts by resolving intersectoral disputes in-house. As a result, these associations can focus on what is best for the economy as a whole and for business as a class (Schneider 1998; Silva and Durand 1998). However, given the break-

11. However, as Evans (1995, 12) notes, a state that is too autonomous lacks "both sources of intelligence and the ability to rely on decentralized private implementation." By extension, a state that is only embedded is ripe for capture, "undercutting development even in the narrow sense of capital accumulation." According to Evans, "only when embeddedness and autonomy are joined together can a state be called developmental."

down of CONFIEP, which had arguably coalesced behind a single encompassing association, it remains to be seen how business-government relations will
progress in the post-Fujimori era. It suffices to say that the governments of
Paniagua and Toledo have been more open to demands from industrialists and
nontraditional exporters, precisely the economic sectors that were abandoned
in Fujimori's version of neoliberalism.

In addition, organizational coherence within the business sector is not a
sufficient condition for successful collaboration between government and
business. According to Schneider (1998, 117), for instance, unrestrained capital
mobility does not facilitate constructive cooperation between government and
business. A fully liberalized capital account, as found in Peru, often favors
foreign investors over domestic capitalists. Not surprisingly, Peruvian business
leaders repeatedly complained about President Fujimori's giving "the red car-
pet treatment" to foreign investors, who are obviously outside the network of
CONFIEP. More important, in the absence of state capacity and autonomy to
monitor business activities and channel business preferences toward socially
constructive ends, increased business organization and professionalization may
only give business the upper hand, undermining the capacity of the state to
formulate and implement policies favorable to development.

It goes without saying that the connections between government and business facilitated collusion and selective rent-seeking behavior (see Diez
Canseco 2002; Durand 2003). And in many cases, Vladimiro Montesinos acted
as a business broker. To name but one example, Dionisio Romero Seminario—arguably the most powerful and influential businessman in Peru—met
privately with Vladimiro Montesinos at least five separate times; issued a public statement, containing questions and answers drafted by Montesinos, supporting the continuation of the Fujimori regime beyond 2000; and, when
government corruption came to light, lent Montesinos his personal airplane
so Montesinos could flee the country.[12] In one of those meetings, Romero
Seminario asked Montesinos for help in reducing import duties on wheat because it affected his "own wallet's interests" (quoted in Bowen and Holligan
2003, 296). The Romero group managed Alicorp S.A., the largest and leading
conglomerate producer of pasta, oils, and other staple food products in Peru.

The banking bailout implemented in the late 1990s is another example of

---

12. This section draws on Bowen and Holligan 2003, 295–97; and Durand 2003, 334. For a
discussion about media collusion during the Fujimori regime, see Conaghan 2002.

mutual back-scratching between state officials and business. The rescue operation spread from smaller banks, such as Banco Latino, with deposits equivalent
to less than 4 percent of the market, to the second largest bank in the country,
Banco Wiese, dubbed the "mafia's bank" because it served as Montesinos's
financial haven. Both banks faced serious financial burdens well before the
1997–98 international financial crisis, which in part served as a justification for
the massive multimillion-dollar bailout operation. The most inconvenient fact
about the bailout operation, however, was and remains the true source of these
unpaid, accumulated debts. Managed by the financial group of Jorge Picasso
Salinas, for instance, Banco Latino lent money to businesses that were also
owned by this financial group. Thus creditor and debtor were one in the
same.[13] Interestingly, Jorge Picasso was president of CONFIEP during the
1996–97 period and was said to be next in line to replace Finance Minister
Jorge Camet. In sum, this pattern of secretive collusion and back-room lobbying between state officials and business interests raises questions about the
extent to which closer cooperation between government and business is likely
to establish a new and stronger basis for economic development or to sustain
market-oriented economic reform.

SUBALTERN ACTORS AND STATE REFORMERS IN THE MARKET ERA

To the extent that market projects have not brought concentrated gains or
losses to elite sectors of society, their impact has been mainly to advance the
interests of state actors. Targeted poverty-alleviation programs are a case in
point. These safety nets have enabled state reformers to obtain short-term electoral support while at the same time presenting an image of state efficacy and
modernity to the international community. In the absence of an organized
response either in favor of or in opposition to these compensatory programs,
targeted assistance mainly only helped to "generate new patronage" (Weyland
1998, 542), bolstering established political leaders at the expense of opposition
challengers. Targeted programs have been widely accepted because of their
effectiveness in assisting the poor while easing fiscal drain. However, it is obvi-
ous that these programs do not represent a long-term policy commitment to

---

13. See "Rescate de la banca: Un secreto billonario," *Actualidad Económica* 204 (February–
March 2000): 6–9; and Pedro Francke and Mariana Ballén, "El rescate continúa," *Actualidad Económica* 209 (September 2000): 10–15. As the story goes, Picasso's own financial brokerage company,
known as Argos S.A., lost millions of dollars by making poor investments on the stock market.

address the problems of the poor, much less broader issues concerning equity or income distribution. As critics have noted, these programs are better described as "band-aids" (Nelson 1989, 103) applied to alleviate adjustment costs than as long-term solutions to pervasive problems of poverty and inequality. It is also likely that grassroots efforts may have been displaced from other traditional organizational activities in order to secure state funding for short-term projects.[14]

Health reform has entailed an entirely different pattern involving the creation of local committees to manage primary-health-care centers as part of a partial health decentralization effort by the national government. The CLAS program has served to empower the members of these local committees by allowing them to make a number of important decisions, "including the hiring and firing of personnel, fiscal management, decisions regarding improvements in center services and the approval of a local health plan" (Ewig 2001, 288). Essentially, the decision-making authority and leadership opportunities provided by the CLAS program have increased the voice of community members, thus permitting them to demand better-quality health services.

With the private sector at the forefront of development in the market era, state actors have granted privileged access to business leaders in the policy-making process. Other sectors of society, notably organized labor, have been excluded and weakened as a result of privatization and labor-deregulation practices. The nucleos and committees resulting from the FONCODES and CLAS programs, respectively, spawned localized and particularistic forms of organization. However, these isolated forms of collective action "will do little to challenge concentrations of private economic power or a logic of capital accumulation that is increasingly transnational in scope" (Roberts 1998, 279). Only stronger forms of organization, such as political parties, are capable of doing that. Thus whereas business leaders have been effectively incorporated as citizens with rights to exercise voice and influence policy under the new economic model, other societal actors have been mainly incorporated as clients of the state.

Before discussing the long-term viability of economic reforms, a couple of observations about the transformation of business and society in Peru as a whole are warranted. First, the number of Peruvian business conglomerates or economic groups (*grupos*) has shrunk considerably. Known as the "twelve apostles" during the García government, there are only four out of these twelve

---

14. I thank an anonymous reviewer for this suggestion.

traditional economic groups remaining.[15] The bulk of these groups have either disappeared or been swallowed up by foreign capital. In many ways, aside from fragmenting the traditional business community represented in CONFIEP (see Chapter 2), the remarkable infusion of private capital flows since the early 1990s has also served to denationalize most of the Peruvian business class.

As for society, clearly traditional collective action by unions has all but disappeared. Whereas in the 1980s the average number of strikes per year was 701, in the 1990s it was 184. Strike activity fell even more beginning in the second half of the 1990s, averaging 59 strikes per year (INEI 2001). However, after the fall of the Fujimori regime, the country experienced an unprecedented rise in mobilizations and protests against neoliberal reforms and their lingering effects (Ballón 2002). According to the Ministry of the Interior, responsible for monitoring public order, there were 1,826 mobilizations and protests in 2001, and 6,240 in 2002.[16] The comparison of strikes and protests reflects a shift in the pattern of social protest, from institutionalized to noninstitutionalized forms of social mobilization. Elements in a new repertoire of social protest include marches, parallel demonstrations, road blockades, and even temporary seizures of state offices.[17] New actors include the unemployed, primarily former state employees from privatized state-owned industries; members of ecological movements, particularly in large mining areas;[18] the landless;[19] and indigenous groups.[20] In all, it appears that neoliberalism has undermined collective action in the labor sphere (Roberts 1998; Zermeño 1999), while increasing collective action through other forms of protest.

15. See Francisco Durand, "Adiós a los 12 apóstoles," *Quehacer*, July–August 2000, 99–105; and "Backus y la desaparición de los apóstoles," *Quehacer*, September–October 2002, 96–104. For an overview of these economic groups, see Durand 1996, 111–67; and Vásquez Huamán 2000.

16. Ministerio del Interior, *Memoria del Servicio Nacional de Inteligencia del Ministerio del Interior 2002*.

17. See "La marcha de no acabar," *Caretas*, August 22, 2002; and "¿El que no llora no mama?" *Caretas*, December 5, 2002.

18. These movements have risen in part as a consequence of environmental contamination caused by mining complexes. The 2000 spill of poisonous mercury from Minera Yanacocha in the city of Choropampa, Cajamarca, is perhaps the most well known case of environmental devastation in Peru. See Muradian, Martinez-Alier, and Correa 2003; and Martín Paredes, "Conflictos entre minería y comunidades indígenas," *Quehacer*, June–August 2001, 95–104.

19. In early 2002, at least twenty people died in the rainforest area of Cajamarca as a consequence of fights over land between native communities and migrants (*colonos*). For further discussion, see Shane Green and Mamais Juep Green, "La jungla sin justicia," *Quehacer*, January–February 2002, 21–23.

20. See, for instance, Eduardo Cáceres, "Los fantasmas del etnocacerismo," *Quehacer*, September–October 2003, 35–40.

THE SUSTAINABILITY OF MARKET REFORMS

Institution Building Revisited

Central to the success of market-oriented economic policies under Fujimori was a far-reaching reform of the state, which helped restore fiscal discipline and increased the efficiency of the state apparatus. Indeed, "Peru's transformation in the 1990s stands on par with that of the 1970s: just as [the twelve-year nationalist military regime] had radically redrawn the lines between state and market in favor of the former, Fujimori reversed them just as radically in favor of the latter" (Wise 2003, 221).

This process of state reengineering began with COPRI, which successfully sold numerous state enterprises. In addition, the Fujimori government created various new state agencies and regulatory bureaus to monitor the activities of the newly privatized industries. Key examples were the consumer-protection agency INDECOPI and several regulatory agencies: OSIPTEL (Supervisory Board for Private Investment in Telecommunications) for telecommunications, OSITRAN (Supervisory Board for Infrastructure Investment in Public Transportation) for public transportation, and OSINERG (Supervisory Board for Investment in Electricity) for electricity.

The transformation of state institutions, however, has been highly selective and uneven, creating "islands of competence" against a backdrop of unreformed sectoral ministries and an ineffective judicial system.[21] Moreover, it appears that the "islands of competence," or enclave, approach to reforming the state may have reached its limits, particularly on the fiscal side. Because of the traditionally low wages of public-sector employees, the bulk of these new state agencies were allowed to recruit personnel using the labor code that applies to the private sector.[22] The tax office, SUNAT, was one of the first state agencies that was allowed to offer private contracts to its personnel, contracts that afforded greater wage flexibility compared to the existing public-sector

21. A January 2004 opinion poll conducted by Apoyo S.A. ranked the judicial system as the most corrupt institution in Peru, followed by the National Police and Congress. For further details, see Proetica 2004.

22. This special labor scheme that applies private law to public employees is known as Regime 728. On average, workers under Regime 728 earn 25 percent more than the rest of the public workforce and account for at least 20 percent of the total number of public-sector employees (World Bank 2003, 116–23).

labor regime (see Chapter 3). Beyond SUNAT, however, private contracts in other public-sector state agencies expanded considerably.[23]

These changes in the structure of the pay scale for government employees have ultimately created a very expensive state bureaucracy, raising questions about the capacity of the government to financially support the emerging state apparatus.[24] Not surprisingly, with tax revenues stagnating and in an effort to maintain fiscal discipline, in late 1999 the government decreed a temporary 15 percent cut for all government workers earning more than 8,000 Peruvian soles per month (about U.S.$2,600).[25] The fragility of government finances suggests that the Peruvian state continues to be "big," but in a way different from that of the past. All told, when private contracts become a surrogate for true civil service or Weberian reforms aimed at enhancing bureaucratic performance, as the Peruvian case suggests, government regulation of business may lead to a different type of state growth.[26]

The institutional implosion experienced by the SUNAT provides a sobering reminder that policy efforts to increase the efficiency and autonomy of the state apparatus remain an uphill struggle. As noted in Chapter 3, in the late 1990s one of the most successful cases of state reform—SUNAT—became a vehicle of corruption and political intimidation. Ironically, the erosion in state capacity was attributable not only to societal opposition to the reform process, but also to activities initiated by the government itself, in particular by the Montesinos mafia. This ultimately undermined compliance with tax laws, generated resistance to tax reform, and eroded the capacity of the collection agency to pursue policy goals. The electoral processes that have followed the collapse of the Fujimori regime, however, have afforded the governments of Paniagua and Toledo the opportunity to make a "clean sweep" (Domínguez

23. Interview by the author with Alberto Rey Rojas, chief researcher of the Economic and Social Studies Division of the SNI, Lima, August 9, 2002. See also "Las mil y una planillas del estado," *Peru Económico*, August 2001, 11–12.

24. Hilderbrand and Grindle (1997, 33) have pointed out that monetary rewards, that is, higher salaries, are not always effective determinants of public-sector performance, yet they have generally been undertaken to improve government output in the developing world.

25. "No se tiene cifra exacta de afectados con reducciones," *El Comercio*, September 21, 1999.

26. A study by the World Bank (2003, 119) notes, "Contrary to common belief, the current [public-sector] employment level is higher than in the early 1990s." Moreover, the true size of public-sector employment in Peru is uncertain. Estimates range from 616,200 to 890,728 workers (World Bank 2003, 116). Even SUNAT was burdened with overstaffing, and in 1997 about eight hundred people were dismissed (see Baca 2000, 187). On Weberian or civil service reforms, see Heredia and Schneider 2003.

1998, 174) and carry out a substantial crackdown on corruption (Durand 2002b, 36–40). The regime change leads us to be cautiously optimistic about the prospects for the sustainability of economic reform.

Democracy and Market Reforms

The Peruvian experience suggests that policy centralization, which became a permanent feature throughout the entire Fujimori regime, does not always deliver effective market change. Consequently, the successful implementation of market reforms may require a broader framework of contestation and accountability rather than centralized policy making (see Haggard and Kaufman 1995; Manzetti 2003). The absence of institutional checks and balances was obviously more acute in Peru than anywhere else in Latin America, which casts doubt on the capacity of insulated decision-making processes to establish the basis for deeper reform.

The exclusionary technocratic decision-making processes that emerged in Latin America during the 1980s and 1990s (Teichman 1997) reached new heights in the Peruvian case. Among other things, the Finance Ministry formulated tax policies, regulated social security pension contributions, and even determined trade tariffs, all with limited input from a broader cross section of society.[27] Further, the Peruvian national legislature became increasingly marginalized from the economic-policy-formation process, and functioned largely as a rubber stamp for executive orders.

A number of general conclusions having broader implications for the politics of marketization may be drawn from the Peruvian experience. First, even when policies appear to be well insulated and highly centralized, the Peruvian case demonstrates that some segments of civil society—notably the business elite—are still able to permeate the policy-making process and obtain concessions by negotiating directly with line ministries. In other words, the marginalization of representative institutions, such as Congress, or more broadly, the weakening of the traditional political party system, have not hindered the capacity of the business elite to reshape policy outcomes in its own interest. This is primarily because the gains and losses resulting from market projects have typically been more concentrated at the elite level as opposed to the middle or lower classes, ultimately strengthening and unifying the business community

---

27. "Rebaja sí, pero no ahora," *Perú Económico*, October 1998, 16.

and thus facilitating collective action. Consequently, by marginalizing deliberative institutions that could potentially be more responsive to popular majorities, exclusionary decision-making processes have mainly served to enhance business influence and dilute reforms unfavorable to the business community. The insulation of the policy process from popular pressures may thus facilitate selective rent-seeking rather than guarantee successful implementation of market-oriented policies.

Second, the Peruvian case suggests that technocratic decision-making processes do not necessarily facilitate sustained structural changes. On the contrary, there is increasing evidence that the process of neoliberal reform under President Fujimori advanced slowly in comparison to other cases from the mid-1990s onward. In 1996, for instance, the Fujimori government announced a major overhaul of the public-sector bureaucracy, but the program never got off the ground, presumably because of the anticipated political costs involved in dismissing public officials (Roca Voto Bernales 2003).[28] The privatization program slowed down considerably after 1996, largely because of labor opposition (Manzetti 1999, 262). And the courageous efforts to reform the fiscal system and combat tax evasion grew significantly weaker during Fujimori's second presidential term (Durand and Thorp 1998, 144–49). If anything, Peru's one-time maverick—the reform-minded political outsider and self-proclaimed "statesman" who challenged vested interests—became a politician, who cautiously weighed the political costs of continuous reform.[29]

Third, the Peruvian experience suggests that the consolidation of market reforms may require broader democratic institutions rather than centralized policy-making to check arbitrary executive actions that are threatening to the coherence and integrity of the policy reform process. As the dominant political figure in Peru, Fujimori greatly exacerbated this exclusionary style of policy formation, often superceding technocratic centralization. Otherwise stated, in the absence of institutionalized consultation or accountability, exclusionary policy making evolved gradually in a highly autocratic and personalistic direction.

There are many examples that reveal the dangers of an autocratic style of policy formulation throughout the Fujimori regime. To diversify risks, for in-

---

28. "Factor humano influyó en retraso de la modernización del estado," *El Comercio*, October 22, 1999.
29. In Arce 2003b I provide an explanation for the slowdown of economic reforms during the Fujimori regime. See also "Fujimori heterodoxo," *Actualidad Económica* 208 (August 2000): 6–9.

stance, the AAFP petitioned the government to allow for a percentage of pension funds under AFP management to be invested abroad. President Fujimori, however, initially vetoed the request, largely for nationalistic reasons.[30] The restrictions to invest outside Peru—according to the AFP industry—made the pension fund particularly vulnerable to domestic shocks, all the while jeopardizing the long-term growth of workers' pensions.

Another example illustrating the risks of an autocratic style of policy formulation is the government's decision to reinstate the so-called development banks, notably the Agrarian Bank. These development banks (including the Mining and Industrial Banks) were liquidated in the early 1990s because of heavy losses resulting from defaulted loans. The government eventually assumed this debt, estimated at U.S.$400 million.[31] As one would expect, technocrats with business interests and the association of private banks—ASBANC—criticized the creation of the Agrarian Bank because of state involvement in financial markets.[32] In contrast, both agrarian producers and populist loyalists led by Absalón Vásquez welcomed the president's initiative; yet the decision to create the Agrarian Bank was never debated, but rather left entirely to the president's sole discretion.

The political manipulation of GDP estimates further underlines the costs of autocratic policy formation. During the Fujimori regime, GDP estimates were calculated on the basis of a 1979 sample of businesses. The original 1979 sample consisted of 275 companies, but because of the economic crisis of the 1980s, in the 1990s only 152 of these businesses (approximately 45 percent) were in operation.[33] Moreover, since 1979 the weight given to various sectors of the economy in GDP estimates did not change to reflect, among other things, increasing informalization and deindustrialization.[34] As a result, GDP figures in Peru were overestimated: 20 percent according to the governor of the Central Bank, or between 14 or 15 percent according to the Finance Ministry.[35]

In 1994, the official statistics bureau INEI began to recalculate GDP esti-

---

30. "Anularán reglamento que permite la inversión en el extranjero de AFPs," *El Comercio*, August 9, 1999.

31. See "Banca de fomento fue un despilfarro total," *El Comercio*, April 4, 2001; and Congreso de la República 2003. See also "Boloña: El ortodoxo," *Caretas*, September 30, 1999.

32. "CONFIEP discrepa con Banco Agrario," *El Comercio*, November 6, 1999.

33. "Solo existe 45% de empresas consideradas para el cálculo del PBI," *El Comercio*, December 6, 1999.

34. "Rumbos y tumbos," *Caretas*, July 22, 1999.

35. "PBI no crecería este año y podría ser negativo," *Gestión*, October 19, 1999. For further discussion, see Cuba 1997 and Jiménez 1997.

mates. The new figures were supposed to be released in 1995, or at the latest in 1996. But despite widespread criticisms from business leaders and academics, the Fujimori government deliberately delayed the publication of these figures, presumably for political reasons. In 1999, for instance, the government projected a 2 percent GDP growth rate. But with a distorted GDP, actual GDP growth was probably close to zero.[36] Revised GDP estimates were only made public once Fujimori's second reelection in 2000 had been secured.

Like GDP figures, poverty estimates were subject to political tinkering. A recent study by the INEI revealed that the percentage of the population living in poverty increased from 42.7 in 1997 to 48.8 percent in 2000. In Lima, the percentage of the poor increased from 25.4 in 1997 to 38.9 percent in 2000.[37] These new poverty figures, which contradicted official accounts put forth by the Fujimori regime, were released during the transitional government of Paniagua.

The lack of credibility and transparency surrounding the economic and social statistics put forward by the government was overwhelming.[38] Business leaders, however, were not able to channel their demands for more reliable GDP estimates, largely because of the increased marginalization of deliberative institutions and constraints on open debate. As noted previously, the tendency to bypass consultative representative institutions was the very mechanism exploited by business leaders to advance their own interests, but the absence of a broader framework of contestation and accountability would also be a major disadvantage to business interests in the long run. As one may expect, segments of the business elite began to look for "an alternative" to President Fujimori, whose authoritarian tendencies increasingly came to be seen as a threat to economic stability (Youngers 2000, 16).

In the absence of institutional checks and balances, exclusionary and con-

---

36. "PBI no crecería este año y podría ser negativo," *Gestión*, October 19, 1999. The business reaction toward the government's political manipulation of GDP estimates was best captured by the testimony of Carlos Bruce, president of ADEX: "In a rather childlike manner that insulted our intelligence, the government told us that they were recalculating the new GDP. They told us this not one nor six months ago, but rather five years ago. It is truly an insult to the intelligence of all Peruvians to claim that it takes five years to recalculate the GDP, without releasing any information since then. If the government's statistics bureau INEI cannot do this calculation, then they should let us do it for them." See "Bruce: Sería una buena señal que Goldenberg informe sobre el nuevo PBI," *Gestión*, October 20, 1999.

37. Instituto Nacional de Estadística e Informatica, *Nota de Prensa* 37, July 2001. See also "Más pobres que antes," *Actualidad Económica* 210 (October 2000): 22–24.

38. An overestimated GDP implies that tax revenues as a percentage of GDP were higher than what the government suggested. For a similar discussion about Argentina, see "Argentina, Not As Big As It Seemed," *The Economist*, June 19, 1999.

centrated decision-making can thus be counterproductive not only to the sustainability and long-term viability of market reforms, but also to democratic consolidation (Haggard and Kaufman 1995, 13). Without institutionalized consultation or accountability, the most likely beneficiaries of exclusionary decision-making are sectors of organized business (at least in the short term) and established political leaders. Business leaders can therefore seek to modify policies by negotiating directly with decision makers in charge of managing the economy, such as the Finance Ministry. In the Peruvian case, exclusionary decision-making strengthened the political hand of the executive, creating possibilities for a personalistic style of policy formation and, subsequently, the political manipulation of reform projects. Unchecked by representative institutions, the partnership of government and business can jeopardize market projects, economic development, and democracy, not least by exposing reform policies to political distortion.

The strengthening of democratic institutions is obviously not a concern of the business community; "the question is not so much whether business will contribute to democracy but whether democracy can guarantee business interests" (Durand 1999, 50). In the end, what appeared to be a symbiotic, proactive relationship between government and business under President Fujimori proved to be a vicious circle of policy decay and depredation. Ironically, organized business benefited from this pattern of centralized authority, mostly through back-room lobbying, and with privileged and easy access to the Finance Ministry. However, when push came to shove, for instance, when business demanded greater transparency in the statistics being released by the government, or the continuation of the privatization program, the impact of business on policy was null.

Crony capitalism, kleptocracy, Vladieconomía (referring to Vladimiro Montesinos's influence on key economic policy-making decisions), and *lumpen capitalists* (suggesting the ethical bankruptcy of the Peruvian business elite), among other terms, have already become common currency to characterize Peru's most recent economic transformation under Fujimori.[39] The debate over whether this is a new phenomenon or simply the continuation of a historical pattern of unfinished transformations and corruption, typical of countries in transition like Peru, has just begun. While recent opinion polls in Peru

---

39. See "Vladieconomía," *Actualidad Económica* 215 (March 2001): 19–21; and Alberto Vergara, "Lumpen-empresariado y derrumbe del Fujimorato," *Quehacer*, January–February 2002, 24–29. Vergara's *lumpen capitalists* (*lumpen-empresariado*) is a variant of the term *lumpen proletariat*, which can be roughly translated as "slum workers."

rank Fujimori as the "best" former president the country has ever had, the international anticorruption watchdog group Transparency International ranked him among the top ten most corrupt political leaders in the world.[40] There is little doubt that the legacy of the Fujimori regime will remain controversial for many years ahead.

40. See "An Ex-president of Peru Plots His Return," *New York Times*, September 29, 2003, A22; and press release from Transparency International's *Global Corruption Report 2004*, March 25, 2004.

BIBLIOGRAPHY

Abusada, Roberto, Fritz Du Bois, Eduardo Morón, and José Valderrama. 2000. *La reforma incompleta: rescatando los noventa.* Lima: Centro de Investigación de la Universidad del Pacífico.
AFP Horizonte. 1996. *Tres años del sistema privado de pensiones: 1993–1996.* Lima: AFP Horizonte.
Aiyer, Sri-Ram. 1997. *Pension Reform in Latin America: Quick Fixes or Sustainable Reform?* Washington, D.C.: World Bank.
Alcázar, Lorena, and Erik Wachtenheim. 2001. "Determinants of Project Success: Case Study of FONCODES." Washington, D.C.: World Bank.
Altobelli, Laura. 2002. "Participación comunitaria en la salud: La experiencia peruana en los CLAS." In *La salud peruana en el siglo XXI: Retos y propuestas de política,* ed. Juan Arroyo, 303–54. Lima: Consorcio de Investigación Económica y Social.
Altobelli, Laura C., and Jorge Pancorvo. 2000. "Shared Health Administration Program and Local Health Administration Associations (CLAS) in Peru." World Bank, Washington, D.C.
Anderson, Karen M. 2001. "The Politics of Retrenchment in a Social Democratic Welfare State: Reform of Swedish Pensions and Unemployment Insurance." *Comparative Political Studies* 34, no. 9 (November): 1063–91.
Apoyo S.A. 1991a. *Informe de opinión* (December). Lima: Apoyo.
———. 1991b. *Informe de opinión* (March). Lima: Apoyo.
———. 1993. *Informe de opinión* (January). Lima: Apoyo.
———. 1995. *Informe de opinión* (March). Lima: Apoyo.
———. 1998a. *Informe de opinión* (February). Lima: Apoyo.
———. 1998b. *Informe de opinión* (October). Lima: Apoyo.
———. 1998c. *Informe de opinión* (September). Lima: Apoyo.
———. 2000. *Informe de opinión* (September). Lima: Apoyo.
———. 2001. *Informe de opinión* (September). Lima: Apoyo.
Arce, Moisés. 1996. "¿Qué tan eficiente es la política social del FONCODES?" *Pretextos* 9 (November): 95–113.
———. 2001. "The Politics of Pension Reform in Peru." *Studies in Comparative International Development* 36, no. 3 (Fall): 88–113.
———. 2003a. "Political Violence and Presidential Approval in Peru." *Journal of Politics* 65, no. 2 (May): 572–83.
———. 2003b. "The Sustainability of Market Reform in a Most Likely Case: Peru." *Comparative Politics* 35, no. 3 (April): 335–54.
Arias, Luis. 1991. "Fiscal Policy." In *Peru's Path to Recovery: A Plan for Stabilization and Growth,* ed. Carlos Paredes and Jeffrey D. Sachs, 200–227. Washington, D.C.: Brookings Institution.

———. 1995. "Un análisis de las modificaciones del impuesto a la renta." *Moneda* 90 (December): 52–55.

Arroyo, Juan. 2000. *Salud: La reforma silenciosa.* Lima: Universidad Peruana Cayetano Heredia.

———, ed. 2002. *La salud peruana en el siglo XXI: Retos y propuestas de política.* Lima: Consorcio de Investigación Económica y Social.

Ascarza, Illich. 1994. "Estadísticas del nivel de vida en el Perú." In *Foro económico: Ataque a la pobreza en el Perú*, ed. Javier Portocarrero, 79–95. Lima: Fundación Friedrich Ebert.

Ausejo, Flavio. 1995. "La reforma del instituto peruano de seguridad social." In *Implementación de políticas públicas en el Perú*, ed. Augusto Alvarez and Gabriel Ortiz, 131–44. Lima: Instituto Apoyo.

Baca, Jorge. 2000. "El ancla fiscal: La reforma tributaria." In *La reforma incompleta: Rescatando los noventa*, ed. Roberto Abusada, Fritz Du Bois, Eduardo Morón, and José Valderrama, 163–218. Lima: Centro de Investigación de la Universidad del Pacífico.

Balbi, Carmen Rosa, and David Scott Palmer. 2001. "Political Earthquake: The 70 Days that Shook Peru." *lasa* Forum 31, no. 4 (Winter): 7–11.

Ballón, Eduardo E. 2002. "El toledismo y el movimiento social." In *Perú hoy: Toledo, a un año de gobierno*, ed. Eduardo Ballón, 13–59. Lima: DESCO.

Banco Central de Reserva del Perú (BCRP). 1994. *Memoria 1994.* Lima: Banco Central de Reserva del Perú.

———. 1995. *Memoria 1995.* Lima: Banco Central de Reserva del Perú.

———. 1996. *Memoria 1996.* Lima: Banco Central de Reserva del Perú.

———. 1997. *Memoria 1997.* Lima: Banco Central de Reserva del Perú.

———. 1998. *Memoria 1998.* Lima: Banco Central de Reserva del Perú.

———. 1999. *Memoria 1999.* Lima: Banco Central de Reserva del Perú.

———. 2000. *Memoria 2000.* Lima: Banco Central de Reserva del Perú.

———. 2001. *Memoria 2001.* Lima: Banco Central de Reserva del Perú.

———. 2002. *Memoria 2002.* Lima: Banco Central de Reserva del Perú.

Baron, David P. 1994. "Electoral Competition with Informed and Uninformed Voters." *American Political Science Review* 88, no. 1 (March): 33–47.

Barrientos, Armando. 2000. "Getting Better After Neoliberalism: Shifts and Challenges of Health Policy in Peru." In *Healthcare Reform and Poverty in Latin America*, ed. Peter Llyod-Sherlock, 94–110. London: Institute of Latin American Studies.

Bergman, Marcelo S. 2003. "Tax Reforms and Tax Compliance: The Divergent Paths of Chile and Argentina." *Journal of Latin American Studies* 35, no. 3 (August): 593–624.

Boloña, Carlos. 1993. *Cambio de rumbo: El programa económico para los '90.* Lima: Instituto de Economía de Libre Mercado San Ignacio de Loyola.

———. 1996. "The Viability of Alberto Fujimori's Economic Strategy." In *The Peruvian Economy and Structural Adjustment: Past, Present, and Future*, ed. Efraín Gonzales de Olarte, 183–264. Miami: University of Miami North-South Center Press.

———. 1998. "Solving the Global Public Pensions Crisis." *cato* Online Policy Report 20, no. 2 (March–April).

———. 2002. *De Paniagua a Toledo: De la confusión al caos.* Lima: Instituto de Economia de Libre Mercado.

Bowen, Sally. 2000. *The Fujimori File: Peru and Its President, 1990–2000.* Lima: Peru Monitor.

Bowen, Sally, and Jane Holligan. 2003. *The Imperfect Spy: The Many Lives of Vladimiro Montesinos.* Lima: Peisa.

Boylan, Delia M. 2001. "Democratization and Institutional Change in Mexico: The Logic of Partial Insulation." *Comparative Political Studies* 34, no. 1 (February): 3–29.

Brooks, Sarah M. 2002. "Social Protection and Economic Integration: The Politics of Pension Reform in an Era of Capital Mobility." *Comparative Political Studies* 35, no. 5 (June): 491–523.

Büchi, Hernan. 1996. "Social Security Reform in Chile." In *Bigger Economies, Smaller Governments: Privatization in Latin America*, ed. William Glade and Rossana Corona, 59–88. Boulder, Colo.: Westview Press.

Cameron, Maxwell. 1994. *Democracy and Authoritarianism in Peru: Political Coalitions and Social Change.* New York: St. Martin's Press.

———. 1998. "Self-Coups: Peru, Guatemala, and Russia." *Journal of Democracy* 9, no. 1 (January): 125–39.

Caretas Dossier. 2001. *Montesinos: Toda la historia.* Lima: Caretas.

Castillo, Manuel. 1995. *De la matriz estado-céntrica a la matriz mercado-céntrica: Régimen y empresarios, 1990–1994.* Working paper no. 5, DESCO, Lima.

———. 1997. "Modelo de reformas liberales y *upper class* empresarial en el Perú: Dilemas y opciones." In *El estado post-ajuste: Institucionalidad, estado, actores y conflictos empresariales*, ed. Manuel Castillo and Andrés Quispe, 19–70. Lima: DESCO.

Castillo, Manuel, and Andrés Quispe. 1996. *Reforma estructural y reconversión empresarial: Conflictos y desafíos.* Lima: DESCO.

Castro, Carlos, and Verónica Zavala. 1996. "Reforma de la administración tributaria." In *Implementación de políticas públicas en el Perú*, ed. Augusto Alvarez and Gabriel Ortiz, 99–112. Lima: Instituto Apoyo.

Chalmers, Douglas A., Scott B. Martin, and Kerianne Piester. 1997. "Associative Networks: New Structures of Representations for the Popular Sectors?" In *The New Politics of Inequality in Latin America: Rethinking Participation and Representation*, ed. Douglas A. Chalmers, Carlos M. Vilas, Katherine Hite, Scott B. Martin, Kerianne Piester, and Monique Segarra, 543–82. New York: Oxford University Press.

Cohen, Jeffrey E. 1986. "The Dynamics of the 'Revolving Door' on the FCC." *American Journal of Political Science* 30, no. 4 (November): 689–708.

Comisión de la Verdad y Reconciliación. 2003. *Informe final.* Lima: CVR.

Conaghan, Catherine. 1996. "A Deficit of Democratic Authenticity: Political Linkage and the Public in Andean Polities." *Studies in Comparative International Development* 31, no. 3 (Autumn): 32–55.

———. 2001. "Making and Unmaking Authoritarian Peru: Re-election, Resistance, and Regime Transition." North-South Agenda Papers no. 47, University of Miami North-South Center, Florida.

———. 2002. "Cashing in on Authoritarianism: Media Collusion in Fujimori's Peru." *Harvard International Journal of Press/Politics* 7, no. 1 (Winter): 115–25.

Conaghan, Catherine, and James Malloy. 1994. *Unsettling Statecraft: Democracy and Neoliberalism in the Central Andes.* Pittsburgh: University of Pittsburgh Press.

Conaghan, Catherine, James Malloy, and Luis Abugattás. 1990. "Business and the Boys: The Politics of Neoliberalism in the Central Andes." *Latin America Research Review* 25, no. 2 (Spring): 3–30.

Congreso de la República. 2002. *Comisión investigadora de los delitos económicos y financieros cometidos entre 1990–2001.* CD-ROM. Lima: Congreso de la República.

———. 2003. *Acciones para erradicar la corrupción en el estado peruano: Comisión investigadora de los casos de corrupción.* CD-ROM. Lima: Congreso de la República.

Confederación Nacional de Instituciones Empresariales Privadas (CONFIEP). 1996. *Opinión de los empresarios sobre las reformas estructurales.* Lima: CONFIEP-USAID, Proyecto PAPI.

———. 1997. *Exportaciones, empleo y tributación: Una propuesta para la generación de un millón de puestos de trabajo.* Lima: CONFIEP-SNE.

Cornelius, Wayne, Anne Craig, and Jonathan Fox. 1994. Introduction to *Transforming State-Society Relations in Mexico: The National Solidarity Strategy,* ed. Wayne Cornelius, Ann Craig, and Jonathan Fox, 3–26. San Diego: University of California Center for U.S.-Mexican Studies.

Cornell, Angela, and Kenneth Roberts. 1990. "Democracy, Counterinsurgency, and Human Rights: The Case of Peru." *Human Rights Quarterly* 12, no. 4 (November): 529–53.

Cortez, Rafael. 1998. *Equidad y calidad de los servicios de salud.* Lima: Centro de Investigación de la Universidad del Pacífico.

Cotler, Julio. 1994. *Política y sociedad en el Perú: Cambios y continuidades.* Lima: Instituto de Estudios Peruanos.

———. 1998. "La articulación y los mecanismos de representación de las organizaciones empresariales." Working paper no. 97, Instituto de Estudios Peruanos, Lima.

Cruz-Saco, María. 1998. "The Pension System Reform in Peru: Economic Rationale Versus Political Will." In *Do Options Exist? The Reform of Pension and Health Care Systems in Latin America,* ed. María Amparo Cruz-Saco and Carmelo Mesa-Lago, 165–85. Pittsburgh: University of Pittsburgh Press.

Cuba, Elmer. 1997. "El recálculo del PBI y sus consecuensias." *Moneda* 102 (April–May): 52–54.

Díaz, Alvaro. 1997. "New Developments in Economic and Social Restructuring in Latin America." In *Politics, Social Change, and Economic Restructuring in Latin America,* ed. William C. Smith and Roberto Patricio Korzeniewicz, 37–53. Miami: University of Miami North-South Center Press.

Diez Canseco, Javier, ed. 2002. *Balance de la inversión y privatización, 1990–2001: Objetivos y resultados.* Lima: Fondo Editorial del Congreso del Perú.

Domínguez, Jorge. 1996. *Technopols: Freeing Politics and Markets in Latin America in the 1990s.* University Park: Pennsylvania State University Press.

———. 1998. "Free Politics and Free Markets in Latin America." *Journal of Democracy* 9, no. 4 (October): 70–84.

Dresser, Denise. 1991. *Neopopulist Solutions to Neoliberal Problems: Mexico's National Solidarity Program.* San Diego: University of California Center for U.S.-Mexican Studies.

Durand, Francisco. 1992. "The Political Formation and Consolidation of Peak Business Associations: The Case of Peru." Working paper no. 170, Helen Kellog Institute for International Studies, University of Notre Dame, Indiana.

———. 1994a. *Business and Politics in Peru.* Boulder, Colo.: Westview Press.

———. 1994b. "The Politics of Tax Revolutions in Peru, Bolivia, and Argentina." Paper prepared for the annual meeting of the Latin American Studies Association, Atlanta, Georgia, March 10–13.

———. 1996. *Incertidumbre y soledad: Reflexiones sobre los grandes empresarios de América Latina*. Lima: Fundación Friedrich Ebert.

———. 1997. "State Institutional Development: Assessing the Success of the Peruvian Tax Reform." Paper prepared for the annual meeting of the Latin American Studies Association, Guadalajara, Mexico, April 17–19.

———. 1998. "Collective Action and the Empowerment of Peruvian Business." In *Organized Business, Economic Change, and Democracy in Latin America*, ed. Francisco Durand and Eduardo Silva, 253–80. Miami: University of Miami North-South Center Press.

———. 1999. "The Transformation of Business-Government Relations Under Fujimori." *Canadian Journal of Latin American and Caribbean Studies* 24, no. 47 (Spring): 29–56.

———. 2002a. "Business and the Crisis of Peruvian Democracy." *Business and Politics* 4, no. 3: 319–341.

———. 2002b. "Desarrollo institucional de SUNAT: Factores de éxito y fracaso." Aportes al Debate no. 6, Fundación Friedrich Ebert, Lima.

———. 2003. *Riqueza económica y pobreza política: Reflexiones sobre las elites de poder en un país inestable*. Lima: Fondo Ediroial de la Pontificia Universidad Católica del Perú.

Durand, Francisco, and Rosemary Thorp. 1998. "Reforming the State: A Study of the Peruvian Tax Reform." *Oxford Development Studies* 26, no. 2 (June): 133–51.

Edwards, Sebastian. 1995. *Crisis and Reform in Latin America: From Despair to Hope*. New York: Oxford University Press.

Edwards, Sebastian, and Daniel Lederman. 1998. "The Political Economy of Unilateral Trade Liberalization: The Case of Chile." Working paper no. 6510, National Bureau of Economic Research, Cambridge, Massachusetts.

Estela Benavides, Manuel. 2001. *Perú: Ocho apuntes para el crecimiento con bienestar*. Lima: Fondo Editorial del Banco Central de Reserva del Perú.

———. 2002. "El Perú y la tributación." Serie Aportes Cuaderno no. 4, Superintendencia Nacional de Administración Tributaria, Lima.

Evans, Peter. 1995. *Embedded Autonomy: States and Industrial Transformation*. Princeton: Princeton University Press.

Ewig, Christina. 2000. "Democracia diferida: Un análisis del proceso de reformas en el sector salud." In *Políticas sociales en el Perú: Nuevos aportes*, ed. Felipe Portocarrero S., 481–518. Lima: Red para el Desarollo de las Ciencias Sociales en el Perú.

———. 2001. "Gender Equity and Neoliberal Social Policy: Health Sector Reform in Peru." Ph.D. diss., University of North Carolina, Chapel Hill.

Fearon, James D. 1991. "Counterfactuals and Hypothesis Testing in Political Science." *World Politics* 43, no. 2 (January): 169–95.

Fondo Nacional de Compensación y Desarrollo Social (FONCODES). 1994. *Nota mensual*, no. 11, December. Lima: Fondo Nacional de Compensación y Desarrollo Social.

———. 1995. *Nota mensual*, no. 17, September–December. Lima: Fondo Nacional de Compensación y Desarrollo Social.

———. 2002. *Memoria 2002*. Lima: Fondo Nacional de Compensación y Desarrollo Social.

———. 2003. "Informe: Los mapas de pobreza de FONCODES." FONCODES, Lima.

Francke, Pedro. 1997. "FONCODES: ¿Llega a los pobres?" *Moneda* 103 (June–July): 44–47.

Frieden, Jeffry. 1991. *Debt, Development, and Democracy: Modern Political Economy and Latin America*. Princeton: Princeton University Press.

Frye, Timothy. 2002. "The Perils of Polarization: Economic Performance in the Postcommunist World." *World Politics* 54, no. 3 (April): 308–37.

Fuentes, Sandro, Luis Alberto Arias, and Francisco Durand. 1996. "Reform of the Tax System and Administration in Peru." In *Reform of Tax Administration in Latin America*, 185–212. Washington, D.C.: Inter-American Development Bank.

García Calderón, Ernesto. 2001. "High Anxiety in the Andes: Peru's Decade of Living Dangerously." *Journal of Democracy* 12, no. 2 (April): 46–58.

Geddes, Barbara. 1990. "Building 'State' Autonomy in Brazil, 1930–1964." *Comparative Politics* 22, no. 2 (January): 217–35.

———. 1994. *Politician's Dilemma: Building State Capacity in Latin America*. Berkeley and Los Angeles: University of California Press.

———. 1995. "The Politics of Economic Liberalization." *Latin American Research Review* 30, no. 2 (Spring): 195–214.

Gómez, Rosario, Roberto Urrunaga, and Roberto Bel. 1997. "Evaluación de la estructura tributaria nacional: 1990–1994." Working paper no. 27, Centro de Investigación de la Universidad del Pacífico, Lima.

Gonzales de Olarte, Efraín. 1998. *El neoliberalismo a la peruana: Economía política del ajuste estructural, 1990–1997*. Lima: Instituto de Estudios Peruanos—Consorcio de Investigación Económica.

Gormley, William T. 1979. "A Test of the Revolving Door Hypothesis at the FCC." *American Journal of Political Science* 23, no. 4 (November): 665–83.

Graham, Carol. 1994. *Safety Nets, Politics, and the Poor: Transitions to Market Economics*. Washington, D.C.: Brookings Institution.

———. 1998. *Private Markets for Public Goods: Raising the Stakes in Economic Reform*. Washington, D.C.: Brookings Institution.

Graham, Carol, and Cheikh Kane. 1998. "Opportunistic Government or Sustaining Reform? Electoral Trends and Public-Expenditure Patterns in Peru, 1990–1995." *Latin American Research Review* 33, no. 1 (Winter): 67–104.

Graham, Carol, and Moisés Naím. 1998. "The Political Economy of Institutional Reform in Latin America." In *Beyond Tradeoffs: Market Reforms and Equitable Growth in Latin America*, ed. Nancy Birdsall, Carol Graham, and Richard H. Sabot, 321–59. Washington, D.C.: Brookings Institution and the Inter-American Development Bank.

Greenberg, George D., Jeffrey A. Miller, Lawrence B. Mohr, and Bruce C. Vladeck. 1977. "Developing Public Policy Theory: Perspectives from Empirical Research." *American Political Science Review* 71, no. 4 (December): 1532–43.

Haggard, Stephan, and Robert Kaufman. 1992. "Institutional and Economic Adjustments." In *The Politics of Economic Adjustment: International Constraints, Distributive Conflicts, and the State*, ed. Stephan Haggard and Robert R. Kaufman, 3–37. Princeton: Princeton University Press.

———. 1995. *The Political Economy of Democratic Transitions*. Princeton: Princeton University Press.

Haggard, Stephan, Sylvia Maxfield, and Ben Ross Schneider. 1997. "Theories of Business and Business-State Relations." In *Business and the State in Developing Countries*, ed. Sylvia Maxfield and Ben Ross Schneider, 36–60. Ithaca, N.Y.: Cornell University Press.

Hagopian, Frances. 2000. "Political Development, Revisited." *Comparative Political Studies* 33, no. 6 (August): 880–911.

Hamann, A. Javier, and Carlos Paredes. 1991. "Economic Characteristics and Trends." In *Peru's Path to Recovery: A Plan for Economic Stabilization and Growth,*ed. Carlos Paredes and Jeffrey Sachs, 41–79. Washington, D.C.: Brookings Institution.

Hays-Mitchell, Maureen. 2002. "Resisting Austerity: A Gendered Perspective on Neo-liberal Restructuring in Peru." *Gender and Development* 10, no. 3 (November): 71–81.

Hellman, Joel S. 1998. "Winners Take All: The Politics of Partial Reform in Postcommunist Transitions." *World Politics* 50, no. 2. (February): 203–34.

Heredia, Blanca, and Ben Ross Schneider. 2003. "The Political Economy of Administrative Reform in Developing Countries." In *Reinventing Leviathan: The Politics of Administrative Reform in Developing Countries*, ed. Ben Ross Schneider and Blanca Heredia, 1–29. Miami: University of Miami North-South Center Press.

Hilderbrand, Mary E., and Merilee S. Grindle. 1997. "Building Sustainable Capacity in the Public Sector: What Can Be Done?" In *Getting Good Government: Capacity Building in the Public Sectors of Developing Countries*, ed. Merilee S. Grindle, 31–61. Boston: Harvard Institute for International Development.

Huber, Evelyne, and John D. Stephens. 2001. *Development and Crisis of the Welfare State: Parties and Policies in Global Markets.* Chicago: University of Chicago Press.

Hurtado Miller, Juan Carlos. 1990. "Statement by the Governor of the Bank for Peru." Summary proceedings of the annual meeting of the Board of Governors. Washington, D.C.: International Monetary Fund.

Instituto Nacional de Estadística e Informática (INEI). 1992. *Perú: Series estadísticas, 1970–91.* Lima: Instituto Nacional de Estadística e Informática.

———. 1997a. *Perú: Compendio de estadísticas sociales, 1996–97.* Lima: Instituto Nacional de Estadística e Informática.

———. 1997b. *Perú: Compendio estadístico, 1996–1997.* Lima: Instituto Nacional de Estadística e Informática.

———. 1998a. *Perú: Compendio estadístico económico financiero, 1997–98.* Lima: Instituto Nacional de Estadística e Informática.

———. 1998b. *Perú: Compendio estadístico socio-demográfico, 1997–98.* Lima: Instituto Nacional de Estadística e Informática.

———. 1999a. *Perú: Compendio estadístico económico financiero, 1998–99.* Lima: Instituto Nacional de Estadística e Informática.

———. 1999b. *Perú: Compendio estadístico socio-demográfico, 1998 –99.* Lima: Instituto Nacional de Estadística e Informática.

———. 2000a. *Perú: Compendio estadístico económico financiero, 1999–2000.* Lima: Instituto Nacional de Estadística e Informática.

———. 2000b. *Perú: Compendio estadístico socio-demográfico, 1999–2000.* Lima: Instituto Nacional de Estadística e Informática.

———. 2001. *Perú: Compendio estadístico, 2001.* Lima: Instituto Nacional de Estadística e Informática.

Instituto Peruano de Economía (IPE). 1997a. *Competitividad y promoción de las exportaciones: Reducción de los sobrecostos tributarios.* Lima: Instituto Peruano de Economía.

———. 1997b. *Reforma del régimen previsional peruano.* Lima: Instituto Peruano de Economía.

Inter-American Development Bank (IDB). 1996. "Tax Reform." In *Economic and Social*

Progress in Latin America, 123–33. Washington, D.C.: Inter-American Development Bank.

———. 2002. "Peru: Stage Three of the National Program to Support Operations of the Compensation and Social Development Fund (FONCODES III)." Washington, D.C.: Inter-American Development Bank.

James, Estelle. 1998. "Pension Reform: An Efficiency-Equity Tradeoff?" In *Beyond Tradeoffs: Market Reforms and Equitable Growth in Latin America*, ed. Nancy Birdsall, Carol Graham, and Robert H. Sabot, 253–72. Washington, D.C.: Inter-American Development Bank.

Jiménez, Félix. 1997. "Sobre la equivocada información oficial del PBI." *Moneda* 102 (April–May): 55–57.

Kaufman, Robert. 1999. "Approaches to the Study of State Reform in Latin American and Postsocialist Countries." *Comparative Politics* 31, no. 3 (April): 357–75.

Kay, Stephen J. 1999. "Unexpected Privatizations: Politics and Social Security Reform in the Southern Cone." *Comparative Politics* 31, no. 4 (July): 403–22.

Kenney, Charles D. 2004. *Fujimori's Coup and the Breakdown of Democracy in Latin America*. Notre Dame: University of Notre Dame Press.

Kingstone, Peter R. 1999. *Crafting Coalitions for Reform: Business Preferences, Political Institutions, and Neoliberal Reform in Brazil*. University Park: University of Pennsylvania Press.

Kuczynski, Pedro-Pablo. 1977. *Peruvian Democracy Under Economic Stress: An Account of the Belaúnde Administration, 1963–1968*. Princeton: Princeton University Press.

Kurtz, Marcus J. 2001. "Understanding and Misunderstanding Democracy in the Open Economy: An Argument with Evidence from the Chilean Case." Paper prepared for the 2001 annual meeting of the Western Political Science Association, Las Vegas, Nevada, March 15–17.

Levitsky, Steven. 1999. "Fujimori and Post-party Politics in Peru." *Journal of Democracy* 10, no. 3 (July): 78–92.

Levitsky, Steven, and Lucan A. Way. 1998. "Between a Shock and a Hard Place: The Dynamics of Labor Backed Adjustment in Poland and Argentina." *Comparative Politics* 30, no. 2 (January): 171–92.

Lewis-Beck, Michael S. 1986. "Interrupted Time-Series." In *New Tools for Social Scientists: Advances and Applications in Research Methods*, ed. William D. Berry and Michael S. Lewis-Beck, 209–40. Beverly Hills: Sage.

Lindblom, Charles. 1977. *Politics and Markets: The World's Political-Economic Systems*. New York: Basic Books.

Lowi, Theodore. 1964. "American Business, Public Policy, Case Studies, and Political Theory." *World Politics* 16, no. 4 (July): 677–715.

———. 1972. "Four Systems of Policy, Politics, and Choice." *Public Administration Review* 32, no. 4 (July): 298–310.

Lustig, Nora, ed. 1995. *Coping with Austerity: Poverty and Inequality in Latin America*. Washington, D.C.: Brookings Institution.

McClintock, Cynthia. 1998. *Revolutionary Movements in Latin America: El Salvador's FMLN and Peru's Shining Path*. Washington, D.C.: United States Institute of Peace Press.

Madrid, Raúl L. 2002. "The Politics and Economics of Pension Privatization in Latin America." *Latin American Research Review* 37, no. 2: 159–82.

Mahon, James E., Jr. 2004. "Causes of Tax Reform in Latin America, 1977–95." *Latin American Research Review* 39 no. 1 (February): 3–30.

Manzetti, Luigi. 1999. *Privatization South American Style*. Oxford: Oxford University Press.

———. 2003. "Political Manipulations and Market Reforms Failures." *World Politics* 55, no. 3 (April): 315–60.

Marcus-Delgado, Jane, and Martín Tanaka. 2001. *Lecciones del final del Fujimorismo: La legitimidad presidencial y la acción política*. Lima: Instituto de Estudios Peruanos.

Mauceri, Philip. 1995. "State Reform, Coalitions, and the Neoliberal Autogolpe in Peru." *Latin American Research Review* 30, no. 1 (Winter): 7–37.

———. 1997. "Return of the Caudillo: Autocratic Democracy in Peru." *Third World Quarterly* 18, no. 5 (December): 889–911.

Maxfield, Sylvia. 1997. *Gatekeepers of Growth: The International Political Economy of Central Banking in Developing Countries*. Princeton: Princeton University Press.

Melo, Marcus A. 2003. "When Institutions Matter: A Comparison of the Politics of Administrative, Social Security, and Tax Reforms in Brazil." In *Reinventing Leviathan: The Politics of Administrative Reform in Developing Countries*, ed. Ben Ross Schneider and Blanca Heredia, 211–49. Miami: University of Miami North-South Center Press.

Mesa-Lago, Carmelo. 1996. "Pension Reform in Latin America: Importance and Evaluation of Privatization Approaches." In *Bigger Economies, Smaller Governments: Privatization in Latin America*, ed. William Glade and Rossana Corona, 89–134. Boulder, Colo.: Westview Press.

———. 1997. "Social Welfare Reform in the Context of Economic-Political Liberalization: Latin American Cases." *World Development* 25, no. 4 (April): 497–517.

Molinar, Juan, and Jeffrey Weldon. 1994. "Electoral Determinants and Consequences of National Solidarity." In *Transforming State-Society Relations in Mexico: The National Solidarity Strategy*, ed. Wayne Cornelius, Anne Craig and Jonathan Fox, 123–41. San Diego: University of California Center for U.S.-Mexican Studies.

Muradian, Roldan, Joan Martinez-Alier, and Humberto Correa. 2003. "International Capital Versus Local Population: The Environmental Conflict of the Tambogrande Mining Project, Peru." *Society and Natural Resources* 16. no. 9 (October): 775–92.

Murillo, Maria Victoria. 2001. *Labor Unions, Partisan Coalitions, and Market Reforms in Latin America*. Cambridge: Cambridge University Press.

———. 2002. "Political Bias in Policy Convergence: Privatization Choices in Latin America." *World Politics* 54, no. 4 (July): 462–93.

Naím, Moisès. 1995. *Latin America's Journey to the Market: From Macroeconomic Shocks to Institutional Therapy*. San Francisco: Institute for Contemporary Studies.

Nelson, Joan M. 1989. "The Politics of Pro-Poor Adjustment." In *Fragile Coalitions: The Politics of Economic Adjustment*, ed. Joan M. Nelson, 95–113. New Brunswick, N.J.: Transaction Books.

———, ed. 1990. *Economic Crisis and Policy Choice: The Politics of Adjustment in the Third World*. Princeton: Princeton University Press.

———. 1999. "Reforming Health and Education: The World Bank, the IDB, and Complex Institutional Change." Washington, D.C.: Overseas Development Council.

Obando, Enrique. 1998. "Civil-Military Relations in Peru, 1980–1996: How to Control and Coopt the Military (and the Consequences of Doing So)." In *Shining and Other Paths: War and Society in Peru, 1980–1995*, ed. Steve J. Stern, 385–410. Durham: Duke University Press.

O'Donnell, Guillermo. 1994. "Delegative Democracy." *Journal of Democracy* 5, no. 1 (January): 55–69.

Olson, Mancur. 1965. *The Logic of Collective Action*. Cambridge: Harvard University Press.

Ortiz de Zevellos, Gabriel, Hugo Eyzaguirre, Rosa María Palacios, and Pierina Pollarolo. 1999. "La economía política de las reformas institucionales en el Perú: Los casos de educación, salud, y pensiones." Working paper no. R-348, Inter-American Development Bank, Washington, D.C.

Oxhorn, Philip, and Pamela K. Starr, eds. 1999. *Market and Democracy in Latin America: Conflict or Convergence?* Boulder, Colo.: Lynne Rienner.

Panfichi, Aldo. 1997. "The Authoritarian Alternative: 'Anti-politics' in the Popular Sectors of Lima." In *The New Politics of Inequality in Latin America: Rethinking Participation and Representation*, ed. Douglas A. Chalmers, Carlos M. Vilas, Katherine Hite, Scott B. Martin, Kerianne Piester, and Monique Segarra, 217–36. New York: Oxford University Press.

Paredes, Patricia, and Carl E. Taylor. 2002. "Peru: Communities and Government Learning to Work Together." In *Just and Lasting Change: When Communities Own Their Futures*, ed. Daniel Taylor-Ide and Carl Taylor, 200–207. Baltimore: Johns Hopkins University Press.

Parodi, Jorge, and Walter Twanama. 1993. "Los pobladores, la ciudad y la política: Un estudio de actitudes." In *Los pobres, la ciudad y la política*, ed. Jorge Parodi, 21–89. Lima: Centro de Estudios de Democracia y Sociedad.

Pastor, Manuel. 1992. *Inflation, Stabilization, and Debt: Macroeconomic Experiments in Peru and Bolivia*. Boulder, Colo.: Westview Press.

Pastor, Manuel, and Carol Wise. 1999. "The Politics of Second-Generation Reform." *Journal of Democracy* 10, no. 3 (July): 34–48.

Perez, José. 1996. "Rondas campesinas: Poder, violencia y autodefensa en Cajamarca central." Working paper no. 78, Instituto de Estudios Peruanos, Lima.

Petrera, Margarita. 1993. "Privatización de la salud." In *La gestión estatal y la privatización en el sector salud, la seguridad social y el sector financiero*, ed. Margarita Petrera, María Antonia Reményi, and Fernando Parodi, 7–9. Lima: Instituto de Estudios Peruanos.

Pierson, Paul. 1993. "When Effect Becomes Cause: Policy Feedback and Political Change." *World Politics* 45, no. 4 (July): 595–68.

Planas, Pedro. 2000. *La democracia volátil: Movimientos, partidos, líderes políticos y conductas electorales en el Perú contemporáneo*. Lima: Fundación Friedrich Ebert.

Proetica. 2004. *Segunda encuesta nacional sobre corrupción*. Lima: Proetica.

Przeworski, Adam. 1993. "The Neoliberal Fallacy." In *Capitalism, Socialism, and Democracy Revisited*, ed. Larry Diamond and Marc F. Plattner, 39–53. Baltimore: John Hopkins University Press.

Reményi, María. 1993. "La gestión estatal de la seguridad social." In *La gestión estatal y la privatización en el sector salud, la seguridad social y el sector financiero*, ed. Margarita Petrera, María Antonia Reményi, and Fernando Parodi,10–13. Lima: Instituto de Estudios Peruanos.

Remmer, Karen. 1998. "The Politics of Economic Reform in Latin America." *Studies in Comparative International Development* 33, no. 2 (Summer): 3–29.

Rey, Nohra. 1996. "Taxation in Latin America and the Caribbean: Achievements and Outlook." In *Reform of Tax Administration in Latin America*, 1–15. Washington, D.C.: Inter-American Development Bank.

Roberts, Kenneth M. 1995. "Neoliberalism and the Transformation of Populism in Latin America: The Peruvian Case." *World Politics* 48, no. 1 (October): 82–116.

———. 1996. "Economic Crisis and the Demise of the Legal Left in Peru." *Comparative Politics* 29, no. 1 (October): 69–92.

———. 1998. *Deepening Democracy? The Modern Left and Social Movements in Chile and Peru.* Stanford: Stanford University Press.

Roberts, Kenneth M., and Moisés Arce. 1998. "Neoliberalism and Lower-Class Voting Behavior in Peru." *Comparative Political Studies* 31, no. 2 (April): 217–46.

Roca Voto Bernales, Leoni. 2003. "Antecedentes del proceso de modernización del estado peruano y propuestas para un nuevo proceso." In *Modernización del estado peruano: Hacia un estado eficiente, democrático, transparente y descentralizado al servicio del ciudadano,* ed. Manuel Bustamante Coronado, 27–70. Lima: Fondo Editorial del Congreso del Perú.

Roggero, Mario. 1993. *Escoja usted.* Lima: Infoser S.A.

Sagasti, Francisco. 1997. *Pobreza, exclusión y política social: Algunas ideas para el diseño de estrategias de desarrollo.* Lima: Agenda Perú.

Schady, Norbert R. 2000. "The Political Economy of Expenditures by the Peruvian Social Fund (FONCODES), 1991–1995." *American Political Science Review* 94, no. 2 (June): 289–304.

Schamis, Hector. 1999. "Distributional Coalitions and the Politics of Economic Reform in Latin America." *World Politics* 51, no. 2 (January): 236–68.

Schneider, Anne, and Helen Ingram. 1993. "Social Construction of Target Populations: Implications for Politics and Policy." *American Political Science Review* 87, no. 2 (June): 334–47.

Schneider, Ben Ross. 1998. "Elusive Synergy: Business-Government Relations and Development." *Comparative Politics* 31, no. 1 (October): 101–22.

Schönwälder, Gerd. 2002. *Linking Civil Society and the State: Urban Popular Movements, the Left, and Local Government in Peru.* University Park: Pennsylvania State University Press.

Schumpeter, Joseph A. 1975. *Capitalism, Socialism, and Democracy.* New York: Harper Brothers.

Sharp, Elaine B. 1994. "The Dynamics of Issue Expansion: Cases from Disability Rights and Fetal Research Controversy." *Journal of Politics* 56, no. 4 (November): 919–39.

Sheahan, John. 1999. *Searching for a Better Society: The Peruvian Economy from 1950.* University Park: Pennsylvania State University Press.

Silva, Eduardo. 1993. "Capitalist Coalitions, the State, and Neoliberal Economic Restructuring: Chile, 1973–88." *World Politics* 45, no. 4 (July): 526–59.

———. 1996. *The State and Capital in Chile: Business Elites, Technocrats, and Market Economics.* Boulder, Colo.: Westview Press.

Silva, Eduardo, and Francisco Durand. 1998. "Organized Business and Politics in Latin America." In *Organized Business, Economic Change, and Democracy in Latin America,* ed. Francisco Durand and Eduardo Silva, 1–50. Miami: University of Miami North-South Center Press.

Smith, William C., and Roberto Patricio Korzeniewicz. 1997. "Latin America and the Second Great Transformation." In *Politics, Social Change, and Economic Restructuring in Latin America,* ed. William C. Smith and Roberto Patricio Korzeniewicz, 1–20. Miami: University of Miami North-South Center Press.

Snyder, Richard. 1999. "Politics After Neoliberalism: Reregulation in Mexico." *World Politics* 51, no. 2 (January): 173–204.

———. 2001. *Politics After Neoliberalism: Reregulation in Mexico.* Cambridge: University of Cambridge Press.

Superintendencia de Administradoras Privadas de Fondos de Pensiones (SAFP). 1997. *Memoria 1997.* Lima: Superintendencia de Administradoras Privadas de Fondos de Pensiones.

———. 1998. *Memoria 1998.* Lima: Superintendencia de Administradoras Privadas de Fondos de Pensiones.

Superintendencia Nacional de Administración Tributaria (SUNAT). 1995a. *Nota tributaria* (June). Lima: Superintendencia Nacional de Administración Tributaria.

———. 1995b. *Tributemos* (June). Lima: Superintendencia Nacional de Administración Tributaria.

———. 1996. *Tributemos* (December). Lima: Superintendencia Nacional de Administración Tributaria.

———. 1997a. *Tributemos* (May). Lima: Superintendencia Nacional de Administración Tributaria.

———. 1997b. *Tributemos* (September–October). Lima: Superintendencia Nacional de Administración Tributaria.

———. 1998a. *Nota tributaria* (December). Lima: Superintendencia Nacional de Administración Tributaria.

———. 1998b. *Tributemos* (November–December). Lima: Superintendencia Nacional de Administración Tributaria.

———. 2000. *Nota tributaria* (December). Lima: Superintendencia Nacional de Administración Tributaria.

———. 2002a. "Estimación del efecto de los convenios de estabilidad jurídica sobre la recaudación." Lima: Superintendencia Nacional de Administración Tributaria.

———. 2002b. "Estimación del efecto de la mayor depreciación de la revaluación sobre la recaudación: Acuerdos de fusión o división, Ley no. 26283 y D.S. no. 120–94-EF." Lima: Superintendencia Nacional de Administración Tributaria.

Swank, Duane. 1998. "Funding the Welfare State: Globalization and the Taxation of Business in Advanced Market Economies." *Political Studies* 46, no. 4: 671–92.

Taliercio, Robert R., Jr. 2001. "Unsustainably Autonomous? Challenges to the Revenue Authority Reform Model in Latin America." Paper prepared for the 2001 annual meeting of the American Political Science Association, San Francisco, August 30–September 2.

———. 2004. "Administrative Reform as Credible Commitment: The Impact of Autonomy on Revenue Authority Performance in Latin America." *World Development* 32, no. 2: 213–32.

Taliercio, Robert R., Jr., and Michael Engelschalk. 2001. "Strengthening Peru's Tax Agency." *prem*notes 60 (November): 1–4.

Tanaka, Martín. 2001. *Participación popular en políticas sociales: Cuándo puede ser democrática y eficiente, y cuándo todo lo contrario.* Lima: Consorcio de Investigación Económica y Social.

Tanzi, Vito. 1996. "Tax Reform in Latin America in the Past Decade." In *Reform of Tax Administration in Latin America,* 17–30. Washington, D.C.: Inter-American Development Bank.

———. 2000. "Taxation in Latin America in the Last Decade." Working paper no. 76, Center for Research on Economic Development and Policy Reform, Stanford University, California.

Tanzi, Vito, and Parthasarathi Shome. 1993. "A Primer on Tax Evasion." *imf* Staff Papers 40, no. 4: 807–28.

Teichman, Judith. 1997. "Mexico and Argentina: Economic Reform and Technocratic Decision Making." *Studies in Comparative International Development* 32, no. 1 (Spring): 31–35.

———. 2001. *The Politics of Freeing Markets in Latin America: Chile, Argentina, and Mexico.* Chapel Hill: University of North Carolina Press.

Tendler, Judith. 2000. "Safety Nets and Service Delivery: What Are Social Funds Really Telling Us?" In *Social Development in Latin America: The Politics of Reform,* ed. Joseph S. Tulchin and Allison M. Garland, 87–115. Boulder, Colo.: Lynne Reinner.

Thorp, Rosemary, and Geoffrey Bertram. 1978. *Peru: 1890–1977 crecimiento y politicas en una economia abierta.* Lima: Mosca Azul Editores SRL.

Torre, Juan Carlos, and Pablo Gerchunoff. 1999. "La economía política de las reformas institutionales en Argentina: Los casos de la política de privatizacíon de Entel, la reforma de la seguridad social y la reforma laboral." Working paper no. R-349, Inter-American Development Bank, Washington, D.C.

Tulchin, Joseph, and Gary Bland. 1994. *Peru in Crisis: Dictatorship or Democracy?* London: Lynne Rienner.

Tulchin, Joseph S., and Allison M. Garland. 2000. *Social Development in Latin America: The Politics of Reform.* Boulder, Colo.: Lynne Reinner.

Urrunaga, Robert. 1994. "Algunos comentarios a las modificaciones tributarias." *Punto de Equilibrio* (February): 2–5.

———. 1995. "Regímenes tributarios especiales: ¿Hasta cuándo?" *Punto de Equilibrio* (February): 17–19.

Vásquez Huamán, Enrique. 2000. *Estrategias del poder: Grupos económicos en el Perú.* Lima: Centro de Investigación de la Universidad del Pacífico.

Vega-Centeno, Máximo, and María Reményi. 1996. "El sistema previsional en el Perú: Sistema nacional de pensiones vs. sistema privado de pensiones." *Economía* 19 (37–38): 291–404.

Verdera, Francisco. 1995. "Nuevo abuso de derecho: Despido arbitrario y pensiones inciertas." *Argumentos* 27: 2–4.

———. 1997. "Seguridad social y pobreza en el Perú: Una aproximación." Working paper no. 84, Instituto de Estudios Peruanos, Lima.

Webb, Richard. 1991. Prologue to *Peru's Path to Recovery: A Plan for Economic Stabilization and Growth,* ed. Carlos Paredes and Jeffrey Sachs, 1–12. Washington, D.C.: Brookings Institution.

———. 1994. "Peru." In *The Political Economy of Policy Reform,* ed. John Williamson, 355–75. Washington, D.C.: Institute for International Economics.

Webb, Richard, and Graciela Fernández. 1990. *Perú en Números, 1990.* Lima: Cuánto.

———. 1996. *Perú en Números, 1996.* Lima: Cuánto.

———. 1999. *Perú en Números, 1999.* Lima: Cuánto.

———. 2000. *Perú en Números, 2000.* Lima: Cuánto.

Weyland, Kurt. 1996. "How Much Political Power Do Economic Forces Have? Conflicts over Social Insurance Reform in Brazil." *Journal of Public Policy* 16, no. 1 (January): 59–84.

———. 1998. "Swallowing the Bitter Pill: Sources of Popular Support for Neoliberal Reform in Latin America." *Comparative Political Studies* 31, no. 5 (October): 539–68.

———. 2000. "A Paradox for Success? Determinants of Political Support for President Fujimori." *International Studies Quarterly* 44, no. 3 (September): 481–502.

Williamson, John. 1990. *Latin American Adjustment: How Much Has Happened?* Washington, D.C.: Institute for International Economics.

Wilson, James Q. 1973. *Political Organizations.* New York: Basic Books.

———, ed. 1980. *The Politics of Regulation.* New York: Basic Books.

———. 1989. *Bureaucracy: What Government Agencies Do and Why They Do It.* New York: Basic Books.

Wise, Carol. 1994. "The Politics of Peruvian Economic Reform: Overcoming the Legacies of State-Led Development." *Journal of Interamerican Studies and World Affairs* 36, no. 1 (Spring): 75–125.

———. 2003. *Reinventing the State: Economic Strategy and Institutional Change in Peru.* Ann Arbor: University of Michigan Press.

World Bank. 1994. *Averting the Old Age Crisis: Policies to Protect the Old and Promote Growth.* Washington, D.C.: World Bank.

———. 1996. *Staff Appraisal Report: Peru, Second Social Development, and Compensation Fund Project.* Washington, D.C.: World Bank.

———. 1997. *World Development Report: The State in a Changing World.* New York: Oxford University Press.

———. 1999. *Poverty and Social Developments in Peru, 1994–1997.* Washington, D.C.: World Bank.

———. 2003. *Restoring Fiscal Discipline for Poverty Reduction in Peru: A Public Expenditure Review.* Washington, D.C.: World Bank.

Yashar, Deborah J. 1999. "Democracy, Indigenous Movements, and the Postliberal Challenge in Latin America." *World Politics* 52, no. 1 (October): 76–104.

Youngers, Coletta. 2000. *Deconstructing Democracy: Peru Under President Alberto Fujimori.* Washington, D.C.: Washington Office on Latin America.

Zavalla, Cynthia. 2003. "Impuestos y equidad: a propósito de las últimas medidas tributarias." In *Perú hoy: La economía bajo presión de la democracia,* ed. Eduardo Toche, 145–212. Lima: DESCO.

Zermeño, Sergio. 1989. "El regreso de líder: Crisis, neoliberalismo y desorden." *Revista Mexicana de Sociología* 51, no. 4 (October–December): 115–50.

———. 1999. "México: ¿Todo lo social se desvanece?" *Revista Mexicana de Sociología* 61, no. 3 (July–September): 183–2000.

INDEX

Note: Page numbers in *italics* indicate figures and tables.

www.ingramcontent.com/pod-product-compliance
Lightning Source LLC
Chambersburg PA
CBHW021921020426
42334CB00013B/520

9 780271 025438